Guided Comprehension

A Teaching Model for Grades 3–8

Maureen McLaughlin
East Stroudsburg University
of Pennsylvania
East Stroudsburg,
Pennsylvania, USA

Mary Beth Allen
East Stroudsburg University
of Pennsylvania
East Stroudsburg,
Pennsylvania, USA

INTERNATIONAL
Reading
Association
®

800 Barksdale Road, PO Box 8139
Newark, Delaware 19714-8139, USA
www.reading.org

The International Reading Association attempts, through its publications, to provide a forum for a wide spectrum of opinions on reading. This policy permits divergent viewpoints without implying the endorsement of the Association.

Director of Publications   Joan M. Irwin
Editorial Director, Books and Special Projects   Matthew W. Baker
Senior Editor, Books and Special Projects   Tori Mello Bachman
Permissions Editor   Janet S. Parrack
Production Editor   Shannon Benner
Assistant Editor   Corinne M. Mooney
Editorial Assistant   Tyanna L. Collins
Publications Manager   Beth Doughty
Production Department Manager   Iona Sauscermen
Supervisor, Electronic Publishing   Anette Schütz-Ruff
Senior Electronic Publishing Specialist   Cheryl J. Strum
Electronic Publishing Specialist   R. Lynn Harrison
Proofreader   Charlene M. Nichols

Project Editors   Matthew W. Baker and Shannon Benner

Art Credits   Cover Design, Linda Steere
Cover Photo, PhotoDisc

Library of Congress Cataloging-in-Publication Data
McLaughlin, Maureen.
    Guided comprehension : a teaching model for grades 3–8 / Maureen McLaughlin, Mary Beth Allen.
        p.   cm.
Includes bibliographical references and index.
    ISBN 0-87207-172-3
1. Reading comprehension—Study and teaching (Elementary)—United States.
    2. Reading (Elementary)—United States.   I. Allen, Mary Beth, 1957–   II. Title.
    LB1573.7 .M35 2001
    372.4--dc21

                                                        2001005664

DEDICATION

For Matt   *MM*

For Jon and Jacquelyn   *MBA*

.

CONTENTS

PREFACE

For all of us who are literacy professionals, reading comprehension seems to hold not only a natural curiosity but also an enduring interest. Seeking a greater conceptual understanding of comprehension as well as knowledge of its practical application are common goals. As a result, reading comprehension is the primary focus of classroom instruction, research, and professional development.

Questions that frequently arise about comprehension include the following:

- What is reading comprehension?
- What are the current beliefs about best practice?
- How can reading comprehension strategies and skills be taught?
- What role does context play?
- How can classrooms be effectively organized and managed to promote reading comprehension?
- How can reading comprehension be assessed?

When we teach our university classes, research aspects of literacy, and conduct professional development sessions, we strive to respond to these inquiries in meaningful ways. Both theory and practice have informed our current thinking, which we detail for you in this book.

We began our investigation of reading comprehension by reviewing current research about best practice in reading comprehension instruction. This revealed that the following elements enhance students' comprehension: direct instruction of comprehension strategies; opportunities to engage with authentic text in a variety of genres; multiple levels of text; dynamic assessment; integration of reading, writing, and discussion; and consistent opportunities for practice and transfer of learning in a variety of settings.

Next, we focused on what we saw happening in literacy classrooms. We observed that comprehension strategies were being "shared" or "gone over" with students, but they were not being taught explicitly. We also noticed that whole class was the instructional setting most frequently used and that many students did not have opportunities to transact with multiple levels of text. Strategy instruction was rarely scaffolded, and there were minimal opportunities for students to apply and transfer their learning. Many of the assessments used were formal in nature and used at the conclusion of learning experiences.

The disparity between what was known about best practice and what we saw happening in literacy classrooms led to our development of Guided Comprehension, a context in which the elements of best practice are easily situated. We also knew that in order for the concept to be effective, it would need to have a viable step-by-step teaching framework. This led to our creation of the Guided Comprehension Model, a framework designed to help students and teachers experience reading as a thinking process. Underpinned by current research and beliefs about best practice, the Model provides a detailed, classroom-tested process for teaching reading from a comprehension-based perspective. It encourages students to become active, strategic readers by providing direct strategy instruction, numerous opportunities for engagement, and a variety of texts and instructional settings.

In this volume we provide a detailed description of the Guided Comprehension Model and suggestions for implementing it in grades 3–8. The book is a practical, easily accessed guide for classroom teachers, staff developers, Title I reading specialists, and teacher educators.

In Chapter 1, we begin by defining Guided Comprehension. Then we introduce the Guided Comprehension Model and discuss the 10 research-based tenets that underpin it.

The next three chapters focus on the stages of the Model. Chapter 2 describes teacher-directed whole-group instruction. Chapter 3 delineates the small-group and independent instructional settings, including teacher-guided small groups and student-facilitated comprehension centers and routines. The final stage, teacher-facilitated whole-group reflection and goal setting, is the focus of Chapter 4. In these chapters we also make connections to supportive information in Appendixes A, B, and C.

Chapter 5 provides the rationale for using leveled texts and suggestions to facilitate leveling narrative and expository works. This chapter also contains descriptions of commercially published leveled texts and makes connections to Appendix D, which features resources for leveled texts.

In Chapter 6, we begin by discussing the multiple roles of assessment in the Guided Comprehension process, then we describe a variety of practical assessments that afford insights into students' thinking and performance. Next, we offer ideas about creating dynamic groups and student-text matches. Throughout the chapter we also make connections to various assessment forms that are included in Appendix E.

Chapter 7 situates Guided Comprehension in grade 3–8 classrooms. In this chapter we illustrate the process by providing teaching plans and student responses, from classrooms in which the Guided Comprehension Model has been used as the focus of reading instruction. We also make connections to Appendix F, which contains additional Guided Comprehension plans.

In the final chapter, we share reflections about Guided Comprehension. These address various aspects of the Model, including its structure, its viability, and its practical application.

Samples of student work are featured in the book and recommendations for further reading appear at the end of the chapters. The appendixes contain a variety of reproducible pages: teaching ideas and blackline masters, forms for organizing and managing comprehension centers and routines, literature response prompts, leveled book resources, assessment forms, and instructional plans.

We have designed this book to be a comprehensive resource that contains everything necessary to implement Guided Comprehension, from detailed explanations of how each stage functions to ideas for facilitating assessment, organization, and management in your classroom.

ACKNOWLEDGMENTS

Although we have authored this book, we have had an impressive supporting cast throughout the research and writing process. We acknowledge them now for their numerous contributions, but most especially for their enthusiasm, their willingness to be action researchers, and their keen ability to find humor in looming deadlines. We are particularly grateful to the following people:

- Everyone who participated in our research study, especially Kim Ware, Meghan Kondisko, Jamie Schuler, and the Pleasant Valley School District
- Barbara Collier, Karen Groller, Joelene Kreitz, Christina Guthrie, Patti Dewitsky, Diane Saylor, Susan Sensinger, Shawn Storm, Melissa Tesche, Mary Ellen Rock, Susan Sillivan, and the graduate students from the Teaching Reading Through Young Adult Literature course at East Stroudsburg University of Pennsylvania
- Victoria Principe and Kim Ware, who worked tirelessly to support the development of the Model, our research, and the writing of this book
- our colleagues Jesse Moore, Fred Fedorko, and Susan Watach
- our graduate assistant Cara Donati
- our families and friends
- Shannon Benner, our production editor
- Matt Baker, Editorial Director, International Reading Association, for his encouragement and editorial expertise

Finally, we thank you, our readers, for joining us in our search for greater understanding of reading comprehension. We hope you find this book to be a valuable teaching resource, one that you and your colleagues will use to further our common goal of enhancing students' understanding of text.

MM and MBA

CHAPTER 1

Guided Comprehension: Helping Students Transact With Text

If you read and comprehend what you read, it stays in your brain. But if you read and don't comprehend what you read, it will just go in one side of your brain and SWOOSH real fast right out the other side.

Jake Scheffler, Grade 7

As literacy professionals, our ultimate teaching goal is to create independent, strategic readers who are capable of engaging in a variety of literacy tasks. Keene and Zimmermann (1997) liken this to a traveler equipped with the necessary tools to make a trip independently. Our role is to equip learners with the proper tools and the ability to select those necessary to reach the predetermined destination. Because it is impossible to anticipate every reading opportunity learners will encounter along the way, readers must learn to use a variety of tools in diverse contexts, thus developing a repertoire of strategies.

In current literacy practice, the destination or goal is for readers to transact with the text and the context in order to comprehend (Rosenblatt, 1978). Transaction implies that a reader's personal experiences shape his or her understanding of narrative and expository text, indicating that response is personal and may vary.

Durkin (1978/1979) defines reading as *comprehension*, indicating that the focus of reading instruction should be on the strategies readers use in order to make sense of text. Smith (1997) extends this idea by defining reading as a thinking process. Suggesting that reading is about cognition indicates that the focus of instruction should not be on the print, but rather on how readers connect with the print. Hiebert, Pearson, Taylor, Richardson, and Paris (1998) endorse this idea, noting, "Teachers support their students' strategic reading through lessons that attend explicitly to how to think while reading" (p. 4).

Describing reading as a thinking process seems quite logical and natural if we examine a reader's transaction with text. To begin, the student contemplates text selection and uses a variety of strategies to make connections to background knowledge. The reader previews the text by activating background knowledge, making predictions about the content, making connections, and setting a purpose for reading. During reading, the student self-questions, visualizes, monitors, thinks about words, and makes connections to self, text, and world. After reading, the learner summarizes, evaluates, and makes connections to self, text, and the world, again engaging in cognitive processes. To successfully transact with text, students need to be thinkers. To effectively think through the reading process and transact with a variety of texts, students need to know how to use comprehension strategies such as previewing, self-questioning, making connections, visualizing, knowing how words work, monitoring, summarizing, and evaluating.

In this chapter we begin by introducing Guided Comprehension, a context in which students and teachers engage in reading as a strategy-based thinking process. We then present the Guided Comprehension Model, a framework designed to help teachers and students engage in reading as a thinking process. Finally, we discuss 10 tenets of reading comprehension and describe their connections to the Model.

WHAT IS GUIDED COMPREHENSION?

Guided Comprehension is a context in which students learn comprehension strategies in a variety of settings using multiple levels and types of text. It is a three-stage process focused on direct-instruction, application, and reflection. In Stage One, teachers directly instruct students using a five-step process. In Stage Two, students apply the strategies in three settings: teacher-guided small groups, student-facilitated comprehension centers, and student-facilitated comprehension routines. In Stage Three, teachers and students engage in reflection and goal setting. Student engagement with leveled text and placement in small groups are dynamic and evolve as students' reading abilities increase.

THE GUIDED COMPREHENSION MODEL

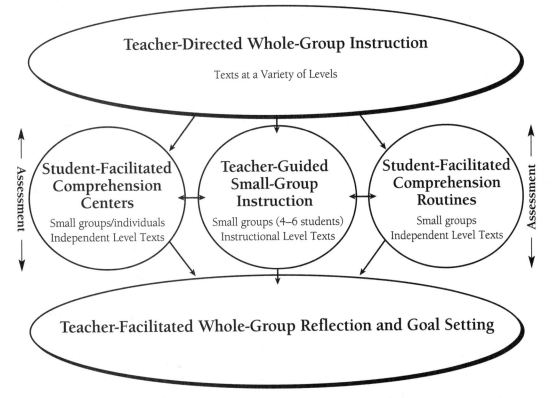

The Guided Comprehension Model is a framework designed to help teachers and students think through reading as a strategy-based process. Designed for use in grades 3–8, the Model is based on what we have learned from existing research, knowledge of best practice, and personal experience. It integrates the following:

- direct instruction of comprehension strategies
- leveled independent, instructional, and challenging texts
- dynamic assessment
- scaffolded instruction (varying levels of teacher support, with eventual relinquishing of control to students)

- various genres and text types
- reading, writing, and discussion
- strategy instruction and application in a variety of settings
- independent practice and transfer of learning in multiple settings
- reflection and goal setting

Structurally, the Model has three stages that progress in the following sequence:

Stage One: Teacher-directed whole-group instruction

Stage Two: Teacher-guided small-group instruction and student-facilitated independent practice

Stage Three: Teacher-facilitated whole-group reflection and goal setting

Naturally situated within the context of balanced literacy, the Guided Comprehension Model is active for both teachers and students. For example, teachers engage in direct instruction and select texts and strategies based on student needs, which are assessed continually. Teachers also participate by facilitating students' engagement in reading, writing, and discussion. Students' active roles in Guided Comprehension include thinking through the reading process, transacting with text in multiple settings, using strategies, and responding in a variety of ways.

The Guided Comprehension Model includes opportunities for whole-group, small-group, paired, and individual reading experiences. Students transact daily with texts at a variety of levels. Teachers direct whole-group instruction, explicitly teach strategies and skills, and work daily with Guided Comprehension small groups. Teachers also observe and assess students as they engage in their independent comprehension activities.

The Model progresses from explicit teaching to independent practice and transfer (see Figure 1). All stages of the Model are necessary to ensure that students can independently apply comprehension strategies in multiple settings. Assessment permeates every aspect of the Model, facilitating our gathering of information about student progress, which continually informs teaching and learning.

We designed this model for use with students in grades 3–8 not to diminish the importance of comprehension in early literacy, but to focus on the direct and often more complex teaching of comprehension strategies needed by more experienced readers. Beyond this philosophical perspective, the need for an effective teaching model clearly exists in grades 3–8, as students move into more challenging and content-based literacy experiences.

In the next section we describe Guided Comprehension's natural emergence from current research on best practice. To illustrate this, we discuss 10 research-based comprehension tenets and describe how they relate to the Model.

Figure 1. Overview of Guided Comprehension Instruction

STAGE ONE

Teacher-Directed Whole-Group Instruction—Teaching a comprehension strategy using easy, instructional, or challenging text.

Explain the strategy of the day and how it relates to the class goal.

Demonstrate the strategy using a think-aloud and a read-aloud.

Guide student practice by reading additional sections of text aloud and having students apply the strategy with support. Monitor students' applications.

Practice by having students apply the strategy to another section of text you have read, providing minimal support. Applications can occur in small groups or pairs.

Reflect by having students think about how they can use this strategy with texts they are reading on their own.

STAGE TWO

Students apply the comprehension strategies in teacher-guided small groups and student-facilitated comprehension centers and routines. In these settings, students work with varying levels of support and use appropriate instructional and independent level texts.

Teacher-Guided Small-Group Instruction—Applying comprehension strategies with teacher guidance using instructional level texts and dynamic grouping (4 to 6 students).

Review previously taught strategies and focus on the strategy of the day.

Guide the students to apply the strategy of the day as well as previously taught strategies as they read a section of the instructional level text. Prompt the students to construct personal meanings. Scaffold as necessary, gradually releasing support as students become more proficient. Encourage discussion and repeat with other sections of text.

Practice by having students work in pairs or individually to apply the strategy. Have students record their applications in their Guided Comprehension Journals and share them during reflection in either small group or whole group.

Reflect and extend by having students share ways in which the strategy helped them to understand the text. Talk about ways in which students can apply the strategy in the comprehension centers and routines.

Student-Facilitated Comprehension Centers and Routines—Applying comprehension strategies individually, in pairs, or in small groups with independent level texts.

Comprehension centers are independent activities to practice strategy application and extend understandings.

Comprehension routines are procedures that foster habits of thinking that promote comprehension of text.

STAGE THREE

Teacher-Facilitated Whole-Group Reflection and Goal Setting—Reflecting on performance, sharing experiences, and setting new goals.

ASSESSMENT OPTIONS

Use authentic measures in all stages.

TENETS OF READING COMPREHENSION

Studies have shown that multiple factors affect successful reading comprehension. The following research-based tenets delineate those we believe to be the most influential:

- Comprehension is a social constructivist process.
- Balanced literacy is a curriculum framework that fosters comprehension.
- Excellent reading teachers influence students' learning.
- Good readers are strategic and take active roles in the reading process.
- Reading should occur in meaningful contexts.
- Students benefit from transacting with a variety of texts at multiple levels.
- Vocabulary development and instruction affect reading comprehension.
- Engagement is a key factor in the comprehension process.
- Comprehension strategies and skills can be taught.
- Dynamic assessment informs comprehension instruction.

Although the tenets have strong research underpinnings, they are also designed to inform instruction. In the section that follows we create connections between theory and practice.

Comprehension Is a Social Constructivist Process

Brooks and Brooks (1993) define constructivism as a theory about knowledge and learning. From a constructivist perspective, learning is understood as "a self-regulated process of resolving inner cognitive conflicts that often become apparent through concrete experience, collaborative discourse, and reflection" (p. vii). Constructivists believe that learners make sense of their world by connecting what they know and have experienced with what they are learning. They construct meaning through these connections when educators pose relevant problems, structure learning around primary concepts, seek and value students' ideas, and assess student learning in context (Brooks & Brooks, 1993).

According to Short and Burke (1996), constructivism frees students of fact-driven curricula and encourages them to focus on larger ideas, allows students to reach unique conclusions and reformulate ideas, encourages students to see the world as a complex place with multiple perspectives, and emphasizes that students are responsible for their own learning and should attempt to connect the information they learn to the world around them through inquiry.

Constructivism is manifested in classrooms that are characterized by student-generated ideas, self-selection, creativity, interaction, critical thinking, and personal construction of meaning (McLaughlin, 2000b). In such contexts, authentic literacy tasks assimilate real-world experiences, provide a purpose for learning, and encourage students to take ownership of learning (Hiebert, 1994; Newmann & Wehlage, 1993).

Constructivists believe that students construct knowledge by linking what is new to what is already known. In reading, this concept is reflected in schema-based learning development, which purports that learning takes place when new information is integrated with what is already known. The more experience learners have with a particular topic, the easier it is for them to make connections between what they know and what they are learning (Anderson, 1994; Anderson & Pearson, 1984). Comprehension is viewed as

> the construction of meaning of a written or spoken communication through a reciprocal, holistic interchange of ideas between the interpreter and the message in a particular communicative context. Note: The presumption here is that meaning resides in the intentional problem-solving, thinking processes of the interpreter during such an interchange, that the content of meaning is influenced by that person's prior knowledge and experience, and that the message so constructed by the receiver may or may not be congruent with the message sent. (Harris & Hodges, 1995, p. 39)

Vygotsky's principles enhance the constructivist perspective by addressing the social context of learning (Dixon-Krauss, 1996). According to Vygotsky, students should be taught within their zones of proximal development (Forman & Cazden, 1994; Vygotsky, 1978). Instruction within the zone should incorporate both scaffolding and social mediation. As Dixon-Krauss notes when explaining this Vygotskian principle, "It is through social dialogue with adults and/or more capable peers that language concepts are learned" (1996, p. 155). Such social interaction encourages students to think and share their ideas.

Guided Comprehension connection: The Guided Comprehension Model is based on the view of comprehension as a social constructivist process. This is evinced in the Model in numerous ways including the ultimate goal of students' transaction with text and the value placed on learning in a variety of social settings.

Balanced Literacy Is a Curriculum Framework That Fosters Comprehension

Balanced literacy is a curriculum framework that

> gives reading and writing equal status and recognizes the importance of both cognitive and affective dimensions of literacy. It acknowledges the meaning-making involved in the full processes of reading and writing, while recognizing the importance of the strategies and skills used by proficient readers and writers. (Au, Carroll, & Scheu, 1997, p. 4)

Authentic texts, print-rich environments, student ownership of learning, and frequent opportunities to read, write, and discuss for a variety of purposes characterize balanced literacy classrooms. Pearson (2001) suggests that the model of comprehension instruction supported by current research actually does more than balance these learning opportunities: It connects and integrates them.

In this integrated view, reading, writing, and discussion are all thinking processes that are focused on the construction of meaning. They are response-related and promote students' transaction with texts and with others. Both direct and indirect instruction are valued components of balanced literacy. In this context, direct instruction is characterized by the teacher purposefully interacting with students and taking an active role in their acquisition of skills and strategies by explaining, modeling, and guiding (Almasi, 1996; Dahl & Farnan, 1998; Duffy et al., 1987; Roehler & Duffy, 1984). Indirect instruction affords students opportunities to make discoveries without teacher guidance (Au, Carroll, & Scheu, 1997).

Balanced literacy has cognitive, social, and affective dimensions. It promotes higher order thinking, interaction, personal response, and comprehension. Situating teaching and learning within this curriculum framework creates an optimal environment for engagement.

Guided Comprehension connection: Guided Comprehension is naturally situated in the framework of balanced literacy for numerous reasons. These include the following shared beliefs: Reading is a meaning-making process; reading, writing, and discussion are integrated; both cognitive and affective aspects of literacy have value; student ownership of learning is critical; and the explicit teaching of comprehension skills and strategies is essential.

Excellent Reading Teachers Influence Students' Learning

Excellent reading teachers are valued participants in the learning process. As the National Commission on Teaching and America's Future (1997) has reported, the single most important strategy for achieving U.S. education goals is to recruit, prepare, and support excellent teachers for every school.

A knowledgeable teacher is aware of what is working well and what each student needs to be successful. A knowledgeable teacher knows the importance of every student having successful literacy experiences, and it is the teacher's knowledge that makes a difference in student success (International Reading Association, 1999).

The teacher's role in the reading process is to create experiences and environments that introduce, nurture, or extend students' abilities to engage with text. This requires that teachers engage in explicit instruction, modeling, scaffolding, facilitating, and participating (Au & Raphael, 1998).

Both reading researchers and professional organizations have delineated the characteristics of excellent reading teachers (Fountas & Pinnell, 1996; International Reading Association, 2000; Ruddell, 1995). The following characterization of such reading teachers integrates their ideas.

Excellent reading teachers believe that all children can learn. They base their teaching on the needs of the individual learner. They know that motivation and multiple kinds of text are essential elements of teaching and learning. They understand that reading is a social constructivist process that functions best in authentic situations. They teach in print-rich, concept-rich environments.

Such teachers have in-depth knowledge of various aspects of literacy, including reading and writing. They teach for a variety of purposes, using diverse methods, materials, and grouping patterns to focus on individual needs, interests, and learning styles. They also know the strategies good readers use, and they can teach students how to use them.

Excellent reading teachers view their teaching as multifaceted and view themselves as participants in the learning process. They integrate their knowledge of the learning cycle, learning styles, and multiple intelligences into their teaching.

These teachers understand the natural relationship between assessment and instruction, and they assess in multiple ways for a variety of purposes. They use instructional strategies that provide formative feedback to monitor the effectiveness of teaching and student performance. They know that assessment informs teaching as well as learning.

Guided Comprehension connection: Teachers who engage in Guided Comprehension are knowledgeable not only about the concept, but also about their students. They know that students read at different levels, and they know how to use the Model to accommodate each reader's needs. These educators are participants in the reading process. They know how to use a variety of materials in a variety of ways, within a variety of settings. Guided Comprehension provides a context for such teaching.

Good Readers Are Strategic and Take Active Roles in the Reading Process

Numerous reading researchers have reported that much of what we know about comprehension is based on studies of good readers (Askew & Fountas, 1998; Keene & Zimmermann, 1997; Pearson, 2001). They describe good readers as active participants in the reading process who have clear goals and constantly monitor the relationship between the goals they have set and the text they are reading. Good readers use comprehension strategies to facilitate the construction of meaning. These strategies include previewing, self-questioning, making connections, visualizing, knowing how words work, monitoring, summarizing, and evaluating. Researchers believe that using such strategies helps students become metacognitive readers (Keene & Zimmermann, 1997; Palincsar & Brown, 1984; Roehler & Duffy, 1984).

Good readers read from aesthetic or efferent stances and have an awareness of the author's style and purpose. Reading from an aesthetic stance is for the emotional, lived-through experience; reading from an efferent stance is for extracting factual information (Rosenblatt, 1978). Good readers read both narrative and expository texts and have ideas about how to figure out unfamiliar words. They use their knowledge of text structure to efficiently and strategically process text. This knowledge develops from experiences with different genres and is correlated with age or time in school (Goldman & Rakestraw, 2000).

These readers spontaneously generate questions at different points in the reading process for a variety of reasons. They know that they use questioning in their everyday lives and that it increases their comprehension. Good readers are problem-solvers who have the ability to discover new information for themselves.

Good readers read widely, which provides exposure to various genres and text formats, affords opportunities for strategy use, increases understanding of how words work, provides bases for discussion and meaning negotiation, and accommodates students' interests.

These readers monitor their comprehension and know when they are constructing meaning, and when they are not. When comprehension breaks down due to lack of background information, difficulty of words, or unfamiliar text structure, good readers know a variety of "fix-up" strategies to use. These include rereading, changing the pace of reading, using context clues, cross-checking cueing systems, and asking for help. Most important, good readers are able to select the appropriate strategies and to consistently focus on making sense of text and gaining new understandings.

Guided Comprehension connection: Creating successful, strategic readers is the ultimate goal of Guided Comprehension, and students fully participate in the process. Students' roles are extensive and include engaging in comprehension as a thinking process and transacting with various levels of text in multiple settings.

Reading Should Occur in Meaningful Contexts

Lipson and Wixson (1997) suggest that the context is a broad concept that encompasses instructional settings, resources, approaches, and tasks. The instructional settings include teacher beliefs, literacy environment, classroom organization, classroom interaction, and grouping. Instructional resources are comprised of elements such as text types and text structures. Instructional approaches include the curriculum, teaching methods, and assessment practices. Task type, content, form, and implementation are the elements of the instructional tasks.

More specific, literacy-based descriptions of context include ideas offered by Gambrell (1996a), Hiebert (1994), and Pearson (2001). They suggest that the classroom context is characterized by multiple factors including classroom organization and authentic opportunities to read, write, and discuss. They further note that the instruction of skills and strategies, integration of concept-driven vocabulary, use of multiple genres, and knowledge of various text structures are other contextual components.

Guided Comprehension connection: Guided Comprehension is a context for learning. Its three stages incorporate a variety of settings, resources, approaches, and tasks.

Students Benefit From Transacting With a Variety of Texts at Multiple Levels

Students need to engage daily with texts at multiple levels. When such levels of text are being used, teachers scaffold learning experiences and students receive varying levels of support, depending on the purpose and instructional setting. For example, when text is challenging, teachers can use a read-aloud to provide full support for students. When the text is just right for instruction, students have support as needed, with the teacher prompting or responding when required. Finally, when the text is just right for independent reading, little or no support is needed.

Transacting with a wide variety of genres enhances students' understanding. Experience reading multiple genres provides students with knowledge of numerous text structures and improves their text-driven processing (Goldman & Rakestraw, 2000). Gambrell (2001) notes that transacting with a wide variety of genres—including biography, historical fiction, legends, poetry, and brochures—increases students' reading performance.

Guided Comprehension connection: In Guided Comprehension, students have opportunities to engage with a variety of genres at independent, instructional, and challenging levels on a daily basis.

Vocabulary Development and Instruction Affect Reading Comprehension

Vocabulary instruction, another valued component of balanced literacy, has strong ties to reading comprehension. As the National Reading Panel (2000) notes, "Reading comprehension is a complex, cognitive process that cannot be understood without a clear description of the role that vocabulary development and vocabulary instruction play in the understanding of what has been read" (p. 13). Snow, Burns, and Griffin (1998) support this view, observing, "Learning new concepts and words that encode them is essential to comprehension development" (p. 217).

In their review of the existing research, Blachowicz and Fisher (2000) identify four guidelines for vocabulary instruction. They note that students should (1) be actively engaged in understanding words and related strategies, (2) personalize their vocabulary learning, (3) be immersed in words, and (4) develop their vocabularies through repeated exposures from multiple sources of information.

Baumann and Kameenui (1991) suggest that direct instruction of vocabulary and learning from context should be balanced. The instruction should be meaningful to students, include words from students' reading, and focus on a variety of strategies for determining the meanings of unfamiliar words (Blachowicz & Lee, 1991). Another important aspect of such teaching is making connections between the vocabulary and students' background knowledge.

Vocabulary growth is also influenced by the amount and variety of text students read (Baumann & Kameenui, 1991; Beck & McKeown, 1991; Snow, Burns, & Griffin, 1998). Teacher read-alouds, which offer students access to a variety of levels of text, contribute to this process (Hiebert et al., 1998).

Guided Comprehension connection: In Guided Comprehension, students are immersed in words. They engage daily with texts at multiple levels in a variety of settings, and they learn words through both direct instruction and use of context. They also learn vocabulary strategies in scaffolded settings that provide numerous opportunities for practice and application, paired and group reading, and teacher read-alouds.

Engagement Is a Key Factor in the Comprehension Process

The engagement perspective on reading integrates cognitive, motivational, and social aspects of reading (Baker, Afflerbach, & Reinking, 1996; Baker & Wigfield, 1999; Guthrie & Alvermann, 1999). Engaged learners achieve because they want to understand, they possess intrinsic motivations for interacting with text, they use cognitive skills to understand, and they share knowledge by talking with teachers and peers (Guthrie & Wigfield, 1997).

Engaged readers transact with print and construct understandings based on connections between prior knowledge and new information. Tierney (1990) describes the process of the mind's eye and suggests readers become a part of the story within their minds. Teachers can nurture and extend this by encouraging students to read for authentic purposes and respond in meaningful ways, always focusing on comprehension, personal connections, and reader response. Baker and Wigfield (1999) note that "engaged readers are motivated to read for different purposes, utilize knowledge gained from previous experience to generate new understandings, and participate in meaningful social interactions around reading" (p. 453).

Gambrell (1996a) suggests that "classroom cultures that foster reading motivation are characterized by a teacher who is a reading model, a book-rich classroom environment, opportunities for choice, familiarity with books, and literacy-related incentives that reflect the value of reading" (p. 20). Gambrell, Palmer, Codling, and Mazzoni (1996) note that highly motivated readers read for a wide variety of reasons including curiosity, involvement, social interchange, and emotional satisfaction.

Motivation is described in terms of competence and efficacy beliefs, goals for reading, and social purposes of reading (Baker & Wigfield, 1999). Motivated readers believe they can be successful and are willing to take on the challenge of difficult reading material. They also exhibit intrinsic reasons for reading, such as gaining new knowledge about a topic or enjoying the reading experience. Motivated readers enjoy the social aspects of sharing with others new meanings gained from their reading.

Guided Comprehension connection: The Guided Comprehension Model is based on students' active engagement. Guided Comprehension is a cognitive experience because students think through the reading process, it is motivational because students' interests and opportunities for success are embedded in the Model, and it is social because students interact with teachers and peers on a daily basis.

Comprehension Strategies and Skills Can Be Taught

Durkin's research in the late 1970s reported that little if any comprehension instruction occurred in classrooms. Instead, comprehension questions, often at the literal level, were assigned and then corrected; comprehension was assessed but not taught. Current studies demonstrate that when students experience explicit instruction of comprehension strategies, it improves their comprehension of new texts and topics (Hiebert et al., 1998). Comprehension strategies generally include

- previewing—activating background knowledge, predicting, and setting a purpose;
- self-questioning—generating questions to guide reading;
- making connections—relating reading to self, text, and others;
- visualizing—creating mental pictures while reading;
- knowing how words work—understanding words through strategic vocabulary development, including the use of graphophonic, syntactic, and semantic cueing systems to figure out unknown words;
- monitoring—asking, "Does this make sense?" and clarifying by adapting strategic processes to accommodate the response;

- summarizing—synthesizing important ideas; and
- evaluating—making judgments.

Fielding and Pearson (1994) recommend a framework for comprehension instruction that encourages the release of responsibility from teacher to student. This four-step approach includes teacher modeling, guided practice, independent practice, and application of the strategy in authentic reading situations. This framework is supported by Vygotsky's (1978) work on instruction within the zone of proximal development, and scaffolding, the gradual relinquishing of support as students become more competent in using the strategy.

Linking skills and strategies can facilitate comprehension. Comprehension strategies are generally more complex than comprehension skills and often require the orchestration of several skills. Effective instruction links comprehension skills and strategies to promote strategic reading. For example, the comprehension skills of sequencing, making judgments, noting details, making generalizations, and using text structure can be linked to summarizing, which is a comprehension strategy (Lipson, 2001). These and other skills—including generating questions, making inferences, distinguishing between important and less important ideas, and drawing conclusions—facilitate students' use of one or more comprehension strategies. Generating questions is an example of a skill that permeates all the Guided Comprehension strategies (see Figure 2).

After explaining and modeling skills and strategies, teachers scaffold instruction to provide the support necessary as students attempt new tasks. During this process, teachers gradually release responsibility for learning to the students, who apply the strategies independently after practicing them in a variety of settings.

Guided Comprehension connection: This tenet is a core underpinning of Guided Comprehension because the Model is designed to promote comprehension as a strategy-based thinking process. It incorporates the explicit teaching of comprehension strategies and the skills that enable their use. The Model also provides multiple opportunities for practice and transfer of learning.

Dynamic Assessment Informs Comprehension Instruction

Dynamic assessment captures students' performance as they engage in the process of learning. It is continuous and has the ability to afford insights into students' understandings at any given point in the learning experience. Dynamic assessment reflects constructivist theory and is viewed not as an add-on, but rather as a natural component of teaching and learning (Brooks & Brooks, 1993).

Dynamic assessments, which are usually informal in nature, can be used in a variety of instructional settings. This includes scaffolded learning experiences in which students have varying degrees of teacher support. Assessing in this context

Figure 2. Generating Questions: A Skill That Supports Comprehension Strategies

Comprehension Strategy	Narrative Text (*The True Story of the Three Little Pigs*)	Expository Text (Chapter: "The American Revolution")
Previewing	What is this story about? What might happen in this story?	What do I already know about the Revolutionary War?
Self-Questioning	Why is the wolf telling this story?	Why did this war occur?
Making Connections	How does this little pigs story compare or contrast to the original?	How does the text description of Washington crossing the Delaware compare or contrast to the film we saw? To the article we read?
Visualizing	Is my mental picture of the wolf still good? Why should I change it?	What did an American soldier look like? A British soldier?
Knowing How Words Work	Does the word make sense in the sentence?	What clues in the text can I use to figure out the word *representation*?
Monitoring	Does what I'm reading make sense? If not, what can I do to clarify?	Does what I'm reading make sense? Did French soldiers fight in this war? How can I find out?
Summarizing	What has happened so far?	What is the most important information in the chapter?
Evaluating	Do I believe the wolf's story? Why? How does this story rank with other little pigs stories I've read?	How would my life be different if we had not won this war?

captures the students' emerging abilities and provides insights that may not be gleaned from independent settings (Minick, 1987). Dynamic assessment is also prevalent in portfolios because it provides an ongoing view of student growth.

Guided Comprehension connection: Assessment permeates the Guided Comprehension Model, occurring for multiple purposes in a variety of settings. Dynamic assessment provides insights into students' thinking as they engage in all stages of the Model. This, in turn, informs future teaching and learning.

The Guided Comprehension Model is dynamic in nature. It accommodates students' individual needs, employs a variety of texts and settings, and utilizes active, ongoing assessment. In Chapters 2, 3, and 4 we detail the stages of the Model: teacher-directed whole-group instruction, teacher-guided small groups and student-facilitated independent practice, and teacher-facilitated whole-group reflection and goal setting.

To learn more about discussion, motivation, and current reading research, read

Gambrell, L.B., & Almasi, J.F. (Eds.). (1996). *Lively discussions! Fostering engaged reading.* Newark, DE: International Reading Association.

Guthrie, J.T., & Alvermann, D. (Eds.). (1999). *Engaged reading: Processes, practices, and policy implications.* New York: Teachers College Press.

Kamil, M.L., Mosenthal, P.B., Pearson, P.D., & Barr, R. (Eds.). (2000). *Handbook of reading research* (Vol. 3). Mahwah, NJ: Erlbaum.

CHAPTER 2

Teacher-Directed Whole-Group Instruction

Reading means the world to me. It's who I am. If anyone ever took all of my books away and there weren't any left in the world, there would be no more me.

Emily Nadal, Grade 3

The first stage of the Guided Comprehension Model, teacher-directed whole-group instruction, is the focus of this chapter. Although the primary purpose of this segment of the Model is the direct instruction of comprehension strategies, we have structured the chapter to address the multiple purposes of Stage One:

- to provide a meaningful, comfortable context for a community of learners;
- to afford students access to multiple levels of authentic text, including those that may otherwise be viewed as challenging; and
- to teach comprehension strategies through direct instruction.

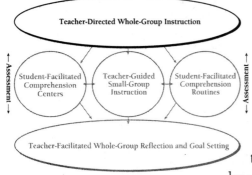

ORGANIZING FOR STAGE ONE

Guided Comprehension is a context that includes a variety of instructional settings, resources, and teaching methods. In Stage One of the Model, we use whole-group instruction to provide students with a positive sense of belonging to a community of learners. Student opportunities to interact with peers of mixed abilities afford additional advantages in this form of grouping. The sense of community also is fostered by student-teacher and student-peer interaction, print-rich environments, numerous opportunities to engage with authentic texts from a variety of genres, students who are active learners, and teachers who are knowledgeable about current best practice.

Because the instruction in Stage One is teacher-directed and allows us to fully support student learning, we can choose to teach from books that range in level from easy to challenging. For example, if we choose a text that is interesting to the students and works well when teaching a particular strategy but is challenging in nature, we can share it with students through a read-aloud. We may also select an easier text as the focus of the lesson because of the full teacher support that characterizes this stage.

ENGAGING IN DIRECT INSTRUCTION

In working with a wide variety of literacy professionals, we have heard many note that reading educators often describe teaching comprehension strategies as "going over" the strategies with students. Effectively teaching comprehension strategies requires more than "going over" these ideas; it requires direct instruction: explaining, demonstrating, guiding, practicing, and reflecting.

We use authentic text to explicitly teach comprehension strategies in Stage One. Assessment is a natural part of this process. The strategies that are incorporated into the Model are previewing (activating prior knowledge, predicting, and setting a purpose), self-questioning, making connections, visualizing, knowing how words work, monitoring, summarizing, and evaluating.

Steps in Direct Instruction

Regardless of the strategy being taught, the direct instruction process remains the same. It includes the following steps:

Explain the strategy. Describe how the strategy works and how it facilitates comprehension. For example, when introducing self-questioning, we ask students how they use questioning in their lives to help them understand. This creates a contextual framework for the strategy.

Demonstrate the strategy. One way to demonstrate strategies is by reading a selection aloud and using a Think-Aloud to share our ideas with our students. As we think aloud, we orally explain precisely what is triggering our thoughts and how it is affecting our understanding. (For a description of the Think-Aloud strategy, see Appendix A, page 133.) This can lead to the development of personal connections, questions for clarification, and refined predictions. When using the Think-Aloud process to demonstrate strategies, we need to explain our thinking so students have a clear idea of the cognitively active process readers experience as they transact with text. For example, when demonstrating self-questioning, we read a text selection and think aloud the questions that come to mind by stating the questions, why they occurred to us, and what responses we expect.

Guide the students to apply the strategy. Read the next section of the read-aloud text or a carefully chosen alternative, and ask the students to apply the strategy just taught. For example, if we modeled self-questioning, we would then read aloud a portion of the text and ask the students to create, orally or in writing, questions about the text. When the students are comfortable successfully composing and responding to questions, they can begin to work in small groups as we gradually relinquish control of the process.

Practice the strategy. Monitor as students work independently in small groups within the whole-group setting. Students use the strategy, in this case self-questioning, to compose and respond to questions using independent level text. Then encourage students to transact with text by using self-questioning when they are reading on their own.

Reflect on strategy use. Have students reflect on how using the strategy helped them to understand the text. Discuss students' reflections.

When engaging in direct instruction, we always focus on

- explaining what the strategy is and how it works;
- providing a good model through demonstration using Think-Aloud;
- offering students multiple opportunities to practice with our guidance;

- providing settings for group, paired, and independent practice; and
- affording opportunities to reflect on strategy use.

We also use multiple authentic assessments in this stage. These often include observation, discussion, and informal writing.

Throughout this stage, students' learning is scaffolded. When students learn how the strategy works, they have our total support. When they engage in guided practice, they have our support as necessary. When they apply the strategy independently, our support is diminished and the students are in control.

Comprehension Strategies: Focus on Teaching

During Stage One of the Model, we use a number of teaching ideas to clarify and reinforce students' understanding and application of the comprehension strategies. Although we initially use these ideas as frameworks for teaching, our goal is for students to eventually use them on their own. In this section, we explain each comprehension strategy and link it to a list of teaching ideas. These lists are not exhaustive, but they do include the ideas we use most frequently. In Appendix A, we examine each idea by describing its purposes and procedures, as well as its links to comprehension strategies, types of text, and reading stages.

Previewing. Previewing is a way of introducing the text. It includes activating background knowledge, predicting, and setting a purpose. The following teaching ideas support this strategy:

- Anticipation/Reaction Guide
- Predict-o-Gram
- Prereading Plan (PreP)
- Probable Passages
- Questioning the Text
- Semantic Map
- Storybook Introductions
- Story Impressions

Self-questioning. Self-questioning involves generating questions to guide thinking while reading. The ability to generate questions is a skill that underpins not only this strategy, but also many of the dimensions of transacting with text. For this reason we always use direct instruction to help our students learn how to generate questions.

When teaching students about questioning, we explain what questions are, discuss their purposes, and delineate their multiple levels. For example, we explain that there are many reasons for generating questions, including information-seeking, connected understanding, psychological and moral reconstruction, historical speculation, imagination, and research. We also immerse students in topics from multiple perspectives by reading, writing, speaking, listening, and viewing to foster their questioning abilities (Busching & Slesinger, 1995).

We teach students how to generate questions at four levels: memory, convergent, divergent, and evaluative. Chiardello (1998) suggests the following signal words and cognitive operations for each category:

Memory Questions

Signal words: *who, what, where, when*?

Cognitive operations: naming, defining, identifying, designating

Convergent Thinking Questions

Signal words: *why, how, in what ways*?

Cognitive operations: explaining, stating relationships, comparing and contrasting

Divergent Thinking Questions

Signal words: *imagine, suppose, predict, if/then*

Cognitive operations: predicting, hypothesizing, inferring, reconstructing

Evaluative Thinking Questions

Signal words: *defend, judge, justify/what do you think*?

Cognitive operations: valuing, judging, defending, justifying

When students become proficient in generating and responding to questions, they apply their knowledge to comprehension strategies, including self-questioning.

The following teaching ideas support self-questioning:

- "I Wonder" Statements
- K-W-L and K-W-L-S
- Paired Questioning
- Question-Answer Relationship (QAR)
- Thick and Thin Questions

Making connections. Making connections occurs when students think about the text in relation to connections they can make to self, to texts, and to others (Keene & Zimmerman, 1997). Teaching ideas that support this strategy include the following:

- Coding the Text: Text-Self (T-S), Text-Text (T-T), Text-World (T-W)
- Connection Stems: That reminds me of…, I remember when…
- Double-Entry Journal

- Drawing Connections
- Save the Last Word for Me

Visualizing.   Visualizing involves picturing in your mind what is happening in the text. Teaching ideas that support this strategy include the following:

- Gallery Images
- Graphic Organizers/Visual Organizers
- Guided Imagery
- Open-Mind Portrait
- Sketch to Stretch

Knowing how words work.   Knowing how words work refers to understanding words through strategic vocabulary development, including the use of graphophonic, syntactic, and semantic cueing systems to figure out unknown words. The graphophonic cueing system involves creating grapheme (written letter)-phoneme (sound) matches. The syntactic cueing system deals with the structure of the language. The semantic cueing system focuses on meaning. Readers use all three of these cueing systems, along with other knowledge of words, to effectively engage with text. Ideas that support this comprehension strategy include the following:

- Concept of Definition Map
- Context Clues
- Decoding by Analogy
- List-Group-Label
- Possible Sentences
- RIVET
- Semantic Feature Analysis
- Vocabulary by Analogy
- Vocabulary Self-Collection

Monitoring.   Monitoring involves asking, "Does this make sense?" and clarifying by adapting strategic processes to accommodate the response. Monitoring is knowing if meaning is being constructed and what to do if it is not. The following teaching ideas support this strategy:

- Bookmark Technique
- INSERT
- Patterned Partner Reading
- Say Something
- Think-Aloud

Summarizing. Summarizing involves extracting essential information—including the main idea and supporting details—from text. Teaching ideas that support this include the following:

- Bio-Pyramid
- Lyric Summaries
- Narrative Pyramid
- Paired Summarizing
- QuIP
- Retelling
- Summary Cubes

Evaluating. Evaluating means making judgments. The following teaching ideas support this strategy:

- Discussion Web
- Evaluative Questioning
- Journal Responses
- Meeting of the Minds
- Persuasive Writing

These strategies and teaching ideas provide the foundation for instruction in Guided Comprehension. It is important to note that although we have organized the teaching ideas by strategy, many of them can be used for more than one purpose. We also often contextualize them in larger teaching routines, which we describe in the next section.

COMPREHENSION ROUTINES

In Stage One we often use larger instructional frameworks. These include comprehension routines such as Questioning the Author, Reciprocal Teaching, Literature Circles, Directed Reading-Thinking Activity, and Directed Reading-Listening Activity. We teach these routines to the students through direct instruction, and when they become proficient they use them independently in Stage Two of Guided Comprehension. Questioning the Author, Reciprocal Teaching, and Literature Circles are delineated in this section. All five comprehension routines are presented in a step-by-step process in Appendix A.

Questioning the Author

Questioning the Author (QtA) (McKeown, Beck, & Worthy, 1993) is a text-based instructional format that helps students build a deeper understanding of texts by learning to query the author. This process helps readers engage with text by considering text ideas in-depth and using a "reviser's eye." QtA can be used with both narrative and expository texts (Beck, McKeown, Hamilton, & Kucan, 1997).

QtA empowers the reader to actively make something understandable. Students learn to construct personal meanings and therefore make texts understandable—something mature readers do when reading (McKeown et al., 1993). When using QtA, students learn that building understanding involves determining what information means, not just extracting it from the text (Beck et al., 1997). In other words, QtA strongly supports the view of reading as a thinking process.

Implementing QtA. For students to use QtA, we need to explicitly teach it. The Guided Comprehension Model provides opportunities not only for this direct teaching, but also for students' transfer and application. To teach students QtA, we follow these steps:

- Explain to students that sometimes readers do not understand what a text says because authors may leave out important details.
- Use an authentic text to model using questions to discern what the author really means. These questions, known as queries, are general probes used to initiate discussion. Queries are essential components of QtA and include the following (Beck et al., 1997):

  What is the author trying to tell us?

  What is meant by that?

  Why is the author telling us that?

  Did the author say it clearly?

  How could the author have said it better?

  Throughout the demonstration, read a portion of text and, using Think-Alouds, verbalize questions that could be posed to the author to help clarify the information presented. Then share possible responses. (See Appendix A, page 133, for details on the Think-Aloud.)

- Guide students to respond to the queries by contributing ideas that can later be refuted, revised, or challenged by other students and/or the teacher.
- Guide the class as a whole to participate in this questioning, and then provide opportunities for practice and transfer in small groups and pairs.
- Work collaboratively with students to discuss ideas and build an understanding of the text.
- Encourage students to reflect on how QtA helps them comprehend and how they can use it in other settings.

QtA helps students learn to ask questions as they read a text. They can work in pairs or small groups to talk about what ideas the author is trying to convey and whether the author has made the ideas clear. This cognitively active process helps students assume a responsible role in understanding text. When students become proficient in using QtA, they can use it with peers as a comprehension routine in Stage Two of the Guided Comprehension Model.

Text selection. Text choices for using QtA can be based on a number of factors. When demonstrating QtA for the class, the text should be one that encourages critical thinking and leaves questions to be answered. The following examples suggest ideas for selecting narrative and expository text:

- For a narrative text, a good choice would be one in which certain aspects of story elements are given, but others are implied. This may be related to plot structure, characterization, decision making, or theme. The goal is to use QtA to help students "read between the lines" and create understandings based on what they think the author meant.
- With an expository text, a good choice would be one that provides some of the information but assumes reader knowledge about other information. Using the QtA process, students can learn to identify what information is missing, implied, and/or needed in order to engage meaningfully with the text.

Another factor to consider when choosing a book to demonstrate QtA is students' background knowledge. It is important to be able to guide them through the process of generating questions for the author. To successfully create questions, students must have some knowledge of content and familiarity with levels of questioning. (For ideas about teaching students how to generate questions, see the discussion of self-questioning earlier in this chapter.)

Assessing QtA. Because assessment in QtA is based on the questions students ask and the conclusions they draw, observation is often the most effective method. We make notes about what the students say and do, which provides the impetus for more demonstrations about the process. (An observation checklist to facilitate this process is included in Appendix E, page 217.) We also ask students to reflect on their questions and subsequent understandings as a way to assess comprehension of the text. We use a self-reflection form to facilitate documentation and provide data for later lessons and demonstrations (see Appendix B, page 166).

After we demonstrate QtA with the whole class, we ask students to practice the process in small groups. An effective way to guide this practice is to provide groups with the same text and guide them through the process of reading, querying, discussing responses in groups, and sharing answers with the class. We scaffold this process until students grasp how to generate the queries. Then we can turn over the responsibility to the students in the group, providing assistance as needed. As the students engage in this process, we observe and probe, helping them move through the text. Once the students understand how to question the author, they can engage in the process independently during comprehension routines.

The process of Questioning the Author helps students become independent thinkers during reading. It promotes questioning and connecting and encourages students to construct understandings in a social context.

Reciprocal Teaching

Reciprocal Teaching is a strategy-based technique that involves discussion of a text based on four comprehension strategies: predicting, questioning, clarifying, and summarizing. The students, as well as the teacher, take on the role of "teacher" in leading the discussion about the text (Palincsar & Brown, 1984).

Reciprocal Teaching has three purposes:

1. to help students participate in a group effort to bring meaning to a text,

2. to teach students that the reading process requires continual use of the four strategies (predicting, questioning, clarifying, summarizing) for effective comprehension, and

3. to provide students with the opportunity to monitor their own learning and thinking.

Implementing Reciprocal Teaching. In order to successfully implement the Reciprocal Teaching procedure, we use direct instruction. The following steps facilitate this process:

- Explain the procedure and each of the four strategies that are part of the dialogue.

- Model thinking related to each of the four strategies using an authentic text and Think-Alouds.

- Within the whole-group setting, guide students to engage in similar types of thinking by providing responses for each of the strategies using verbal prompts, such as those suggested by Mowery (1995):

    Predicting:

        I think _____

        I bet _____

        I wonder _____

        I imagine _____

        I suppose _____

        I predict _____

    Questioning:

        What connections can I make?

        How does this support my thinking?

Clarifying:

I did not understand the part where _____

I need to know more about_____

Summarizing:

The important ideas in what I read are _____

- Place the students in groups of four and provide each group with a text to read and use as the basis of their Reciprocal Teaching.
- Assign one of the four strategies and suggested prompts to each group member.
- Have students engage in Reciprocal Teaching using the process modeled.
- Provide time and forms for students to reflect on the process and their comprehension (see Appendix B). This leads to further goal setting.

This process provides students with opportunities to share their thinking in a reciprocal fashion. While students are participating in their groups, we can monitor their activity and scaffold the dialogue when appropriate. Once the students are skilled at using Reciprocal Teaching, they can use it as an independent comprehension routine.

Studies by Palincsar and Brown (1984) demonstrate that students with a wide variety of abilities can use Reciprocal Teaching successfully. Although originally designed to help students who could decode well but had weak comprehension skills, Reciprocal Teaching benefits all students because it allows them to read, effectively use the strategies, and understand more challenging texts.

Text selection. The level of the text is determined by students' abilities and the instructional setting in which Reciprocal Teaching is being used. Narrative texts should have complex story lines that require critical thinking. Expository texts should have complex organizations and enough information for students to distinguish essential from nonessential content.

Assessing Reciprocal Teaching. We can assess students in Reciprocal Teaching groups by observing their conversations and documenting their ability to successfully execute the strategies. (An observation checklist for Reciprocal Teaching is included in Appendix E, page 218.) Students may use a form to self-reflect on their contributions (see Appendix B) or they may keep notes of the ideas they contributed in their Guided Comprehension Journals. Guided Comprehension Journals are used for recording students' ideas. They can be any kind of notebook. Students use the journals in all stages of the Model. For example, when engaging in Reciprocal Teaching, students can use their journals to record ideas, to respond to prompts, or to reflect on new insights. This information promotes discussion and informs future instruction.

Literature Circles

Groups of students can share their insights, questions, and interpretations of the same or similar texts in Literature Circles. The basic goal of using Literature Circles is to help students converse about texts in meaningful, personal, and thoughtful ways (Brabham & Villaume, 2000).

Implementing Literature Circles. To facilitate students' use of Literature Circles, we need to explicitly teach the concept and engage in active demonstration. Brabham and Villaume (2000) caution against a "cookie-cutter" approach to implementing Literature Circles and instead recommend designing and using them in ways that emerge from our students' needs and challenges. These circles may not all have the same format, but they all encourage the implementation of grand conversations about the texts (Peterson & Eeds, 1990). Although the procedural decisions about the implementation of Literature Circles need to emerge from specific classrooms, there are some guidelines that do facilitate their use.

It is important to remember that the students' personal interpretations drive the discussion. There is not a list of questions to be answered, but rather a focus on students' inquiries, connections, and interpretations. We may need to model how to converse in critical ways by doing some class demonstrations or using Think-Alouds.

Daniels (1994) and Tompkins (2001) suggest guiding principles for using Literature Circles. We have incorporated their ideas into our process for direct instruction, which includes the following steps:

- Explain that Literature Circles are discussion formats for sharing meaningful ideas about books that group members have selected to read. Note that groups are formed based on book selections and meet on a regular basis according to predetermined schedules.

- Demonstrate how Literature Circles work by describing one and thinking out loud for the class. Use an overhead to share responses from the perspective of roles used in Literature Circles. Think aloud about how the information students recorded contributes to the discussion.

- Guide students to engage in Literature Circles by having students form groups and choose roles. Read aloud another brief text and encourage students to jot or sketch notes or reactions they have in their Guided Comprehension Journals. Then guide students to use the information they recorded to facilitate their discussions. Monitor students' abilities to engage in meaningful discussion. Support or prompt as needed. Discuss the process with the whole group.

- Practice by having students self-select brief texts and engage in Literature Circles.

• Reflect on Literature Circles and how they help us comprehend by facilitating discussion of text.

Choice, literature, and response are Tompkins's (2001) suggestions for the key features of Literature Circles.

Choice. Students make many choices within the framework of Literature Circles: They choose the books they will read, the group they will join, the schedule of their reading, and the direction of the conversation. We can set the parameters for students to make these choices by providing a variety of texts for student selection, setting minimum daily or weekly reading requirements, and prompting ideas for conversations. However, the ultimate responsibility for the group rests with the students.

Literature. The books from which the students choose should be high-quality, authentic literature that relates to their experiences. Texts should also help students make personal connections and prompt critical reflection (Brabham & Villaume, 2000). The books should include interesting stories with well-developed characters, rich language, and relevant themes that are engaging, meaningful, and interesting for students (Noe & Johnson, 1999; Samway & Wang, 1996).

Response. After reading, students gather in their small group to share understandings from the text and make personal connections. This public sharing, in the form of a conversation, helps students broaden their interpretations and gain new perspectives from the other group members.

Organizing and managing Literature Circles. There are several ways to structure and manage Literature Circles. There is no "right" way, but rather choices must be made to accommodate the needs and challenges of each student in the class. Any of the existing plans for Literature Circles may be used to create successful formats (see Figure 3). Once we have determined a meaningful plan, we make decisions about text choice, forming groups, and structuring the conversations.

Text selection. Texts for Literature Circles can be novels, picture books, poetry books, magazine articles, information books, or selections from anthologies. Students in Literature Circles may read the same text, similar texts about the same theme, or a variety of theme-related genres on multiple levels. The material that is selected will need to accommodate a wide range of student interests and abilities.

There are several ways to select texts for Literature Circles. One way is to choose books that relate to a theme, topic, genre, or author (Noe & Johnson, 1999). When using this method we choose several texts on varying levels and the students make reading choices based on interest and ability. Another way to select text is to create collections of text sets related to a theme or topic (Short, Harste, & Burke, 1996). Texts within each set are related but can vary in levels

Figure 3. Literature Circle Formats

OPTION 1 (Daniels, 1994)
Roles:

Required	*Optional*
Discussion director	Researcher
Literary luminary/passage master	Summarizer/essence extractor
Connector	Character captain
Illustrator/artful artist	Vocabulary enricher/word master
	Travel tracer/scene setter

Books: All participants use the same text.
Process:
- Meet to set reading goals.
- Read independently, complete role sheets.
- Meet to discuss role sheets and other text connections.
- Set new reading goals, rotate roles.
- Read independently, complete role sheets.
- Meet to discuss role sheets and other text connections.

Continue this process until finished.
Celebrate by class sharing of project related to the book.

OPTION 2 (Klein, 1995)
Books: Teacher selects and introduces several according to theme; students make choices.
Group: Teacher composes groups based on student text choices.
Process:
- Groups meet, choose format for reading: whole group—read aloud; independently—silently
- Weekly—each group reads 4 days, responds 2 days, meets to talk about the book 1 day.
- Groups prepare response projects to share books with the class.

of difficulty. Students select the theme or topic and then choose the reading material from within that set. For example, text sets might focus on the theme of survival, include a variety of versions of a fairy tale, or be comprised of a group of biographies. A third way to choose reading material is to allow students to self-select from a predetermined list of titles.

Introducing text. After selecting the texts to be used in Literature Circles, we introduce the books to readers. Although there are various methods for doing this, we have found these two to be especially effective:

Book talks: This is a short oral overview of the book, focusing on the genre, the main characters, and the plot.

Book pass: Several books are passed among students. Each peruses a book for a few minutes, noting the title, reading the book cover, and leafing through the opening chapter. If the students find a book appealing, they jot the title in their notebook and pass the book to the next person. After previewing several titles, students make choices. Groups are formed on the basis of book selections.

It is important to remember that we may need to guide some students in making appropriate text choices. If text sets are used, we will want to introduce the theme of the set and the kinds of texts that are in it. If selections are used from an anthology, we can use them as the basis for book talks.

Grand conversations: Schedules, talk, and roles. Once the
groups are formed, students meet and develop a schedule to determine how much they will read and to create meeting deadlines. At first, we can provide the schedule as a way to model how to set these goals. After reading goals have been set, students read independently or with a buddy. At the designated group meeting time, the students gather to discuss the texts. Notes from their reading that have been recorded in their Guided Comprehension Journals inform this discussion. Prior to this point we model how to respond to text and how to use these responses to get the group conversations started.

The time spent in Literature Circles varies by length of text, but usually 10 to 20 minutes is sufficient. We can use a minilesson to demonstrate a particular literary element—such as plot, theme, or characterization—on which the students may focus their discussion. It is important, though, that we allow each group's conversation to evolve on its own.

Gilles (1998) has identified four types of talk that often occur during Literature Circles: (1) talk about the book, (2) talk about the reading process, (3) talk about connections, and (4) talk about group process and social issues. Teachers can encourage all types of talk with demonstrations and gentle prompts during the Literature Circle conversations.

Some teachers prefer to use assigned roles and responsibilities as a way to guide the conversations. Daniels (1994) has found that the following roles, which students rotate, provide a wide level of conversation within the Literature Circle:

Discussion director—takes on the leadership of the group and guides the discussion. Responsibilities include choosing topics for discussion, generating questions, convening the meeting, and facilitating contributions from all members.

Literary luminary/passage master—helps students revisit the text. Responsibilities include selecting memorable or important sections of the text and reading them aloud expressively.

Connector—guides the students to make connections with the text. Responsibilities include sharing text-self, text-text, and text-world connections and encouraging others to do the same.

Illustrator/artful artist—creates a drawing or other symbolic response to text. Responsibilities include making the visual response and using it to encourage others to contribute to the conversation.

The advantage of using these roles is that they represent response in a variety of learning modes, including linguistic, dramatic, and visual. The disadvantage is that this structure may stifle responses. We have found that starting with clearly defined roles and then relaxing or relinquishing them as the students gain competence in Literature Circles is effective. Daniels (1994) concurs, noting that role-free discussions are the ultimate goal.

Assessment in Literature Circles. There are several ways to assess the students' comprehension, contributions, and cooperation within Literature Circles. Options include self-reflection, observation, and response sheets or journal entries.

- Students may self-reflect on their contributions to the circle. Students can reflect on their contributions to the group and the group's ability to function. To record this information, we can provide forms for students to complete (see Appendix B).

- Although the students meet independently, we can observe their conversations and make anecdotal notes or keep a checklist of the content and depth of discussions. For example, we can note who is contributing to the discussion; if full participation is lacking, we can use this data to teach the students additional ways to include all members. We can also observe the scope of the discussion. If the students are focused on basic recall of story events, we can choose to do a minilesson on making meaningful connections with texts.

- Students' response sheets or book journals provide another opportunity for assessment. In this format students take notes about the text, document understandings, and make personal connections to bring to the discussion. These written artifacts provide a window into the students' thinking about the text.

The most important thing to remember about assessment in Literature Circles is to use the assessment results. These should influence future instructional decisions.

Using teaching routines such as Questioning the Author, Reciprocal Teaching, and Literature Circles not only provides us with frameworks for teaching, but also helps students understand how these routines work. When students become proficient, they can use QtA, Reciprocal Teaching, or Literature Circles as independent comprehension routines in Stage Two of the Model.

When reviewing the components of the Guided Comprehension Model, it is important to acknowledge that in addition to daily whole-group instruction in

Stage One, all students participate in teacher-guided small groups and experience small-group, paired, and independent practice and transfer on a regular basis. This assures that students transact with multiple levels of text in a variety of settings.

Once Stage One of the Model is completed, the class progresses to Stage Two, which is the focus of the next chapter. This stage is comprised of three different instructional settings: teacher-directed small groups, student-facilitated comprehension centers, and student-facilitated comprehension routines.

To learn more about Questioning the Author, Literature Circles, and Reciprocal Teaching, read

Beck, I.L., McKeown, M.G., Hamilton, R.L., & Kucan, L. (1997). *Questioning the author: An approach for enhancing student engagement with text*. Newark, DE: International Reading Association.

Daniels, H. (1994). *Literature circles: Voice and choice in the student-centered classroom*. York, ME: Stenhouse.

Palincsar, A.S., & Brown, A.L. (1986). Interactive teaching to promote independent learning from text. *The Reading Teacher, 39*, 771–777.

CHAPTER 3

Teacher-Guided Small Groups and Student-Facilitated Independent Practice

Reading means an only-in-your-mind adventure told by words. Sometimes I feel like I'm in the book. I experience what's happening in the book because I can relate to a lot of things in it.

Korin Butler, Grade 6

I n this chapter we delineate Stage Two of the Guided Comprehension Model. Although the primary purpose of this segment of the Model is student application, we have designed the chapter to address the multiple purposes of Stage Two:

- to provide meaningful, comfortable settings for a community of learners;
- to afford students a variety of opportunities to apply strategies; and
- to provide students with occasions to work with teacher support, with peer support, and independently.

ORGANIZING FOR STAGE TWO

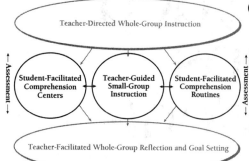

In Stage Two of Guided Comprehension, students are in three different instructional settings: teacher-guided small groups, student-facilitated comprehension centers, and student-facilitated comprehension routines. In this stage we provide students with opportunities to apply the comprehension strategies in a variety of settings with varying levels of support. Texts in this stage vary from the instructional level texts used in the teacher-guided small groups to the independent level texts used when students work independently in comprehension centers and routines.

Because students are working in three different settings in this stage, having an organizational plan is essential. One way to manage this time is to use a chart that illustrates the settings in which students should be at given times (see Figure 4). Other organizational plans can be found in Appendix B.

TEACHER-GUIDED SMALL-GROUP INSTRUCTION

Although Stage Two of Guided Comprehension is characterized by three different settings, only one is teacher-guided. In this small-group setting, students of similar abilities apply their knowledge of strategies to leveled texts to become active, engaged readers. Students are dynamically grouped and progress at individual rates, changing groups as they become prepared to transact with increasingly challenging levels of text.

When organizing for teacher-guided small-group instruction, we need to consider the following factors:

- All students in the group need to have similar instructional levels; this means that all students in this Guided Comprehension setting should be able to read the same texts with some teacher support.
- What we are teaching is determined by students' needs and use of strategies while constructing meaning.

Figure 4. Organizing for Stage Two

Centers	Session 1	Session 2
Partner Reading	▢ ▢ ▢ ▢	▢ ▢ ▢ ▢
Mystery	▢ ▢ ▢	▢ ▢ ▢
Poetry	▢ ▢ ▢	▢ ▢ ▢
Making and Writing Words	▢ ▢	▢ ▢
Writing	▢ ▢ ▢	▢ ▢ ▢

Routines	Session 1	Session 2
Literature Circles	▢ ▢ ▢ ▢	▢ ▢ ▢ ▢
Reciprocal Teaching	▢ ▢ ▢	▢ ▢ ▢
Questioning the Author	▢ ▢ ▢	▢ ▢ ▢

Teacher-Guided Small Groups		
	▢ ▢ ▢ ▢ ▢ ▢	▢ ▢ ▢ ▢ ▢ ▢

• While teaching in this setting, we also need to monitor students who are working independently.

Once the small groups are formed and the appropriate texts are matched to students' abilities (see Chapter 6 for assessments to facilitate grouping; see Chapter 5 for text leveling processes), we meet with one or more guided small groups every day. During our time with the students, we use the Guided Comprehension small-group lesson format, which progresses in the following manner:

Review previously taught strategies and focus on the strategy of the day.

Guide the students to apply the strategy of the day, as well as previously taught strategies, as they read a section of the instructional level text. Prompt the students to construct personal meanings. Scaffold as necessary, gradually releasing support as students become more proficient. Encourage discussion and repeat with other sections of text.

Practice by having students work in pairs or individually to apply the strategies. Have students record their applications in their Guided Comprehension Journals and share them during reflection in either small group or whole group.

Reflect and extend by having students share ways in which the strategy helped them to understand the text. Talk about ways in which students can apply the strategy in the comprehension centers and routines.

Review the Strategies

Each guided group begins with the teacher reminding students about strategies that have been taught previously. It is helpful to have these posted on a chart in the classroom or to have them listed on a bookmark or other quick reference for the students. This review serves to remind students and also helps them prepare for what is expected of them as they read; our goal is for students to build a repertoire of strategies they will use to facilitate their construction of meaning. After this quick review, our focus shifts to revisiting the strategy taught in that day's whole-group setting.

Guide Students

We begin by introducing the text and helping students preview. Then each student reads silently or in whisper tones a designated portion of the text. We sometimes ask the students to read in whisper tones so we can check for fluency and observe strategy use. During reading we guide students to use all appropriate comprehension strategies. After reading, we guide the students to discuss understandings. To facilitate this, we may revisit predictions, verbalize connections, or share visualizations. We may ask "What does this remind you of?" "Have you ever had an experience like this?" "How is this character like...?" We can also revisit students' original predictions and have students determine why their thinking has changed or remained the same. After this, the students read another pre-determined section of the text and stop for more guided discussion.

Practice

When we believe the students are actively engaging with the text and constructing meaning, we have them practice. For example, we may have them finish reading the text independently and then discuss it with members of the small group. If the text appears challenging for the students, we may continue guiding their comprehension until they are more successful.

Reflect and Extend

The final component of the Guided Comprehension group is to discuss the text as a whole. Students may make personal responses, retell portions of the text, share new information or insights, or reread favorite or interesting parts. This is also when we guide students to make broader connections to other texts and extend their understandings. These may be documented through writing, drawing, dramatization, or oral discourse. This is a good time for us to observe student responses and connections; this information will inform dynamic grouping, future student-text matches, and instructional planning. During discussion, it is important to ask students to reflect on their reading and review the strategies they used to make sense of the text. This will remind students to transfer what they have learned in whole-group instruction and in their Guided Comprehension small groups to their reading of other texts. The Guided Comprehension Model provides students with two settings for such independent practice: comprehension centers and comprehension routines. These components are detailed in the next two sections of this chapter.

STUDENT-FACILITATED COMPREHENSION CENTERS

Comprehension centers provide purposeful, authentic activities that students can engage in either individually or in small groups. Activities in these centers emerge from balanced literacy and promote the integration of reading, writing, and discussion. The centers are related to the texts students are reading and the strategies and skills that have been taught in whole-group settings.

The centers offer multiple ways in which students can practice various aspects of comprehension. They are usually located around the perimeter of the classroom and away from the Guided Comprehension area. They vary in appearance from a table-top display to file folders, pizza boxes, or gift bags. It is important to remember that the content of the center is more important than its physical appearance.

Students can move from center to center in a variety of ways, depending on the structure of the literacy schedule and the independence of the students. One way to organize the center time is to use a chart that provides a visual organizational system of the day (see Figure 4, page 39). This chart shows where each student is during Stage Two. Center options are included on the chart and student names can be placed in the spaces provided. The number of students who may work at a given center or at a given activity is designated. For example, there are three designated spaces provided on the chart for the poetry center; therefore, three students may choose that center. When students complete their work at the poetry center, they may move on. For example, a student may write a poem at the poetry center and then choose to work on a project at the research center. This assures that student choice is being accommodated on multiple levels: They can choose what goals they are trying to achieve that day, which centers to visit, how long to stay, and how to manage their time. We can also provide students with a framework for required and optional centers (see Appendix B, page 186). Sometimes we may choose to assign students to the centers where they will start and then students can move as they complete their tasks, and there are openings at other centers.

Some teachers prefer to move the students using a rotational schedule. With this, students move periodically among three or four activities (see Appendix B, page 169). This rotational format provides maximum control by the teacher, but limits students' opportunities for choice and learning to manage their own time.

Student Accountability

It is important to have accountability for the time students spend at the centers. It is helpful for the teacher to have a record-keeping system to keep track of what centers each student visits during the week. We can use a whole-group chart to monitor who visits which centers each week, or we can place charts at individual centers for students to record their visits. Students may also keep track of their work in their Guided Comprehension Journals, or they can use response sheets to self-reflect on what they have learned at each center and how they have progressed toward their goal for the day (see Appendix B, page 167).

We can keep student work and reflections in a two-pocket folder and review them weekly or biweekly. Students can also share their work in individual conferences. Including a rubric or other evaluative tool at each center facilitates this process (see Appendix B, page 168).

Ideas for Creating Comprehension Centers

Many activities can be completed in comprehension centers. We believe the most important thing to remember is that these activities should be helpful in the students' development or application of using comprehension strategies. We use several types of centers when implementing the Guided Comprehension Model.

Some centers may be specific to a content area being studied or to a genre of books the students are reading. These may include projects, literature extensions, or research directly related to the topics. Other centers may be permanent throughout the year, except to change their themes and resources. For example, we have an alphabet book center, in which students create their own books. During the course of the year, the topic of this center as well as the resources provided could change from whales to deserts, depending on current content area study.

During comprehension center time, students can work independently or in small groups to complete projects, research, or extensions related to the topics they are studying or the books they are reading. We like to provide a structure for these projects, but we make sure that the activity is open-ended to allow for students to apply thinking and personal interpretations. Some suggestions for centers and accompanying open-ended projects, extensions, and research activities are listed here.

Making books center. Students can retell key events from stories, gather data and create reports on content area topics, or write creative pieces that can be published. These pieces may be self-created or follow a familiar structure, such as alphabet books or biographies. The following is a list of books and suggestions for using them (see Appendix B, page 173, for directions for making books):

Accordion books: retellings, content area facts, creative stories with illustrations

Origami books: retellings, facts, short stories, story elements

Flip/flap books: word work (parts of speech, antonyms, synonyms, rhymes, story elements, prefixes/suffixes), story elements, character traits

Slotted books: journals, reading response, word books, alphabet books

Dos à dos books: dialogue or buddy journals, research and report, compare/contrast

Stair-step books: riddle books, sequence story events, time lines

Pattern book center. Students use a pattern from a familiar book and retell their story or share information using the pattern. Some effective patterns to use are from *Fortunately* (1993) by Remy Charlip, *The Important Book* (1990) by Margaret Wise Brown, *Animal Fact/Animal Fable* (1979) by Seymour Simon, or any alphabet book. We have found it helpful to provide specific organizers to help students plan these books (see Appendix B, pages 180–182).

Art center. Provide materials and specific art techniques for students to use to demonstrate understandings of texts or illustrate original books. Have a variety of materials and examples of specific art techniques (drawing, collage, painting, printmaking, puppetry, etc.) handy at this center. We like to include the following materials:

- All kinds of paper—colored, lined, construction, large, textured, adhesive notes
- All kinds of writing and illustrating utensils—markers, crayons, paints, colored pencils, pencils, water colors
- Scraps of fabric
- Glue sticks, white glue, tape
- Scissors—straight and patterned, hole punches
- Stamps—textures, symbols, designs, alphabet
- Printmaking supplies
- Wire, yarn, sticks
- Magazines, catalogs

We encourage and teach students how to use materials at the art center to visually represent their ideas and create illustrations for the texts they are writing.

Writing center. This is a place for free and structured writing. Students who are motivated to write can take pieces through various writing stages. You may also structure the writing using one or more of the following strategies:

Patterned Writing: Provide forms based on pattern books, poetry, fractured fairy tales, and nursery rhymes (see Appendix B, pages 183–184 for poetry form).

Story Bag: Put a variety of items in a bag. Students pull out one item at a time and build a story using these props to stimulate thinking.

Sticker or Stamp Stories: Use stickers or stamps to create an illustration with action. Write a story to accompany the picture.

Journals:

Free writing: Students write daily about self-selected topics.

Prompted writing: Students write about provided topics.

Story Impressions: Students write a story based on approximately 10 clues from a story. Each clue is from 1 to 5 words. The clues are placed sequentially and connected with downward arrows. The title of the original story may or may not be shared. When the story is completed and the student shares his or her story, the original author's story is read for comparison or contrast (see Appendix A, page 118).

Story Collages: Instead of writing a story and then illustrating it, students create textured illustrations first and then develop stories based on them. Because the illustrations are textured (using pine cones, aluminum foil, felt, sand), students can use their tactile modalities (Brown, 1993).

Vocabulary center. This center might have a word wall or other display of words that can be the focus of study. These words may be structurally similar (rhymes, prefix, suffix, roots) or may be theme related. This may also include interesting word books (such as *The Weighty Word Book* [1990] by Paul Levitt, *Anamalia* [1996] by Graeme Base, or books by Fred Gwynne, Ruth Heller, or Marvin Terban) that can provide the impetus for word study. Students work on learning, using, and making connections to these new vocabulary words. The following is a list of activities students can complete at the vocabulary center:

Word Sorts: Students sort vocabulary words into categories provided by the teacher (closed sort) or by self-selected categories (open sort). These might include rhyming words, parts of speech, vowel sound, syllables, and specific content subtopics. This may be completed in a hands-on fashion using word cards, and then students can record on a word-sort sheet. This activity also may be completed in writing on a web or other organized structure.

Word Storm: A visual display—such as a picture from a book, a piece of art, or a poster—provides the impetus for word brainstorming. Students look at the visual, and brainstorm and record words that come to mind. Then they use some or all the words to create a detailed sentence or paragraph about the visual.

Word Bingo: Students put 16 vocabulary words on a Bingo sheet. Clues—such as definitions, synonyms, antonyms, or rhymes—are listed on cards and placed in a bag or box. One at a time, a student pulls out a card, reads the clue, and students cover the word with a marker. The first student to get four in a row wins.

Acrostics: Students write the name of a topic or character vertically and then write words or phrases to describe the topic, each description starting with one of the letters in the name. The focus can include characters, places, people, or any other topic related to areas of study. The following is a seventh-grade acrostic based on Anne Frank:

Another Holocaust victim

Not deserving of how she was treated

Noted her feelings in her diary

Ever interested in life

Friend to Peter

Reflective

Amsterdam was her home

Never had a chance to grow old

Knowledgeable

Students can use acrostics to retell key events of a story in sequential order. The following example on Goldilocks was developed by a third-grade student:

G goes for a walk

O on her own in the woods

L looks in the cottage

D dines on porridge

I investigates the rest of the house

L lounges in baby's chair

O opens the door to the bedroom

C catches some Z's in the baby's bed

K knows bears see her

S screams and runs away

Word Riddles: Students can make riddles for others to solve. The process includes

- choosing your answer to the riddle,

- finding synonyms for words in the answer, and

- substituting the synonyms for the words in this question: What do you call a _____ _____?

> *Examples:*
>
> Hink Pink
>
> > Answer = chunky monkey
> >
> > Riddle = What do you call a plump primate?
>
> Homophones
>
> > Answer = sail sale
> >
> > Riddle = What do you call a canvas bargain?
>
> Alliteration
>
> > Answer = dainty daffodil
> >
> > Riddle = What do you call a delicate jonquil?

Invent a Word: Students use their knowledge of prefixes, suffixes, and roots to create new words and their meanings.

Reading response center. Students respond to texts they are reading in a journal or on a graphic organizer. Sometimes we prompt with specific stems or questions connecting to the strategy lesson that day; other times we encourage a free response.

Example stem: This text reminds me of _____ because _____.

Example question: What did you think was most important in the story? Why?

We keep a fresh list of literature response prompts at this center. These can be used at any time for responding to text. Students can then share responses in small groups and during the whole-group reflection time. These responses also may be turned in as documentation of thinking and connections.

Making and writing words center. For making and writing words (Rasinski, 1999), we use a mystery word related to the theme we are studying and provide the letters in random order on a chart or on a sheet for recording words. Students use the letters to make as many words as they can. Younger students may need to manipulate letter cards or tiles as they begin to make words; older student can write them as they think of them. We can provide clues to specific words or just let the students create as many as they can (see Appendix B, page 177). For example, if we are studying life cycles, we might use the word *caterpillar* as the mystery word. Then we would ask the students to make and write as many words as they can using the letters in that word. These words can be recorded for future use.

- Two-letter words: *at, it*
- Three-letter words: *cat, rat, pat, pit, lit, car, par, tar, all, ill, lip, tip, rip, air, act, ape, are, arc, art*
- Four-letter words: *rate, late, care, rare, pare, pear, pair, tall, call, clip, trip, pill, pact, cape, ripe, cart, race*
- Five-letter words: *trail, liter, alert, peril, price, alter, plate, trial, pleat, pearl, petal, relic, taper, crate, crept, crier, lilac, alert, later*
- Six-letter words: *pillar, carpet, pirate, taller, triple, parcel, caller, cellar, crater*
- Seven-letter words: *trailer, erratic*

Poetry center. Keep a large supply of poetry books and poetry cards at this center. Have lots of copies of poems that students can read, act out, or illustrate. The following is a list of activities our students enjoy completing at the poetry center:

Poetry Theater: In small groups, students plan and practice dramatizing a poem. These dramatizations include minimal theatrics and props, and maximum expression through voice and actions.

Poetry Frames: Students create their own versions of published poems. We create frames in which students can write their own words, keeping the structure but changing the content of the original poem. (A poetry frame for "If I Were in Charge of the World" is included in Appendix B, page 175.)

Poetry Forms: Students create their own poems using structured formats. Provide blacklines and examples including bio-poems, cinquains, and diamantes (see Appendix B, pages 183–184).

Poem Impressions: Students write poems based on a series of clues provided from an existing poem. Then students share their poems. Finally, the original poem is read and discussion focuses on comparison or contrast of the impressions and the original poem.

Research center. Students work on research specific to content literacy studies. Various reference materials, from encyclopedias to books to the Internet, are readily available. Our students' favorite research center activities include the following:

Data Disks (Lindquist, 1995): Students collect data and record it on a disk with predetermined subtopics. For example, a data disk about a state might include the name of the state; the state motto, symbols, and flowers; population; natural resources; leading businesses; major cities; famous residents; or historical significance. Data disks can be used to write paragraphs or create exhibitions.

The Classroom Times: Students write a variety of newspaper articles related to the topic and publish in a newspaper format; write an article and contribute to a class newspaper; or create "period" newspapers (e.g., history or geographic or the setting of a novel).

Press Conference (McLaughlin, 2000b): This is an inquiry-based activity that promotes oral communication. Students choose a topic to investigate, then peruse newspapers, magazines, or the Internet to find at least two sources of information about the topic. After reading the articles, focusing on essential points, raising questions, and reflecting on personal insights, the student presents an informal summary of his or her research to a group of classmates or the entire class. Members of the audience raise questions that can lead to "I Wonder" Statements that they can record in their investigative journals.

Questions Into Paragraphs (QuIP): Students ask questions related to a chosen topic and use two or more sources to find answers to each question. The information is recorded on a QuIP graphic organizer and then used to write a summary paragraph or to organize research for a press conference (see Appendix A, page 161).

ReWrite (Bean, 2000): In this activity students write songs before and after content area study. For example, students write a song based on what they think they know about bats. Then they read to learn about bats and rewrite their lyrics based on the new information. The rewrite represents how students' knowledge, perceptions, and feelings have changed after studying the topic. Tunes may include familiar songs or instrumental tapes.

The Rest of the Story (McLaughlin, 2000b): This inquiry-based investigation encourages the researcher to go beyond the basic facts generally known about a person, discovery, invention, or event in content area study. For example, students could choose a famous inventor such as Alexander Graham Bell and use The Rest of the Story to learn about his life. Students use numerous resources to locate information, including the Internet. Technology also plays a role in the way students choose to format their investigations to share them with the class; they may elect to design a home page or create software. Audiotapes or videotapes are other popular formatting selections. When using videotapes, students may report their research as a news story or choose to dramatize the results of their investigation.

Genre center. We maintain a genre center that changes as the year progresses. Examples of topics include science fiction, biography, folk tales, mythology, historical or realistic fiction, legends, fantasy, mysteries, or poetry. For examples of how to create a genre center, see the mystery center and poetry center sections.

Mystery center. Students use the mystery center to engage in inquiry-based learning and problem solving. When using this center, students question, read, write, solve, and dramatize to extend their understandings.

Create-a-Mystery: Label bags or boxes with the major components of a mystery (i.e., suspects, clues, victims, detectives, criminals, motives, crimes, and crime scenes). The students will record on index cards examples of each from mystery novels they have read. Then they will place the index cards in the appropriate bag or box. Other students will select one index card from each box and use that information to create another mystery. After writing their mystery, they can illustrate it and share it with the class. The students can extend this activity by participating in a mystery theater.

Suspicious Suspects: The students will organize their thoughts of the suspects in a novel by completing the suspect organizer (see Appendix B, page 179). Based on the clues, the students can easily come to a conclusion about who committed the crime. This organizer also can be completed before writing a mystery.

Write Your Own Mystery: The students will use the Write Your Own Mystery graphic organizer to help create a new mystery story (see Appendix B, page 189). On the organizer they will draw, describe, or explain the crime scene. They will write four clues and describe a main character. They will also write a brief description of how the mystery is solved. The students may also use this activity to retell mysteries they have read. As an alternative writing activity, students can read the introduction to *The Mysteries of Harris Burdick* and choose a picture and story starter from the book. Then they can either write a solution to what happened to Harris Burdick or write a story based on the picture they selected. Figure 5 contains a mystery that Erin Riley, a seventh-grade student, wrote based on a Harris Burdick picture and story starter.

Poetry: Using different poetry formats such as cinquain, diamante, bio-poem, and definition poems, have students write about various aspects of a mystery novel (see Appendix B, pages 183–184, for poetry forms). Students can then use their poems for a poetry theater presentation.

Acrostics: Students can write an acrostic about one of the suspects in a mystery novel. The name can be written vertically. The letters in the suspect's name can be starters for the clues related to this suspect.

Mystery Pyramid: Students can summarize or manipulate language by trying to fit all the elements of a mystery into a Mystery Pyramid (see Appendix B, page 178).

Figure 5. Mystery Center Seventh-Grade Writing Sample

Mr. Linden's Library

He had warned her about the book. Now it was too late. Mr. Linden, a librarian, had given a lady a book from his library. Mr. Linden had warned her about this book for some reason. This book had a mystery about it. There was something unusual about it that was different from all of the other books.

So the lady had checked the book out of the library, and brought it home. Later that night, as she was lying in bed she picked up this unusual book, and began to read it. All of a sudden, she got a weird feeling throughout her body. She stopped breathing. She wasn't moving anymore. She was dead.

At the end of the third week of June, the library book that the lady had checked out of the library was due back. But she never brought the book back, because she was dead. Mr. Linden did not know this.

One week later, Mr. Linden had looked up her information in the computer. He had found, and wrote down her information on a piece of notebook paper. Then Mr. Linden called her home phone number. He waited. After four rings, there was no answer. Later that night, after the library had closed, Mr. Linden walked to her house, which was directly down the road from the library. He rang the doorbell, but nobody answered. So then he banged on the door. Yet again, nobody answered but the door flew right open. He walked through the door, and began to look around. It seemed as though nobody was home. So he slowly walked up the stairs and into the very last bedroom at the end of the hallway. He saw a dead body. It was the woman's body from the library. She had died and he knew that she died from the book.

That very next morning, Mr. Linden took her body and found a quiet place in the forest and buried her body and the mysterious book. He laid beautiful flowers around her burial place.

From that day forward, Mr. Linden never had to warn anybody about any books.

Sample in response to Van Allsburg, C. (1984). *The mysteries of Harris Burdick*. Boston: Houghton Mifflin.

Mystery Theater: The students can script and practice a scene from a mystery to perform to the class. The students will try to guess what mystery the scene is from and the characters involved.

Word Detective: Using the Sequential Roundtable graphic organizer, the students can create a master list or word wall of mystery words from novels read (see Appendix B, page 188). This can then serve as a writing tool or be used for word sorts.

Drama center. Students use drama to demonstrate understandings of stories and content area topics. While students are working at this center, they can be creating, planning, and rehearsing for the dramatic performance. The following list offers some ideas for implementing drama in the classroom:

Dinner Party (Vogt, 2000): Students choose people—such as characters from novels or short stories, scientists, presidents, military leaders, artists, explorers, or authors—from content areas of study. They then have a dinner party and act out the conversation that the guests would be having. Dialogue must relate to information gained in their studies.

You Are There (Vogt, 2000): Students select a content area event that they will research. After they gather information, they select a character that was important in the event. They then create interview questions and responses related to that person. Pairs of students reenact the event through this interviewer-interviewee format.

Readers Theatre: Students either transcribe a story or other text into a play format or use an existing one to dramatize stories. Then they rehearse the dramatization using voice, facial expressions, and movement to portray characterizations. They use scripts during the performance. There are several Web sites that provide scripts for Readers Theatre. The following are among our favorites:

http://www.aaronshep.com
> Author Aaron Shepherd's Web site on Readers Theatre contains resources, stories, scripts, and more.

http://www.lisablau.com/scriptomonth.html
> Lisa Blau's Web site features monthly Readers Theatre scripts and access to archived scripts.

http://bsuvc.bsu.edu/home/00mevancamp/rt.html
> This site contains information about Readers Theatre and links to sites that provide scripts.

http://www.geocities.com/Athens/Thebes/9893/readerstheater.htm
> Many Readers Theatre scripts are available for classroom use.

http://www.proteacher.com/070173.shtml
> This site provides a listing of Web sites that provide suggestions for writing scripts, ideas for using Readers Theatre, and scripts for classroom use.

Project center. Students work on specific extensions or projects related to literature or the content area of study. These may include multiple modes of response including reading, writing, illustrating, dramatizing, or other modes of investigation. Here are some projects our students have enjoyed the most:

Bookmarks: Students create bookmarks about the book they read. We can set the criteria or give students a choice about what to include on the bookmark. Some suggestions for narrative texts are title, author, main characters, critique, and illustrations of characters or events. For informational texts, students can include title, author, and key ideas they learned and their reactions or reflections.

Literature Response Projects: Students may self-select a project from an extensive list of literature response ideas (see Appendix C, pages 191–194). They may work on these projects over time and may choose whether to work individually or with a partner. We add literature response ideas throughout the year.

Open-Mind Portraits: Students draw two or more portraits of one of the characters in the story. One is a regular face of the character; the others are one or more pages that represent the mind of the character at important points in the story. The mind pages include words and drawings representing the character's thoughts and feelings (Tompkins, 2001).

Choose Your Own Project: Students make selections from the project chart to design their own product or performance related to a theme or text. The teacher has demonstrated all choices in previous lessons. A chart listing students' options facilitates this process (see Appendix B, page 172).

Regardless of what the centers include or how they are managed, it is important to remember that these are places for independent exploration by students. The centers should have clear directions and activities that are familiar to students so they can apply skills and strategies with little or no teacher support.

STUDENT-FACILITATED COMPREHENSION ROUTINES

After we teach and model a variety of comprehension strategies, students practice and transfer what they have learned in other settings, including comprehension routines. Comprehension routines are those habits of thinking and organizing that facilitate reading and response in authentic contexts. These are independent settings. This implies that students are knowledgeable about the strategies and routines, they are provided with texts at their independent levels, and they have ample time for practicing and transferring these processes.

Routines are courses of action that are so ingrained that they can be used successfully on a regular basis. The routines we find most effective for promoting comprehension in both whole-group and small-group settings are Questioning the Author, Reciprocal Teaching, and Literature Circles. Before students can use these comprehension routines independently, they need to understand why they are engaging in the routines and how each functions. We accommodate these needs by explicitly teaching Questioning the Author, Reciprocal Teaching, and Literature Circles. Detailed descriptions of the routines and ideas for teaching them can be found in Chapter 2. As the learning process progresses, we gradually release control of the routines to the students.

Questioning the Author

QtA is a text-based instructional format that helps students build a deeper understanding of texts by learning to query the author (Beck et al., 1997). We explicitly teach QtA to enable students to gain a complete understanding of the process before engaging in it independently.

Reciprocal Teaching

Reciprocal Teaching is a comprehension routine that is strategy based and involves discussion of text. When using it as a comprehension routine, the students take turns assuming the role of "teacher" in leading the discussion (Palincsar & Brown, 1984). Teaching this strategy through direct instruction allows students to become proficient in using it before they apply it as an independent comprehension routine.

Literature Circles

Literature Circles are group discussions in which students share meaningful ideas about texts they have read (Brabham & Villaume, 2000). We introduce Literature Circles through direct instruction, so students can gain an in-depth understanding of how they function before using them independently.

Comprehension routines are directly taught in Stage One and used independently by students in Stage Two. Questioning the Author, Reciprocal Teaching, and Literature Circles, along with other comprehension routines, are described in a step-by-step process in Appendix·A (pages 139–141).

At the conclusion of Stage Two, we encourage students to reflect on their performances. This facilitates their transition into Stage Three, which is the focus of the next chapter. In it we address teachers' and students' roles in the reflection and goal-setting processes.

To learn more about innovative teaching ideas and connections to the arts, read

Buehl, D. (2001). *Classroom strategies for interactive learning* (2nd ed.). Newark, DE: International Reading Association.

McLaughlin, M., & Vogt, M.E. (Eds.). (2000). *Creativity and innovation in content area teaching.* Norwood, MA: Christopher-Gordon.

Pinciotti, P. (2001a). *Art as a way of learning: Explorations in teaching.* Bethlehem, PA: Northampton Community College.

CHAPTER 4

Teacher-Facilitated Whole-Group Reflection and Goal Setting

To me reading is like dreaming because most of the time I read books without pictures and just make up the pictures in my head.

Jamie Juchniewicz, Grade 3

I n Stage Three of the Guided Comprehension Model, participants engage in reflection, sharing, and goal setting. We have structured this chapter to address the multiple purposes of this stage:

- to provide a meaningful, comfortable setting for a community of learners;
- to afford students opportunities to monitor learning by engaging in self-reflection;
- to encourage students to share their thinking; and
- to create connections between self-reflection and goal setting.

ORGANIZING FOR STAGE THREE

In this setting we encourage students to think about what they have accomplished in the first and second stages of the Model. We want them to actualize their learning and be accountable for it. Bringing the class together also provides opportunities for closure and celebration of new knowledge.

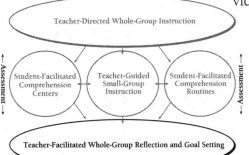

In Stage Three, students actively engage in reflection, sharing, and goal setting. The cyclical process of setting goals, engaging in learning experiences, reflecting on performance, and setting new goals helps students to perceive themselves as empowered, successful learners. It encourages students to think critically, observe progress, and take ownership of their learning.

It is these active roles that students are taking, not reflection itself, that is new to the educational process. In 1933, Dewey suggested that teachers become reflective practitioners to gain a better understanding of teaching and learning. In 1987, Schon noted that reflection offers us insights into various dimensions of teaching and learning that can lead to better understanding. In the 1990s, when reflection became a valued component of evolving assessment practices, students were encouraged to actively engage in the process (Darling-Hammond, Ancess, & Falk, 1995; Hoyt & Ames, 1997; McLaughlin, 1995).

Self-reflection focuses on what students have learned and how they feel about their learning (Cooper & Kiger, 2001). It includes both self-assessment, which addresses process and product, and self-evaluation, which makes judgments about performance. Questions raised for self-assessment purposes include "What is confusing me?" and "How did I contribute to the discussion?" Questions that foster self-evaluation include "What did I do well?" and "Did I achieve my goal?"

Self-reflection offers insights into students' thinking. It not only illustrates that they are thinking, but also details *how* they are thinking. According to Hoyt and Ames (1997), "Self-reflection offers students an opportunity to be actively involved in internal conversations while offering teachers an insider's view of the learning and the student's perception of self as learner" (p. 19). This focus on internal conversations parallels Tierney and Pearson's (1994) idea that "literacy learning is an ongoing conversation with oneself.... If we view learning as dynamic in character, as that evolving dialogue with oneself, then even major shifts become little more than the natural, almost inevitable, consequence of human reflection" (p. 514).

Goal setting is a natural outgrowth of reflection. As Hansen (1998) notes, "learning proceeds from the known to the new" (p. 45). What students have learned to a given point influences what they learn next; this is the foundation of goal setting. Students reflect on what they have learned and set future personal goals for continuous improvement. When students actively engage in creating both personal and class goals, they appear to be more motivated and take more responsibility for their learning (Clemmons, Laase, Cooper, Areglado, & Dill, 1993; Hill & Ruptic, 1994).

REFLECTION AND GOAL SETTING IN GUIDED COMPREHENSION

In Guided Comprehension, we engage in both whole-group and personal goal setting. Because our ultimate goal is using comprehension strategies to transact with text, our whole-group and personal goals often focus on comprehension. Examples of whole-group goals include "We will use a variety of methods to preview text," and "We will use multiple approaches to evaluate text." Students engage in evaluation by sharing their work with peers and discussing everyone's progress. Students and teachers then decide if progress has been made in attaining the goal, if the goal has been achieved, and if a new goal needs to be set.

Because direct instruction of reflection and goal setting is necessary, we apply the steps we shared in Chapter 2 to this process. We often use nonacademic topics such as hobbies or special interests to introduce strategies or concepts (McLaughlin, 1995). This works especially well in this stage, because many students do not have strong background experiences in reflection; in fact, many may not even be familiar with the concept. The following is an excerpt from directed instruction of reflection and goal setting. Although students participated in this process through discussion, the excerpt focuses on our "thinking aloud" during the process.

- *Explain*: We explain to the students what reflection is and how it works.

  Today we're going to learn about reflection, a special kind of thinking that allows us to examine something that we've done or something that we've learned. It can help us to understand how we learned and how well we learned.

- *Demonstrate*: We show our students what reflection in action is like and use a Think-Aloud to share our reasoning process with students.

For example, tennis is a sport that I have learned to play. I'm going to demonstrate what reflection is by telling you about the last time I played tennis. It was a close match. My serve was OK and I moved well to be able to return all the shots that my opponent hit. In the end, she won one set, and I won the other. I think I played pretty well, but I think it would help my game if I could find more time to practice and make my serve faster and more powerful. I'm going to make those my two goals to improve my tennis.

- *Guide*: We guide students to apply reflection to something they have learned. We often use reflection forms to facilitate this process (see Appendix E).

  The forms I'm distributing are going to help you with your reflections. Remember how I reflected on my tennis match? Well, now it's your turn to reflect on something you have learned to do. First, you'll need to think of a hobby, sport, or special interest that you have. Now focus on the last time you did it and think about what it was like. Consider these questions: How well did it go? What did you do well? What do you think you could do to improve your performance next time? What will your new goal be?

- *Practice*: After students reflect on their hobbies and special interests and share their goals, we transfer the reflection and goal-setting process to reading.

  Now that we've shared our reflections and new goals for our hobbies and special interests, let's try to reflect on our reading. For example, today we were all engaged in Stage Two of Guided Comprehension. Let's use our reflection and goal-setting sheets to help us think about something we did in Stage Two, how well we did it, what we could do to improve it next time, and what our new goal will be.

During this teaching and learning experience, students situated reflection and goal setting in a wide variety of hobbies that included dancing, basketball, hockey, cooking, babysitting, playing musical instruments, and making crafts. Their new goals included learning to dance in toe shoes, to shoot three-point baskets, to train more consistently, to read directions before beginning to cook, to make sure the children go to bed on time, to practice more, and to plan better.

When they transferred their reflecting and goal setting to Guided Comprehension, students focused either on the process as a whole or on a particular component. The following are examples of new goals created at various grade levels:

My goal for next time is ask bigger questions, ones that have bigger answers. (Grade 3)

Next time I want to read for a longer time without my mind wandering. (Grade 4)

My new goal is to write a better summary, one that has all the main points. (Grade 5)

Next time I want to say more when I'm in my Literature Circle. (Grade 6)

My new goal is to use more than one source for my research. (Grade 7)

My new goal is to go to the poetry center because I haven't done that yet. (Grade 8)

When students become comfortable with reflection and goal setting, they engage in transfer of their learning. For example, they can analyze their performance in all stages of Guided Comprehension, which means that they can reflect on their performance as a member of a whole group, small group, or pairs as well as individually (see Appendix E).

Because reflection and goal setting are essential components of Guided Comprehension, it is important to maintain student interest in them. The following are other teaching ideas we use to foster students' engagement in these processes.

Vary the Components

When planning reflection and goal setting, we make selections from the following four categories:

1. Type of goal: individual or whole class, short term or long term
2. Reflection setting: whole group, small group, paired, or individual
3. Reflection mode: speaking, writing, illustrating, or dramatizing
4. Sharing setting: whole group, small group, paired, or individual

Choices can vary according to lesson content, student learning styles, or student interest. For example, students can create new personal goals by working in pairs to reflect on their learning, create sketches to illustrate their thinking, and then share them with a small group.

There are several formats for engaging students in written reflection. Two we find effective are Guided Comprehension Journals and Tickets Out.

Guided Comprehension Journals. Guided Comprehension Journals are provided for students to use during all stages of the Model. For example, they can use them to record notes for Literature Circles, store their word choices from vocabulary self-selection, jot down questions that arise during Guided Comprehension, and engage in reflection. In Stage Three, they can use the journals to record their reflections and set new goals.

Tickets Out. Tickets Out is one of our favorite teaching ideas because it fosters reflection, helps us monitor students' learning, and takes very little time. It is called Tickets Out because students hand their tickets to us as they exit the classroom at the end of the period or the day. To participate in this activity, students use a half sheet of paper. On the first side, they write the most important thing they learned that day. On the other side, they write one question they have about something they learned that day. Whether students put their names on their tickets is the teacher's choice.

To complete this activity students need only about 5 minutes. When students have left the room, we read side one of their tickets first. This is not a time-consuming process, but it does provide valuable information. For example, it offers insight into what students valued about their learning and also gives us an opportunity to monitor and clarify any misconceptions they may have. During this part of Tickets Out, we set aside any tickets that need clarification.

Next, we turn over the entire pile of tickets and read the questions students have about their learning. Some days more than one student will raise the same question, and other days not every student will have a question. During this part of Tickets Out, we set aside questions that we think address significant topics. We respond to these questions, which usually number between four and six, at the start of the next day's class. This helps students understand that we value their thinking and also enhances the continuity from class to class. (A graphic organizer for Tickets Out can be found in Appendix E, page 225.)

Provide Prompts

Providing prompts can assist students when reflecting and creating new goals in a variety of settings. Prompts help to focus students' thinking on various dimensions of learning.

Questions to guide reflection:

- What was your goal today?
- What did you learn today?
- What did you do today that you have never done before?
- What strategies did you find most helpful?
- What confused you today? How did you figure it out?
- How did your group do? What contributions did you make to your group? What contributions did others make?
- What questions do you have about what you learned today?
- How do you think you will use what you learned today?

Questions to guide goal setting:

- What do you need to work on?
- Where will you start next time?
- What do you hope to accomplish?
- What is your new goal?

Reflection stems:

- I was really good at _____.
- The best thing was _____.
- I found out that _____.

- I contributed _____ to our literature discussion.
- I read _____ and found out that _____.
- When I was confused today, I _____.

Goal-setting stems:

- I need more work on _____.
- Tomorrow I hope to _____.
- My goal for tomorrow is to _____.

Students can think about one or more of these prompts and then share their responses. Sharing can take place with a partner, small group, or the whole class. We often use Think-Pair-Share (McTighe & Lyman, 1988) as a framework for this. Students *think* about their learning, *pair* with a partner to discuss ideas, and then *share* their thoughts with the class. Students can also write their reflections in their Guided Comprehension Journals and then use Think-Pair-Share. This technique can also be adapted for goal setting. First, students think about their performance and new goal(s), then they write the goal(s). Next they pair with a partner to discuss their new goal(s). Finally, they share their goal(s) with the whole class. Sharing with the whole class is beneficial because it shows that everyone values reflection and goal setting and provides good models for the other students.

Accessible text is another factor that affects student reflection and goal setting. In the next chapter we take a closer look at the roles of multiple levels of text in Guided Comprehension and examine related issues including leveled texts and creating student-text matches.

To learn more about reflection and goal setting, read

Courtney, A.M., & Abodeeb, T.L. (2001). *Journey of discovery: Building a classroom community through diagnostic-reflective portfolios.* Newark, DE: International Reading Association.
Hansen, J. (1998). *When learners evaluate.* Portsmouth, NH: Heinemann.
Hill, B.C., Ruptic, C.A., & Norwick, L. (1998). *Classroom based assessment.* Norwood, MA: Christopher-Gordon.

CHAPTER 5

Leveled Texts: A Factor in Student Accessibility

You will lose interest in the story if it is not to your liking, so you have to choose a good book to be a good reader.

Sara Bogaert, Grade 7

Authentic text is a mainstay of Guided Comprehension. It is motivational, dynamic, exciting, fascinating, and real, but none of these characteristics matter if the text is not accessible to students. Readers need opportunities to engage with multiple levels of texts in a variety of instructional settings. This means that even though whole-group instruction is part of the Guided Comprehension Model, it should not be the only setting used. Similarly, small-group guided instruction, another component of the Model, should not be the only setting used. Multiple instructional settings—whole group, small group (guided and independent), paired, and individual—afford student accessibility to a variety of text levels.

In this chapter, we discuss making text accessible to students. We begin by describing the various levels at which text can be accessible. Then we discuss the reader and text factors that influence accessibility. Next we provide the rationale for using leveled texts, ideas for text organization, and suggestions to facilitate leveling. We also describe commercially published leveled texts and make connections to Appendix D, which features leveled book resources.

STUDENTS' READING LEVELS AND ACCESSIBLE TEXTS

Students can usually engage with multiple levels of text if they have appropriate teacher support. Students can engage with independent level or easy text when working on their own; they can engage with instructional level or "just right" text when they have some teacher support; they can engage with independent, instructional, and challenging texts when they have full teacher support, such as during teacher-directed whole-group instruction. This means that even though students should work with independent level texts when reading on their own, they can engage with text at a challenging level if we share it through a read-aloud. Figure 6 illustrates how these texts are generally situated in the Guided Comprehension Model. It is important to remember that descriptions of texts at these levels are approximations, and that factors beyond the text influence student accessibility.

Accessible text is a core component of comprehension instruction. For students to learn to use reading strategies to enhance comprehension, it is important that they learn within their zone of proximal development (Vygotsky, 1978), the context in which learners can be successful if their learning is scaffolded by a more knowledgeable other. In Guided Comprehension, teachers are the more knowledgeable others, and we can scaffold students' learning in a variety of ways including the use of modeling, thinking aloud, prompting/reminding, or coaching (Brown, 1999/2000; Roehler & Duffy, 1991).

Figure 6. Accessible Texts

Text Level	Teacher Support	Guided Comprehension
Independent	No teacher support needed.	Stage Two: Independent Centers and Routines
	Just right when students are reading on their own and practicing strategy application.	
Instructional	Some teacher support needed.	Stage Two: Teacher-Guided Small Groups
	Just right when guiding small groups.	
Challenging	Full teacher support needed.	Stage One: Teacher-Directed Whole Groups
	Just right when doing read-alouds in whole group.	
	(*Note*: Because full teacher support characterizes this setting, independent and instructional level texts also can be used.)	

FACTORS THAT INFLUENCE ACCESSIBILITY

There are several factors that influence the accessibility of a text; some reside in the reader, others are determined by the text. Reader factors include background knowledge and prior experience with language and types of texts, motivation, and critical thinking. Text factors include type and structure, page layout, content, and language structure (Fountas & Pinnell, 1999; Weaver, 2000).

Reader Factors

Background knowledge. Readers' background knowledge of text content, language, and text type influence accessibility. If students have background knowledge, they will be more familiar with vocabulary and concepts. This would also provide a greater brain framework to make relevant connections to the new information. This is true for both narrative and expository texts, and is influenced by the amount of time spent reading each type.

Motivation to read. This factor also is influenced by students' previous experience with texts. Students who have spent years reading textbook chapters and answering the questions at the end can have negative feelings when asked to read for information. This is also true for students who have had stories so chopped up for vocabulary study or detail recall that the major themes and meaning have been lost. Students who have had positive, successful experiences with texts have greater motivation to try more challenging or longer texts.

Critical thinking. Once students begin to read more challenging or longer texts, thinking critically and reading between the lines become essential for comprehension. Texts that have supports, such as pictures and examples, may be a better match for students who lack higher levels of critical thinking. On the other hand, students who have the ability to make connections and inferences will be able to read more challenging texts.

Text Factors

Text type and structure. Students' knowledge of and experience with text type and structure can affect accessibility. This means that if students have a greater background in reading narrative text—which is generally based on characters, setting, problem, attempts to resolve, and resolution—they may find reading expository text more difficult. One reason for this may be that expository text has a greater variety of structures including problem-solution, comparison-contrast, sequence, description, and cause and effect (Vacca & Vacca, 1999). Students' familiarity with these structures facilitates their transaction with texts.

Goldman and Rakestraw (2000) have drawn the following three conclusions from existing research on students' knowledge of text structure:

1. Readers use their knowledge of structure in processing text.
2. Knowledge of structural forms of text develops with experience with different genres, and is correlated with age/time in school.
3. Making readers more aware of genre and text structure improves learning. (p. 321)

Page layout. The size of print, the number or availability of pictures or other visual cues, the range of punctuation, the layout and organization of print, and the number of words per page are the influential factors in this category.

Text content. Often the text requires background knowledge by the reader in order to be fully interpreted. Students who have a vast amount of knowledge of a specific topic—for example, whales—will find the text more accessible simply because the vocabulary and concepts are familiar. This will allow them to make interpretations and connections with the information provided. Similarly, with narrative texts, a student who has good experience reading mysteries will be able to read many levels of mysteries, because the process of looking for clues and an unlikely suspect is familiar.

Language structure. Texts with unfamiliar, difficult, or technical vocabulary tend to be more difficult for students to read and comprehend. When the vocabulary is challenging, readers often spend more energy decoding, thereby decreasing fluency and comprehension. Similarly, texts with complex and unusual sentence structures pose challenges for readers if they lack the background knowledge or language familiarity to make connections and interpretations. The use of literary language and devices—such as metaphor, simile, or onomatopoeia—also may be challenging for readers unfamiliar with them (Fountas & Pinnell, 1999).

Considering all these text features is essential when we choose texts and create student-text matches. Because some of these features may pose challenges to the reader, we need to be familiar with the texts and what, if any, supports each has to offer students.

Supports include illustrations, support information (such as table of contents or book jacket summary), text set up (including font size and sentence layout), dialogue, book and chapter leads, and chapter formats (such as continuation from chapter to chapter and length) (Szymusiak & Sibberson, 2001). Harvey (1998) suggests supports specific to nonfiction texts: fonts and special effects, textual cues ("similarly," "for instance"), illustrations and photographs, graphics, and text organization.

We need to help students understand these supports and how to use them to facilitate comprehension. The more blatant the supports, the easier it is for the reader to understand and make connections.

CHOOSING TEXTS TO PROMOTE STUDENT SUCCESS

The process of choosing appropriate text for each student is challenging because there are so many variables to consider. Assuring that text is accessible involves not only leveling the texts themselves, but also making good matches between the readers and the texts. Two factors that influence these decisions are student information and text information.

Student Information

Before planning meaningful Guided Comprehension instruction, we need to determine each student's independent and instructional level. We use this information for two purposes: to form teacher-guided small groups and to inform teacher-directed whole-group instruction. Miscue analysis (Goodman, 1997), which assesses students' oral reading and comprehension, is a viable source of this information. (For further discussion of a variety of assessments, see Chapter 6.)

Hunt (1996/1997) suggests that students also contribute to determining text accessibility. He recommends that students engage in self-evaluation during independent reading by responding to questions such as

- Did you have a good reading period today?
- Were you able to concentrate as you read independently?
- Did the ideas in the book hold your attention?
- Were you bothered by others or outside noises?
- Could you keep the ideas in the book straight in your mind?
- Did you get mixed up in any place? Were you able to fix it?
- Were there words you did not know? How did you figure them out?
- Were you hoping the book would end, or were you hoping it would go on and on?

Although these queries require only yes or no responses, they do provide insights into students' perceptions of their performance. This information can be useful when determining the appropriateness of a text for the reader.

We also need to gather data on student experiences and interests. This can be accomplished through interviews, observations, or interest inventories. In addition, students can complete self-perception scales. (See Chapter 6 for a list of diagnostic measures.)

Text Information

Once information about each student is gathered, we need to consider what texts we will use. We use the following steps to facilitate this process:

1. *Identify the texts already available in the classroom.* These may include basals, anthologies, trade books, textbooks, magazines, poetry books, and picture books.

2. *Organize the texts to facilitate Guided Comprehension.* We use the following questions to accomplish this:

   - Does this text add to existing content area study or knowledge?
   - Can this text be used in a genre study?
   - Does this text exemplify a particular style, structure, language pattern, or literary device? Can this text be used to teach a comprehension strategy?
   - Are there multiple copies of the text available?
   - Does this text match a particular student's interests?
   - Is this a good example of a text structure?
   - Is this text part of a series?
   - Is it written by a favorite author?

These questions can be used with both narrative and expository texts. This includes individual stories in literature anthologies, as well as individual articles within magazines.

3. *Acquire additional materials to assure ample accessible texts for all readers.* It is important to have some small sets of books to use during teacher-guided comprehension groups, but it is also necessary to have a wide array of texts, varying in type, genre, length, and content. All students must have a multitude of accessible books within the classroom. These books must represent a wide range of readability and genre. It is important to include novels of varying lengths, nonfiction trade books, picture books, poetry books, and magazines.

We keep in mind the following ideas when adding to classroom collections:

- Content areas—nonfiction and narrative text to supplement studies in math, science, and social studies
- Student interests—a variety of texts (fiction, nonfiction, poetry) to match students' interests
- Read-aloud—texts that offer examples of a variety of text structures and engaging story lines to be used to demonstrate comprehension processes and fluency
- Anchor books—texts used in whole-group and small-group instruction to demonstrate a specific strategy or routine
- Sets of books—small sets (four to six copies) of books to be used in Guided Comprehension groups; these should be based on students' levels as well as the strategies that can be taught and used
- Text sets—series books, favorite author, genre, topic; several books that have a common characteristic

Once we have accumulated the texts, we need to organize them to accommodate all stages of the Model.

METHODS FOR LEVELING TEXTS

All text levels are approximations, and there is no specific rule for determining them. Text ease or difficulty is determined by both text and reader factors. Each text will need to be evaluated with specific readers in mind. Leveling systems, teacher judgment, paralleling books, and using leveled lists developed by others facilitate this process.

Leveling Systems

Several systems exist that will help determine the approximate level of a text. These take into consideration factors such as format, language structure, and content (Weaver, 2000). The following are examples of these formulas: the Primary Readability Index (Gunning, 1998), Reading Recovery (Clay, 1985), and the Fountas and Pinnell Leveling System (1996).

Teacher Judgment

Although these leveling systems provide a starting point for leveling texts and have been used in the primary grades, teacher judgment may be the most often used method in leveling texts for the upper grades. In grades 3–8, it is important to identify reader factors, such as familiarity with content or genre, as well as motivation to read, when trying to match a text with a reader.

We can use the following processes for leveling texts:

- Separate books into fiction, nonfiction, and poetry.
- For each type of book, divide the books into harder and easier.
- Take each pile of books and sort by hardest to easiest (repeat this process as necessary).
- Label or color code levels for student access.

The process of leveling texts works best when several teachers work together and discuss the decision-making process.

Paralleling Books

Another way to level texts is to parallel classroom books with titles from published lists. Factors such as length, font size, number of illustrations, and type of text can be matched with lists of published leveled books to determine approximate levels. The lists provide model books to represent approximate levels (see Appendix D).

Published Lists and Web Sites for Leveled Books

Using published resources is another method of leveling books. These collections provide titles at various levels that we can use in creating student-text matches and in all stages of Guided Comprehension. We can use these lists as resources for identifying anchor books as well as assessment purposes. Many of these sets of leveled books, which include narrative and expository texts, are available for purchase. (Information about these sources, including Web sites, is detailed in Appendix D.)

CLASSROOM TEXT ORGANIZATION

Once we have leveled our classroom collections, our goal is to organize the texts efficiently to promote their optimum use. This includes texts for use in whole-group and small-group teaching, as well as texts for students to use during comprehension centers and routines.

To facilitate accessing text for our teaching, Harvey and Goudvis (2000) suggest accumulating a master list of titles and organizing them according to what they have to offer as teaching models. Figure 7 illustrates three different approaches to such organization: listing books by strategy to be modeled, by book title, and by sample teaching plan.

Figure 7. Approaches to Organizing Text

Listing by Strategy to Be Modeled
Example:

Strategy	Text	Teaching Idea
Previewing	*The Empty Pot* (Demi, 1990)	Predict-o-Gram
	Charlie Anderson (Abercrombie, 1995)	Story Impression

Listing of Books by Title
Example:

Text	Strategies	Teaching Idea
The Empty Pot	Previewing	DR-TA
	Visualizing	Sketch to Stretch

Sample Teaching Plan
Teaching Routine: DR-TA

Explain: Tell students that we're going to read this book together and work on predictions because predicting helps us understand the text better and gives us reasons to keep reading.

Demonstrate: Show the cover of the book and think out loud about what the book might be about. Encourage students to share their predictions.

Guide: Read to page _____. Think out loud to confirm or disconfirm predictions using information from the text. Encourage students to make new predictions. Read another section of text and have students provide evidence from the text to confirm or disconfirm predictions. Prompt if necessary.

Practice: Finish reading the story in a similar way. Encourage students to use evidence from text to confirm or modify predictions. Have students share with partners or in small groups. Write a response to the story. Discuss the moral. Make personal connections to times we did or did not tell the truth, and what consequences or rewards we experienced.

Reflect: Encourage students to think about how predicting and using authors' clues helped them to engage with the text. Have them share their reflections and determine how they can use this process when they read on their own.

To provide accessible texts for student-facilitated comprehension routines and centers, we use the following methods of organization:

Class book baskets: Creating book baskets by author, series, content, or approximate reading level is one method. With our help, students can then make selections from a whole collection of books in the basket.

Individual book baskets: We can also help students to create individual book baskets in which they keep an ongoing collection of books they want to read. This eliminates any "down time" when students need to select text for independent reading.

Individual student booklists: Students keep these lists in the back of their Guided Comprehension Journals. Titles can be added to the list in an ongoing manner to accommodate student progress. These books would be stored in the classroom book baskets.

To further facilitate text organization, Szymusiak and Sibberson (2001) recommend that books in classroom collections be placed face out so that readers can easily see the covers and preview the texts and that sections for fiction, nonfiction, and poetry be marked clearly.

The two most important factors in making appropriate text selections are the level of the text and the reading level of the student. We can determine students' range of approximate reading levels by using informal assessments. This information helps us to create meaningful matches between students and texts. In the next chapter, we describe a variety of measures we can use for this purpose, as well as for formative and summative purposes.

To learn more about leveling text, read

Fawson, P.C., & Reutzel, D.R. (2000). But I only have a basal: Implementing guided reading in the early grades. *The Reading Teacher, 54,* 84–97.

Fountas, I.C., & Pinnell, G.S. (1999). *Matching books to readers: Using leveled books in guided reading, K–3.* Portsmouth, NH: Heinemann.

Weaver, B.M. (2000). *Leveling books K–6: Matching readers to text.* Newark, DE: International Reading Association.

CHAPTER 6

Assessment in Guided Comprehension

Reading is exercise for your brain.

Ashley Todd, Grade 4

**W**hen beginning to teach any aspect of literacy, it is important that we focus on the end result.

To begin with the end in mind means to start with a clear understanding of the destination. It means knowing where we're going so that we better understand where we are now and so that the steps we take are always in the right direction. (Covey, 1989, p. 98)

If we do not teach with the end in mind, we may find ourselves wandering through a string of unrelated activities that have no ultimate purpose.

As reading teachers, our ultimate goal is that our students will be able to comprehend. To determine student progress in attaining this goal we use a variety of assessments. Before teaching we use *diagnostic* assessments to determine what students know; while teaching we use *formative* assessments to document student progress; after teaching we use *summative* assessments to determine what students have learned. We use the results of these measures to inform teaching and learning.

In this chapter we present a practical approach to student assessment. We begin by focusing on the dynamic nature of assessment and its multiple roles in Guided Comprehension. Then we discuss how the Model supports student performance on state assessments. Next, we present a number of practical, informative assessments. We describe their purposes and their connections to Guided Comprehension, including grouping and making student-text matches. Following this we introduce Guided Comprehension Profiles, tools to organize and manage student progress, and explain how they function. Throughout the chapter we also make connections to Appendix E, which contains a variety of reproducible assessment forms.

THE MULTIPLE ROLES OF ASSESSMENT IN GUIDED COMPREHENSION

Assessment in Guided Comprehension is dynamic in nature. It occurs in an ongoing manner, offers insights into process, chronicles student development, and is a natural component of teaching and learning (McLaughlin, 2002). This aligns with constructivist thinking that purposeful assessments should be a natural part of teaching and learning (Brooks & Brooks, 1993; Tierney, 1998). It also supports Vygotsky's belief that assessment should extend to scaffolded experiences to capture students' emerging abilities (Minick, 1987).

Assessment in Guided Comprehension has several purposes, including the following:

- to provide an approximate range of reading levels for students
- to offer insights into student attitudes and interests

- to facilitate student-text matches
- to inform grouping for teacher-guided instruction
- to provide windows to students' thinking
- to document students' performance
- to provide information for evaluation

Assessment permeates every stage of the Model and occurs in a variety of forms and settings. For example, we use diagnostic assessments to initially group students for the teacher-guided instruction in Stage Two. We employ formative measures to monitor student learning in a continuous, ongoing manner in all stages, and we use summative assessments to examine what students have learned over time. The measures we use for diagnostic and formative purposes tend to be informal and flexible, focused on process. Summative assessments are often more formal and fixed, focused on product (McMillan, 1997).

CONNECTIONS TO STATE ASSESSMENTS

Students in the United States are required to take state assessments at multiple points during their K–12 careers. In fact, students' engagement with high-stakes testing often extends beyond their school years to university entrance and professional certification requirements. Although our thinking about these measures is more closely aligned with the position statements issued by the American Education Research Association (AERA), the International Reading Association (IRA), and the National Council of Teachers of English (NCTE), we know that student performance on state assessments affects schools, curricula, teachers, and students. For these reasons, we are demonstrating how Guided Comprehension supports student performance on these measures.

Some state departments of education are taking active roles in making connections between the state assessments and students. For example, the Pennsylvania Department of Education has created the Pennsylvania Classroom Connections Home Page (http://www.pde.psu.edu/connections), which provides teachers with access to a variety of ideas to help make classroom connections to the Pennsylvania System of School Assessment (PSSA). One of the links is to intermediate assessment, which in turn links to the Reading Rubric for Student Use (1998). This rubric has been restated from the more complex version that is shared with teachers. What follows is our adapted version of level 4 of that rubric (our primary adaptation was expanding the original language "story" to "story or article" to reflect the rubric's applicability to both narrative and expository text):

- You show a complete understanding of what you have read.
- You get all the facts about the story or article right.

- You go beyond the story or article to connect it to what you have learned and/or you can explain why you agree or disagree with the text.
- You use examples from the story or article and can tell how it connects to other things you know and what you think about the story.

All of these criteria address elements of comprehension: understanding, making connections, accessing background knowledge, and using text to support responses. These same elements are components of Guided Comprehension. The Model has a comprehension focus, promotes knowledge of text structure, encourages question generation at multiple levels, and supports making connections—text-self, text-text, and text-others.

The state assessment criteria address valued aspects of comprehension. We assess for similar purposes during Guided Comprehension. In the next section, we discuss many of the measures we use.

PRACTICAL ASSESSMENT MEASURES

When preparing to teach Guided Comprehension, we assess to gather information about students' reading backgrounds to determine approximate range of reading levels, and to gain insights into students' knowledge of strategies and ability to apply them. Results of these assessments inform several aspects of our planning, including lesson content, student-text matches, and grouping students for guided instructional settings.

In this section we present a number of practical, effective assessments. We provide a description of each measure, briefly explain its functions, and note its connection to Guided Comprehension.

Assessments to Learn About Students' Backgrounds

Some assessments provide insights into students' pasts that enable us to better understand their present attitudes toward and performance in reading. Examples of these measures include attitude surveys, interest inventories, literacy histories, motivation profiles, and reader and writer self-perception scales. (Reproducible copies of these measures are included in Appendix E.)

Attitude surveys. Attitude surveys are designed to illuminate students' feelings about their literacy experiences. The most common formats are question and response, sentence completion, and selected response. How students feel about various aspects of reading and writing, how they would define reading and writing, and how they would describe successful readers and writers are topics that are addressed commonly. Information gleaned from these surveys also provides insights into factors that may have contributed to students' current attitudes toward literacy. (Reproducible reading and writing attitude surveys can be found in Appendix E, pages 201–202.)

Guided Comprehension connection: Completed surveys contribute to our understanding of students' perceptions of literacy and resulting motivational needs.

Interest inventories. Interest inventories are informal surveys designed to provide information about students' literacy habits and general backgrounds. Topics typically addressed include students' reading preferences, hobbies, and special interests. The most common formats for interest inventories are question and response or incomplete sentences. These surveys are relatively easy to complete and provide information about numerous topics including the following: genre and author preferences, what students are currently reading, and whether students choose to read beyond required assignments. (An example of an interest inventory appropriate for grades 3–8 can be found in Appendix E, page 204.)

Guided Comprehension connection: Completed inventories inform our decisions about text selection and student-text matches.

Literacy histories. Literacy histories chronicle students' literacy development from earliest memory to present day (McLaughlin & Vogt, 1996). They facilitate students' ability to make connections between their past literacy experiences and their current beliefs.

To create their personal literacy histories, students engage in questioning and reflection. Sources they use to construct their histories range from family memories to early grade writing samples to copies of favorite books. Students can choose the mode of presentation, and we have received everything from time lines to scrapbooks replete with family photos. To model this assessment, we share our literacy histories and provide students with prompts to guide the process. (Reproducible copies of the literacy history prompts are included in Appendix E, page 205.)

Guided Comprehension connection: Literacy histories offer insights into students' development that contribute to our understanding of them and their current attitudes toward literacy.

Motivation to Read Profile. The Motivation to Read Profile (Gambrell, Palmer, Codling, & Mazzoni, 1996) consists of two instruments: the Reading Survey and the Conversational Interview. The cued response survey, which requires 15 to 20 minutes for group administration, assesses the self-concept of a reader and value of reading. The interview, which features open-ended free response questions and requires 15 to 20 minutes for individual administration, assesses the nature of motivation, such as favorite authors and interesting books. The Conversational Interview (included in Appendix E, pages 213–215) has three emphases: narrative text, informational text, and general reading.

Guided Comprehension connection: Knowledge of what motivates students to read both narrative and informational text enhances our understanding of our students and informs meaningful text selection.

The Reader Self-Perception Scale. The Reader Self-Perception Scale (Henk & Melnick, 1995) offers insights into how students think about themselves as readers. When responding, students indicate how strongly they agree or disagree with each of 33 statements. Sample items include "I think I am a good reader" and "Reading is easier for me than it used to be." (A reproducible copy of this measure is available in Appendix E, pages 219–221.)

Guided Comprehension connection: This scale helps us understand students and help them perceive themselves as better readers.

The Writer Self-Perception Scale. The Writer Self-Perception Scale (Bottomley, Henk, & Melnick, 1997/1998) provides information about how students feel about their writing abilities. The students respond to 38 statements, indicating how strongly they agree or disagree. Sample items include "I am getting better at writing" and "I enjoy writing." (A reproducible copy is available in Appendix E, pages 226–229.)

Guided Comprehension connection: This scale helps us understand students and help them perceive themselves as better writers.

Attitude surveys, interest inventories, literacy histories, motivation profiles, and self-perception scales provide background information that informs our understanding of individual students and their literacy needs. These measures contribute vital information as we seek to provide optimum literacy experiences for our students. These assessments are easy to administer, require little time, and provide insights that may not be discerned from other literacy assessments.

Assessing to Learn About Students' Reading Levels and Use of Strategies

Some assessments provide insights into students' strategy use while reading and their ability to comprehend text. Examples of these measures include metacognitive strategy inventories, miscue analysis, student writing samples, and observation. (Reproducible copies of many of these measures are included in Appendix E.)

Metacognitive Reading Awareness Inventory. The Metacognitive Reading Awareness Inventory (Miholic, 1994) is designed for students from seventh grade through college. It consists of 10 statements with selected responses. The focus of this measure is how students use strategies to respond to difficulties they encounter while reading. Students select all the responses that they think are effective.

Guided Comprehension connection: This inventory informs our understanding of seventh- and eighth-grade students' strategy use.

Metacognitive Strategy Index. The Metacognitive Strategy Index (Schmitt, 1990) is a questionnaire that contains 25 items with selected responses. It is designed to evaluate elementary students' awareness of before-reading, during-reading, and after-reading metacomprehension strategies when reading narrative text.

Guided Comprehension connection: This measure informs our understanding of elementary students' metacognitive strategy knowledge and application.

Miscue analysis. Miscue analysis (Goodman, 1997) assesses students' use of the graphophonic, syntactic, and semantic cueing systems. Miscues indicate how a student's oral reading varies from the written text. We use miscue analysis for three purposes: to determine oral reading accuracy, to code and analyze miscues to determine needs for strategy instruction, and to evaluate the retelling for insights into student comprehension.

To analyze miscues, Goodman, Watson, and Burke (1987) suggest we use the following four questions:

1. Does the miscue change the meaning?
2. Does the miscue sound like language?
3. Do the miscue and the text word look and sound alike?
4. Was an attempt made to self-correct the miscue?

To facilitate the use of the miscue analysis we select some "anchor books"—both fiction and nonfiction—and have students do an informal oral reading, which we tape record. At this point we code and analyze their miscues. The students also do a brief retelling based on this text. These two pieces of information provide approximate student reading levels and insights into their strategy use and comprehension. There are some defined accuracy percentages that may influence the determination of a reader's range of levels: below 90%, frustration; 90–95%, instructional; 96–100%, independent. However, when assessing students' levels we also need to consider factors such as background experience with the content, interest in the text, and supports within the text.

There are a number of published resources that facilitate administering the miscue analysis. The Qualitative Reading Inventory, which ranges from preprimer to high school, is detailed in the next section. Other published resources include the following:

Leveled Reading Passages Assessment Kit (Houghton Mifflin, 2001): This assessment offers word lists, leveled reading passages, benchmarks, and scoring forms for levels ranging from Kindergarten/beginning Grade 1 to Grade 6.

PM Benchmark Introduction Kit (Rigby, 2000): This assessment includes leveled reading passages, benchmarks, and scoring forms for grades K–5.

Guided Comprehension connection: Miscue analysis provides approximate reading levels, helps us make matches between readers and texts, and informs instruction.

Qualitative Reading Inventory–3. The Qualitative Reading Inventory-3 (Leslie & Caldwell, 2000) is a comprehensive assessment that ranges from preprimer to high school. It includes fluency and comprehension measures that enable us to estimate students' reading levels, match students with appropriate texts, and verify suspected reading difficulties. Because there are so many components to this measure, we need to make choices when using it. For example, we may choose to do the miscue analysis and then use either the retelling checklist or the comprehension questions that accompany each leveled passage to determine students' instructional levels.

Guided Comprehension connection: The QRI provides information necessary to place students in teacher-guided small groups and create student-text matches.

Student writing. Student writing is a flexible assessment. It can be used for numerous purposes including applying strategies, recording personal responses, and as a mode of reflection and goal setting. We observe and analyze student writing for multiple purposes including language structure, use of vocabulary, knowledge of sight words and spelling patterns, and organization.

Guided Comprehension connection: Writing is a mode of expression for students' thinking that informs all stages of the Model.

Observation. Observation is one of the most flexible assessments because it can offer information about virtually any aspect of literacy in which our students engage. For example, we can observe if we want to assess students' fluency, record ideas about their engagement, or comment on their roles in cooperative learning activities.

Before we begin observing, we need to establish a purpose and determine how we will record the information gleaned from this measure. For example, if we are observing a student who is doing an oral retelling, we can use a checklist that includes information such as the characters, setting, problem, attempts to resolve, resolution, and a section for us to record additional comments. In contrast, if we are observing a student's contribution to a cooperative activity, our checklist might include items such as the student's preparation for the group's work, engagement with peers, and contributions. (Reproducible observation checklists can be found in Appendix E, pages 216–218.)

Guided Comprehension connection: This informal technique can be used in all stages of the Model to gain insights into students' performance.

What we want to know about our students determines which assessments we use. Therefore, our goal is not to use all these measures to assess each reader, but rather to make choices and use the measures that provide the information we need. The assessments we have described are practical, can be used for multiple purposes, and offer valuable insights into students' backgrounds and abilities.

In addition to the measures described, informal assessment opportunities are embedded in all stages of the Guided Comprehension Model. These formative measures are situated in a variety of instructional settings and provide occasions for students to demonstrate what they know through multiple modes of response including reading, writing, discussion, illustration, drama, and music. For example, one of the most authentic measures of students' abilities to use the comprehension strategies is simply evidence of their application. We can observe students using the strategies while reading and we can also review their applications in formats such as Concept Maps, Story Impressions, INSERTs, Retellings, or Lyric Summaries.

USING ASSESSMENT TO CREATE DYNAMIC GROUPS AND STUDENT-TEXT MATCHES

Once students' approximate reading levels are determined, we can group students for teacher-guided small-group instruction, placing students of similar abilities together. It is important to remember that grouping in this stage of the Model is dynamic in nature; students will move to groups using more challenging levels of text as they become more proficient.

Assessment results also inform student-text matches. When students' approximate reading levels and interests are known, we can make meaningful matches to encourage student engagement in all stages of the Model. Student access to a variety of genres and levels of text is an essential component of this process.

For example, a third-grade student may have a fifth-grade instructional level and a fourth-grade independent level. This student's book basket would contain both levels of text: fifth-grade books for guided small-group instruction and fourth-grade books for independent practice. Similarly, if an eighth-grade student has a sixth-grade instructional level and a fifth-grade independent level, he or she would need access to sixth-grade texts for guided small-group instruction and fifth-grade texts for independent practice.

As the students become more proficient and move to groups using more challenging text, their access to texts would change accordingly.

GUIDED COMPREHENSION PROFILES

We use Guided Comprehension Profiles to organize and manage student assessments. These profiles are strategy-based collections of assessments and indicators of student progress. Maintaining the profiles is an active process for both the students and teacher. As our students transact with texts and people in multiple settings in a variety of modes, we collect information to document their progress. Although Guided Comprehension offers numerous opportunities for assessment, there are some measures such as student writing, oral reading fluency, and comprehension that we systematically include. We use the results of these assessments to document student progress, refine guided instruction groups, and inform future instruction.

We store the students' assessments and work samples in pocket folders and we use a Profile Index to organize assessment information. This offers an at-a-glance overview of student progress and facilitates reporting student progress. (A reproducible copy of this organizer is included in Appendix E, page 203.)

In Guided Comprehension, assessment is viewed as a natural part of instruction, a dynamic process in which both students and teacher actively participate. In the next chapter, we journey inside Guided Comprehension classrooms to observe their structure and learn how teachers at various grade levels use the Model to plan instruction.

To learn more about reading assessment, read

Barrentine, S.J. (1999). *Reading assessment: Principles and practices for elementary teachers*. Newark, DE: International Reading Association.

Griffin, P.E., Smith, P.G., & Burrill, L.E. (1995). *The American literacy profile scales: A framework for authentic assessment*. Portsmouth, NH: Heinemann.

McLaughlin, M. (2000a). Assessment for the 21st century: Performance, portfolios, and profiles. In M. McLaughlin & M.E. Vogt (Eds.), *Creativity and innovation in content area teaching* (pp. 301–327). Norwood, MA: Christopher-Gordon.

CHAPTER 7

Classroom Applications of Guided Comprehension

Reading is like an adventure. You can use your imagination to see the story in your own way. If you like reading, then you must have a huge imagination. If you don't like reading, you're wasting your life.

Eric Pritchard, Grade 6

In this chapter we tie together all aspects of Guided Comprehension. We begin by presenting a brief overview of a Guided Comprehension classroom, including physical attributes of the environment and the social nature of the learning. Then we use fourth-, sixth-, and eighth-grade classroom planning examples to illustrate how the teachers developed all stages of Guided Comprehension. These are followed by teacher reflections and sample student responses. We also make connections to Appendix F, which contains Guided Comprehension plans for other strategies and grade levels.

INSIDE A GUIDED COMPREHENSION CLASSROOM

Imagine that we are walking into Kim Ware's fourth-grade classroom. It is difficult to see Kim because she is working with a small group of readers in a corner of the room. There are small groups of engaged readers, writers, and talkers all over the room. In one area, four students are engaged in a conversation about who committed the crime in the mystery they are reading. Several students are around the room working at various literacy centers—two students are practicing for a Readers Theatre performance, two are publishing the alphabet books they have just finished writing, three are making and writing words using the letters from a mystery word Kim has chosen, and four students are working on a PowerPoint presentation to share the research they have just completed. In another section of the room, four students working in a Reciprocal Teaching group after reading a story are sharing predictions, summaries, questions, and clarifications. The students do not even look up when we walk in because they are so engaged in their work.

The room is filled with print. There are poetry charts, a word wall of theme-related vocabulary words, original student writing, a class library, book baskets on students' desks, self-selected vocabulary books, and Guided Comprehension Journals. The class is abuzz with conversation, reading, and writing. Students are engaged and helping one another learn. It is a lively literacy context.

The students in Kim's class are engaged in Guided Comprehension. They have learned how to work in whole groups, small groups, and independently. When they need help, they usually turn to one another instead of Kim; she has taught them to be independent workers. Kim has taught her students to use comprehension strategies to read successfully and to take active roles in learning. She also has taught them how to work at literacy centers and has held them accountable for what they have learned.

How did Kim get to this place? Are her students gifted? No. These students are like any other fourth graders. Some are excellent readers while others are not at grade level. Some students are mature and others are naïve. Although they are quite diverse, they are engaging in meaningful literacy activities.

We worked in the field with Kim and her colleagues to pilot and refine the Guided Comprehension Model. We introduced the Model through direct instruction. Kim's reflection contains her thoughts about using the Model in her teaching. Kim and her colleagues provided periodic feedback and student samples that informed the refinement of the Model.

The learning environment in Kim's classroom is the result of detailed preparation. Even before school officially started, she was busy preparing her Guided Comprehension classroom. She worked with several other fourth-grade teachers in her school to

- group books by genre, author, and approximate level;
- prepare a variety of theme-related and ongoing learning centers;
- choose and label books that would provide good examples for directly teaching comprehension skills; and
- develop a record-keeping system for students to use and for Kim to monitor.

Once these beginning projects were completed, Kim spent the first month of school preparing her students to work in small groups. She introduced the framework, and modeled step by step what was expected in each stage. She introduced several comprehension centers, and, using whole-group instruction, taught her students how to complete a variety of tasks independently in that setting. She also showed the students how to be effective participants in Literature Circles, how to maintain a Guided Comprehension Journal, and how to assume discussion roles. Then she modeled how each role might contribute to discussion, and created a rubric for successful participation. Kim knew that if she wanted her students to engage successfully in independent routines, she had to teach them how to do it by modeling, guiding, and allowing them time to practice with one another and independently.

During this first month, Kim was also busy determining the strengths and needs of her students by gathering assessment information. She learned about students' self-perceptions through the reader and writer self-perception scales. She found out about their interests and hobbies so she could make sure she had many books they would enjoy. Kim also needed to find out the students' reading levels and what strategies they used to help them make sense of text. For this information, she tape recorded each student reading several short passages of narrative and expository texts and retelling key points. She then analyzed these for accuracy, fluency, and strategy use. Kim used her findings to inform instructional planning and organize guided small groups, knowing that her ongoing assessments would help her to modify groups and lessons to continually meet the needs of her students.

Although the first month of school was a busy time for Kim, she knew that if she spent time teaching her students to work independently and finding out about their literacy competencies, she could spend the rest of the year helping them to engage in meaningful reading and writing activities.

Once Kim had gathered information about her students, knew what kinds of books were accessible to them, and determined what they needed to learn, she was ready to plan for Guided Comprehension. Kim realized that her students were not previewing or monitoring in successful ways, so she made that the focus of one of her first Guided Comprehension whole-group lessons. She selected a book she had identified as a good one to model previewing. Then she chose the teaching idea that she thought would be most helpful to her students. Next, she determined how to help students gain more in-depth understanding of previewing and monitoring in guided small groups. She also decided on the tasks in which her students could engage when they participated in literacy centers and comprehension routines that would allow them to practice previewing and monitoring in independent settings. Figure 8 shows Kim's plans for this process.

Although Kim has planned her Guided Comprehension lessons based on the information she has gathered about her students, she knows that she can adapt her teaching based on how quickly students become more competent. Therefore, she uses her plan as a guide but views it as flexible and adapts it to best meet the needs of her students. She observes their oral and written responses in whole-class and small groups to help her make decisions about student progress and planning subsequent Guided Comprehension lessons.

GUIDED COMPREHENSION PLANS

Although we visualized Kim's classroom, our visions would have been strikingly similar if we had journeyed into the classrooms of other teachers who are using Guided Comprehension. All the contexts are lively, engaging, and authentic; they are literacy communities in which both students and teachers are active participants.

When thinking about instruction, these teachers base their plans on the Guided Comprehension Model (see Appendix F for planning form, page 251). Their lessons focus on how they can use comprehension strategies, multiple settings, and accessible texts to enhance their students' understanding. In this section we take a closer look at sample plans used in grades 4, 6, and 8. In each case, the teacher shares the plan, engages in a Think-Aloud, and provides samples of student responses. Guided Comprehension plans addressing other strategies, topics, and grade levels are included in Appendix F.

Beth's Fourth-Grade Guided Comprehension Plan

In Figure 9, Beth Gress, a fourth-grade teacher, plans how she will teach previewing using Anticipation/Reaction Guides with the theme of Native Americans. After the planning example, Beth engages in a Think-Aloud (presented here in the first person) that gives a step-by-step account of how the activity unfolded. Topics she addresses include links to content literacy and multiple instructional settings.

Figure 8. Guided Comprehension Planning Sheet

Teacher-Directed Whole-Group Instruction

Comprehension Strategies: Previewing and Monitoring

Book: *Armadillo Tattletale* (Kettleman, 2000)

Explain by reviewing all strategies we've learned so far and focusing on how to use "I Wonder" Statements to help preview the text and monitor reading.

Demonstrate by looking at the book cover and using an "I Wonder" Statement. Think aloud about what you are wondering. Read the first page and say, "I wonder...." Share your thoughts aloud again. Talk about the importance of thinking about the text and making predictions before and during reading.

Guide students by reading additional sections of text and encouraging them to create "I Wonder" Statements. Prompt as necessary. Discuss why they are wondering those things.

Practice by reading additional sections of text and having students create "I Wonder" Statements. Have students share their wonderings and reasons with the whole group. Use a Think-Pair-Share to complete the story this way.

Reflect by asking students how "I Wonder" Statements helped them to preview the text and monitor their reading.

Teacher-Guided Small-Group Instruction

Review previously taught strategies and focus on the strategy of the day.

Guide the students to read a section of the text silently. Have students take turns saying "I wonder..." and explaining their thinking. Encourage discussion and repeat with other sections of text.

Practice by having students finish reading the selection on their own. Have them write "I Wonder" Statements in their Guided Comprehension Journals and share them at the next group meeting.

Reflect by having students think about how using "I Wonder" Statements helped them engage with the text. Extend by having students share how they can use this process with texts in other settings.

Student-Facilitated Comprehension Centers

Students engage in reading picture books at the genre or library centers. They write "I Wonder" Statements on sticky notes and place them in the books they are reading. Other students can also add their wonderings. Students discuss the wonderings they placed in the books.

Student-Facilitated Comprehension Routines

In Literature Circles, students will read different selections and write "I Wonder" Statements about them. Then they will all play the role of discussion director as they explain the text they read and share their wonderings with the circle members.

Whole-Group Reflection and Goal Setting

Discuss how using "I Wonder" Statements helped students to preview text and monitor what they were reading. Have students share examples of their wonderings in pairs or small groups. Encourage students to reflect on the whole group's progress of attaining its goal.

Assessment Options

Use observation as the primary mode of assessment.

Figure 9. Comprehension Strategy: Previewing—Anticipation/Reaction Guide

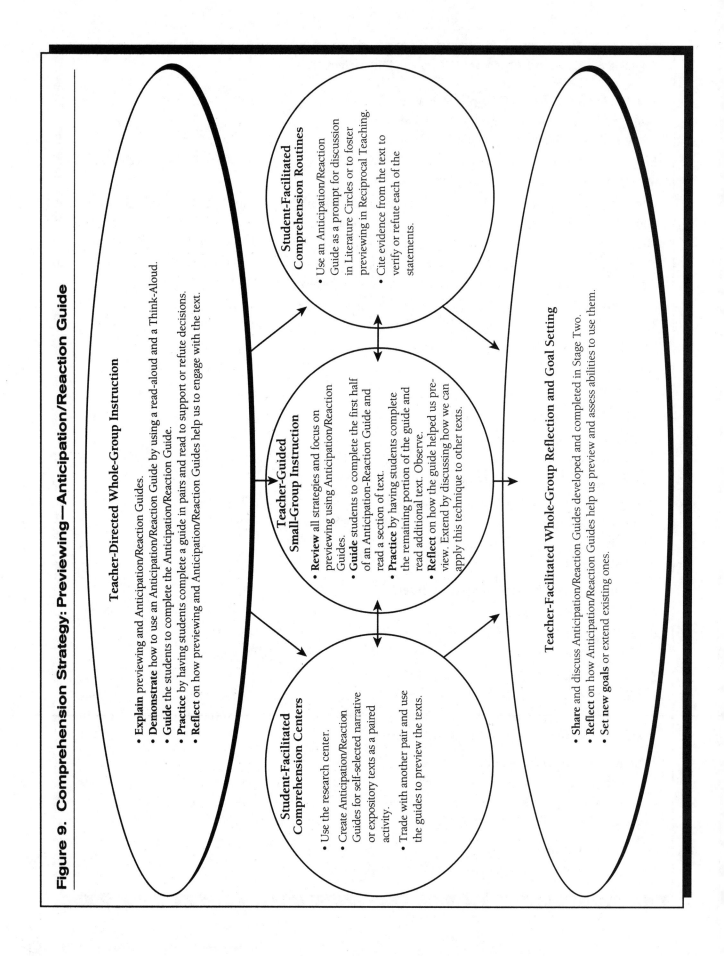

Teacher-Directed Whole-Group Instruction

- **Explain** previewing and Anticipation/Reaction Guides.
- **Demonstrate** how to use an Anticipation/Reaction Guide by using a read-aloud and a Think-Aloud.
- **Guide** the students to complete the Anticipation/Reaction Guide.
- **Practice** by having students complete a guide in pairs and read to support or refute decisions.
- **Reflect** on how previewing and Anticipation/Reaction Guides help us to engage with the text.

Student-Facilitated Comprehension Routines

- Use an Anticipation/Reaction Guide as a prompt for discussion in Literature Circles or to foster previewing in Reciprocal Teaching.
- Cite evidence from the text to verify or refute each of the statements.

Teacher-Guided Small-Group Instruction

- **Review** all strategies and focus on previewing using Anticipation/Reaction Guides.
- **Guide** students to complete the first half of an Anticipation-Reaction Guide and read a section of text.
- **Practice** by having students complete the remaining portion of the guide and read additional text. Observe.
- **Reflect** on how the guide helped us preview. Extend by discussing how we can apply this technique to other texts.

Student-Facilitated Comprehension Centers

- Use the research center.
- Create Anticipation/Reaction Guides for self-selected narrative or expository texts as a paired activity.
- Trade with another pair and use the guides to preview the texts.

Teacher-Facilitated Whole-Group Reflection and Goal Setting

- **Share** and discuss Anticipation/Reaction Guides developed and completed in Stage Two.
- **Reflect** on how Anticipation/Reaction Guides help us preview and assess abilities to use them.
- **Set new goals** or extend existing ones.

Teacher-directed whole-group instruction. *Knots on a Counting Rope* (Archambault & Martin, 1987)

Explain: I reviewed strategies previously taught and introduced previewing as the strategy of the day and focus of our class goal. I explained how previewing helps us to activate our prior knowledge, predict, make connections, and set purposes for reading.

Demonstrate: I read the first two statements on the Anticipation/Reaction Guide and used a Think-Aloud to demonstrate accessing prior knowledge. Based on that knowledge, I made an educated decision about each concept on the Anticipation/Reaction Guide.

Guide: We read the next statement and I guided the students to agree or disagree with the statement based on their prior knowledge. We discussed responses and repeated the process with the next statement. Then I read the text aloud. As I read, I stopped to think aloud, emphasizing the information that supported or refuted the statements in the Anticipation/Reaction Guide.

Practice: As I continued to read aloud, I invited the students to support their choices with evidence from the text. After reading the book, we revisited the Anticipation/Reaction Guide to verify our decisions and make appropriate changes.

Reflect: I encouraged students to reflect on how using an Anticipation/Reaction Guide helped focus their reading and encouraged them to transact with the text. Then we talked about how the text confirmed some of our initial beliefs and how it surprised us with other information.

Teacher-guided small-group instruction. In one of my small groups I used a four-step guided instruction process (Review, Guide, Practice, Reflect and Extend) to guide students in using Anticipation/Reaction Guides. As we read *Sees Behind Trees* (Dorris, 1997), students discussed possible changes to their responses and supported them with information from the text.

By the end of our lesson, my students seemed comfortable with this aspect of previewing. They did a good job of making connections between their thinking and supportive ideas in the text. They also reflected on how this helped their reading and made connections to other settings.

Student-facilitated comprehension centers. Various fiction and nonfiction books on Native Americans were placed in the literacy center. The students read books and created an Anticipation/Reaction Guide to which other students could respond. I encouraged them to focus on the social studies content. The Anticipation/Reaction Guide that appears here is one they designed for the book *Little Firefly: An Algonquin Legend* (Cohlene & Reasoner, 1991).

	Agree	Disagree
1. Algonquins live in wigwams.	_____	_____
2. Young girls learn the same roles as the women.	_____	_____

3. Native Americans use parts of animals to build tools. _____ _____

4. Algonquins eat corn and moose meat. _____ _____

Student-facilitated comprehension routines. Some of the students completed an Anticipation/Reaction Guide prior to participating in Literature Circles using books about Native Americans. Titles included *Guests* (Dorris, 1994), *The Sign of the Beaver* (George & Speare, 1984), *Morning Girl* (Dorris, 1999), and *Squanto, Friend of the Pilgrims* (Bulla & Williams, 1990). After discussing their books, the students made connections between the text and the Anticipation/Reaction Guide to explain their answers. The Anticipation/Reaction Guide and some of the students' responses follow:

	Agree	Disagree
1. Native Americans have ceremonies to receive their names.	_____	_____
2. Native Americans tell legends to explain the unknown.	_____	_____
3. People see without using their eyes.	_____	_____
4. Native Americans respect nature.	_____	_____

> I believe that Native Americans do have ceremonies to receive their names because Moss earns his new name after going on away time. (Jamel)
>
> I believe that Native Americans do tell legends to explain the unknown because they tell the guests a story about "The People Who Lost Each Other." They think that the guests may be the children of Never Enough. (Marco)
>
> I believe Native Americans respect nature because in the legend "The People Who Lost Each Other" adults were assigned to make sure the area was left as it was found. Also, the children were told to leave everything as it is, but Never Enough had to have the deer antlers. That is why the people lost each other. (Chandra)

Teacher-facilitated whole-group reflection and goal setting.
Students reflected on how the Anticipation/Reaction Guide prepared them for reading about the topic; they used it to make connections to their background knowledge and set purposes for reading. This led to whole-group sharing and goal setting.

Assessment opportunities. There are multiple opportunities to assess during this lesson. Observation and informal written response work well in all stages. Examples of particular assessments include completed Anticipation/Reaction Guides and student-designed Anticipation/Reaction Guides.

Jacquelyn's Sixth-Grade Comprehension Plan

In Figure 10, Jacquelyn Seaborg, a sixth-grade teacher, plans how she will use texts about the Holocaust as the basis for teaching evaluative questions. Her Guided Comprehension plan includes a variety of texts, multiple settings, and the comprehension strategy. Jacquelyn walks us through her lesson by sharing a Think-Aloud.

Teacher-directed whole-group instruction.

Explain: I reminded students of all the strategies we've learned and introduced evaluating through Evaluative Questioning. I explained that when we evaluate we make judgments and this helps us express our thinking.

Demonstrate: I then applied the concept of Evaluative Questioning to a section of *Anne Frank* (McDonough, 1997), which I had just finished reading aloud. I thought out loud about the questions the book made me think about. I discussed how I thought of the questions and how I could find the answers, using the text and my own ideas.

Guide: Next, I guided the students, in small groups, to generate two questions the book made them think about. I encouraged them to explain why they thought of the questions and how they could figure out the answers.

Practice: I read the next section of text out loud and asked the students to generate evaluative questions and responses. I continued this process through a portion of the text. The following are samples of the questions the students created:

> How would you defend what the Frank family did to avoid being sent to the concentration camp?
>
> How would you justify Hitler's actions to someone had you been part of the Nazi army?
>
> What do you think happened to the friends that helped smuggle food and clothing to the Frank family?

Reflect: We discussed the importance of Evaluative Questioning and how it helps us understand the text better and make judgments. Then we talked about how we could use Evaluative Questioning while reading other types of text.

I think the students performed well. Next, pairs of students practiced creating evaluative questions with additional sections of text and shared them with the whole group. Other class members responded to the questions. At the end of our lesson we reflected on how we used Evaluative Questioning, how it helped us understand text, and how we will use it when we read other texts.

Teacher-guided small-group instruction.
In one of my small groups, I reviewed Evaluative Questioning and reminded students of the keywords used in evaluative questions. Then I guided students' reading of selections from *Number the Stars* (Lowry, 1990), and helped with their creation of evalua-

Figure 10. Comprehension Strategy: Evaluating—Evaluative Questioning

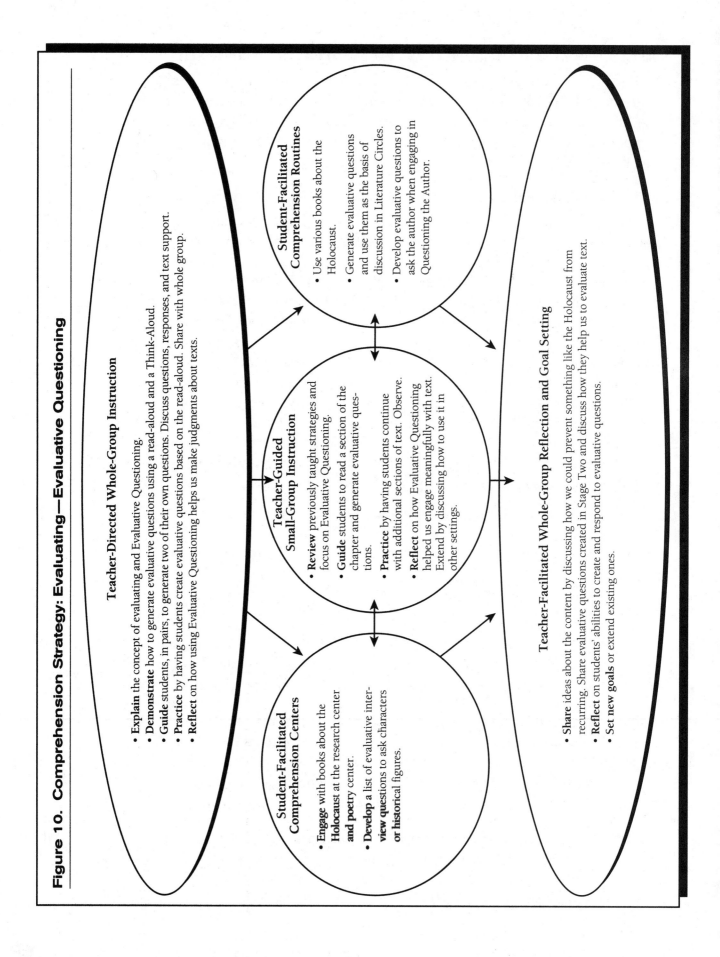

Teacher-Directed Whole-Group Instruction

- **Explain** the concept of evaluating and Evaluative Questioning.
- **Demonstrate** how to generate evaluative questions using a read-aloud and a Think-Aloud.
- **Guide** students, in pairs, to generate two of their own questions. Discuss questions, responses, and text support.
- **Practice** by having students create evaluative questions based on the read-aloud. Share with whole group.
- **Reflect** on how using Evaluative Questioning helps us make judgments about texts.

Student-Facilitated Comprehension Routines

- **Use** various books about the Holocaust.
- **Generate** evaluative questions and use them as the basis of discussion in Literature Circles.
- **Develop** evaluative questions to ask the author when engaging in Questioning the Author.

Teacher-Guided Small-Group Instruction

- **Review** previously taught strategies and focus on Evaluative Questioning.
- **Guide** students to read a section of the chapter and generate evaluative questions.
- **Practice** by having students continue with additional sections of text. Observe.
- **Reflect** on how Evaluative Questioning helped us engage meaningfully with text. Extend by discussing how to use it in other settings.

Student-Facilitated Comprehension Centers

- **Engage** with books about the Holocaust at the research center and poetry center.
- **Develop** a list of evaluative interview questions to ask characters or historical figures.

Teacher-Facilitated Whole-Group Reflection and Goal Setting

- **Share** ideas about the content by discussing how we could prevent something like the Holocaust from recurring. Share evaluative questions created in Stage Two and discuss how they help us to evaluate text.
- **Reflect** on students' abilities to create and respond to evaluative questions.
- **Set new goals** or extend existing ones.

tive questions. The following is a student-generated question and a few student responses:

> How would you justify the fact that Papa told Annemarie and Ellen to lie about being sisters so Ellen wouldn't be relocated?
>
> • My parents always tell me not to lie, but in some situations you may need to.
>
> • The lie protected an innocent young child from being harmed.

At the end of our lesson we reflected on how we used Evaluative Questioning, how it helped us understand text, and how we will use it when we read other texts.

I think the students performed well. They created viable questions, and they supported their thinking with connections to the text and their own lives. Once again they seemed to appreciate using the signal words that I shared when I taught them how to generate questions.

Student-facilitated comprehension centers. The students read books about the Holocaust at the research and poetry centers and developed a list of evaluative interview questions that could be asked of characters from those books. The following questions are examples of those student-generated questions and the people to whom the questions were addressed:

> German soldier, how can you defend your actions during WWII?
>
> Anne Frank, what experiences do you value most from when you stayed in the attic?
>
> Miep, how can you defend your position as someone who helped the Jewish community during the Holocaust? When reflecting on helping the Jewish families, what are some things you value about that experience?

Related books on this topic include *A Picture Book of Anne Frank* (Adler, 1994) and *Four Perfect Pebbles* (Perl & Lazan, 1999).

Student-facilitated comprehension routines. The students participated in a Literature Circle about various books on the Holocaust theme, including *Terrible Things: An Allegory of the Holocaust* (Bunting, 1995), *The Devil's Arithmetic* (Yolen, 1990), and *The Diary of Anne Frank* (Goodrich, 1993). The discussion directors presented evaluative questions to the group. The students in the group discussed those questions based on information from the books they were reading. Then students generated their own evaluative questions for peers to answer. The following example is from Kevin, a student who had read *Terrible Things*:

> The author of this book used animals as a symbol for humans during the Holocaust. How can you justify the author using animals to portray this horrible historical event?

Teacher-facilitated whole-group reflection and goal setting.
In this stage, our reflections addressed both the content and the strategy. First we reflected on how we could prevent something like the Holocaust from recurring and created goals that will help accomplish that. This helped students to make text-world connections. Then students used a Think-Pair-Share to reflect on their abilities to create and respond to evaluative questions. Finally, we engaged in goal setting.

Assessment opportunities. I observed students' discussions and used their creation of and response to evaluative questions to assess during this lesson.

Richard's Eighth-Grade Guided Comprehension Plan

In Figure 11, Richard Watkins, an eighth-grade teacher, plans how he will teach the comprehension strategy *evaluating* using a variety of texts, multiple settings, and a Discussion Web. He uses a Think-Aloud to take us through his lesson.

Teacher-directed whole-group instruction. The students and I discussed the concepts of opinions and persuasion at the start of class. Then I read the article "The Right to Bear Arms" to the students, and we talked about it in terms of our opinions and how we might persuade others to think about the topic in the same way we did. I provided them with the Discussion Web format and engaged in direct instruction. As part of this process I began a Discussion Web based on the following question: Should the U.S. Constitution be changed to prevent private ownership of guns? I cited examples from the text to support both positive and negative responses (see Figure 12). I guided the students to extend the discussion by finding more text examples for each side. Next, students worked in groups to come to a consensus. Ideas and supports were shared with the whole class. Finally, we discussed the importance of using a discussion guide to look at both sides of an issue, examine the facts for both, and make informed decisions and opinions.

Teacher-guided small-group instruction. In this setting, I began by reviewing the comprehension strategies, including evaluating. Then I guided students through the reading of an informational article about school violence. After modeling two different positions and use of text supports, I asked the students to provide additional text support for each position. After discussion, the group came to consensus. Then we reflected and extended our thinking.

Student-facilitated comprehension centers. In one group, students used the research center to read information about school violence from the Web site http://www.dosomething.org. Then they completed a Discussion Web

Figure 11. Comprehension Strategy: Evaluating—Discussion Web

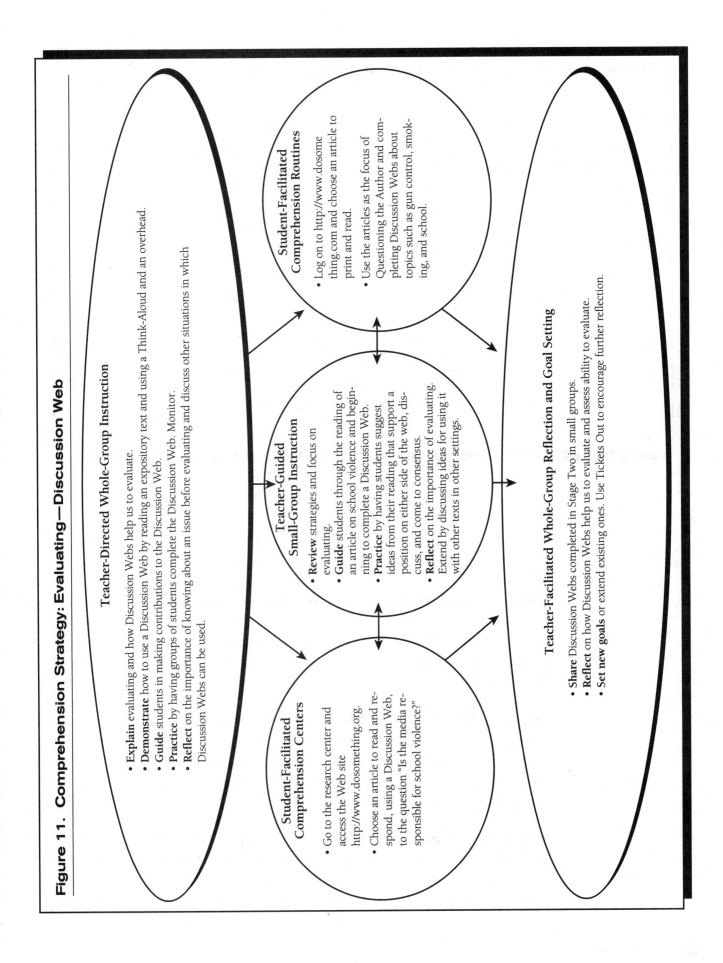

Teacher-Directed Whole-Group Instruction

- **Explain** evaluating and how Discussion Webs help us to evaluate.
- **Demonstrate** how to use a Discussion Web by reading an expository text and using a Think-Aloud and an overhead.
- **Guide** students in making contributions to the Discussion Web.
- **Practice** by having groups of students complete the Discussion Web. Monitor.
- **Reflect** on the importance of knowing about an issue before evaluating and discuss other situations in which Discussion Webs can be used.

Student-Facilitated Comprehension Routines

- Log on to http://www.dosome thing.com and choose an article to print and read.
- Use the articles as the focus of Questioning the Author and completing Discussion Webs about topics such as gun control, smoking, and school.

Teacher-Guided Small-Group Instruction

- **Review** strategies and focus on evaluating.
- **Guide** students through the reading of an article on school violence and beginning to complete a Discussion Web.
- **Practice** by having students suggest ideas from their reading that support a position on either side of the web, discuss, and come to consensus.
- **Reflect** on the importance of evaluating. Extend by discussing ideas for using it with other texts in other settings.

Student-Facilitated Comprehension Centers

- Go to the research center and access the Web site http://www.dosomething.org.
- Choose an article to read and respond, using a Discussion Web, to the question "Is the media responsible for school violence?"

Teacher-Facilitated Whole-Group Reflection and Goal Setting

- **Share** Discussion Webs completed in Stage Two in small groups.
- **Reflect** on how Discussion Webs help us to evaluate and assess ability to evaluate.
- **Set new goals** or extend existing ones. Use Tickets Out to encourage further reflection.

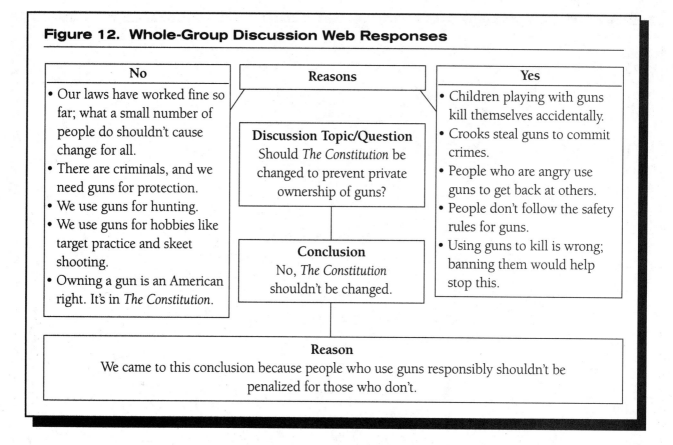

Figure 12. Whole-Group Discussion Web Responses

No	Reasons	Yes
• Our laws have worked fine so far; what a small number of people do shouldn't cause change for all. • There are criminals, and we need guns for protection. • We use guns for hunting. • We use guns for hobbies like target practice and skeet shooting. • Owning a gun is an American right. It's in *The Constitution*.	**Discussion Topic/Question** Should *The Constitution* be changed to prevent private ownership of guns? **Conclusion** No, *The Constitution* shouldn't be changed.	• Children playing with guns kill themselves accidentally. • Crooks steal guns to commit crimes. • People who are angry use guns to get back at others. • People don't follow the safety rules for guns. • Using guns to kill is wrong; banning them would help stop this.

Reason
We came to this conclusion because people who use guns responsibly shouldn't be penalized for those who don't.

based on the following question: Are the media responsible for school violence? Figure 13 shows sample Discussion Web responses.

Student-facilitated comprehension routines. Students logged onto http://www.dosomething.org and chose an article to print and read. They then used these articles as the focus of Questioning the Author and completed Discussion Webs about such topics as gun control, advertising, school violence, and smoking.

Teacher-facilitated whole-group reflection and goal setting. In Stage Three we reflected on our abilities to use the Discussion Web to choose our positions, support our thinking, and persuade others to share our views. We used a modified Tickets Out activity for reflection and sharing, then we created new goals.

Assessment opportunities. During this lesson, I observed students negotiating what information would be included in the positive and negative views of the Discussion Web and how they came to consensus. I also used completed Discussion Webs, Tickets Out, and student writing as informal measures.

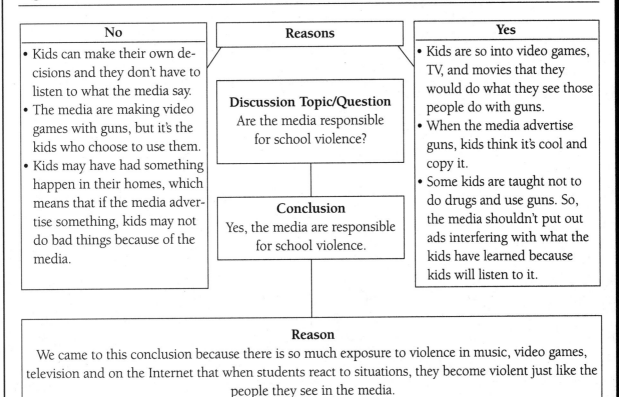

Figure 13. Teacher-Guided Small-Group Discussion Web Responses

No	Reasons	Yes
• Kids can make their own decisions and they don't have to listen to what the media say. • The media are making video games with guns, but it's the kids who choose to use them. • Kids may have had something happen in their homes, which means that if the media advertise something, kids may not do bad things because of the media.	**Discussion Topic/Question** Are the media responsible for school violence? **Conclusion** Yes, the media are responsible for school violence.	• Kids are so into video games, TV, and movies that they would do what they see those people do with guns. • When the media advertise guns, kids think it's cool and copy it. • Some kids are taught not to do drugs and use guns. So, the media shouldn't put out ads interfering with what the kids have learned because kids will listen to it.

Reason

We came to this conclusion because there is so much exposure to violence in music, video games, television and on the Internet that when students react to situations, they become violent just like the people they see in the media.

At the conclusion of their lessons, Beth, Jacquelyn, and Richard engaged in assessment updates. This involved including evidence such as observations and comments in selected students' Guided Comprehension Profiles. These teachers have found that doing daily updates for a few students facilitates organization and management. By the end of the week, they have current assessment information in all their students' profiles.

The examples in this chapter have illustrated how Guided Comprehension functions when situated in fourth-, sixth-, and eighth-grade classrooms. Plans that demonstrate the Model's use at other grade levels with other strategies complete with teacher reflections and sample student responses can be found in Appendix F. A sample 60- and 90-minute class schedule for using Guided Comprehension is also included in Appendix F (page 252).

In the final chapter, we extend the role of reflection by sharing teachers' and students' reactions to Guided Comprehension. We also reflect on what we have learned from designing and implementing the Model.

To learn more about planning innovative literacy instruction, read

Kaywell, J. (Ed.). (1993). *Adolescent literature as a complement to the classics.* Norwood, MA: Christopher-Gordon.

Richardson, J.S. (2000). *Read it aloud! Using literature in the secondary content classroom.* Newark, DE: International Reading Association.

Tierney, R.J., & Readence, J.E. (2000). *Reading strategies and practices* (5th ed.). Needham Heights, MA: Allyn & Bacon.

CHAPTER 8

Reflections on the Guided Comprehension Model

I think reading is something teachers
use to get us hooked on school.

Rosie Parker, Grade 3

I n this final chapter we bring the book full circle by sharing a variety of reflections about Guided Comprehension. We begin by presenting ideas from teachers, then we offer students' reactions. We conclude by sharing our thoughts about the development and implementation of the Model.

TEACHERS' REACTIONS TO GUIDED COMPREHENSION

The reflections presented here are from teachers in grades 3–8 who had either implemented the Model or reviewed it in a focus group. The reflections included both oral and written comments directed to fellow teachers and to us as the creators of the Model. We collected the teachers' ideas about the Guided Comprehension process to help refine the Model. Those engaging in written reflection had the option of including their names.

Teachers commented on a number of different aspects of the Model, including its structure and accessibility, planning format, assessment options, and time constraints.

We begin by presenting a detailed reflection written by Kim Ware, then provide brief excerpts from other teachers' reflections.

Kim's Reflection

Many reading programs and strategies have been introduced in the past few years. I enjoy learning new ways to teach reading, but lately I had been feeling that these methods were not helping me to truly *teach* my students what they needed to know.

I find this to be especially true in the upper grades. By the time they reach this level, most students have learned to read fluently, and it is more difficult to recognize and track their growth. That is why I am truly excited about the Guided Comprehension Model. When I used it with my students, I was able to see that they were developing good comprehension strategies and successfully applying them. I was impressed with the level of independence in reading that my students gained. Most of all I was surprised by the amount of literacy-based discussion that took place every day among the students. In the past, it was like pulling teeth to spark a conversation about a novel; now classroom talk is a natural part of our learning experiences.

When I first started implementing Guided Comprehension, I was concerned about the time it required. I found that it actually took me 2 or 3 days to complete the entire process. However, after directly teaching the Model, its independent applications, and its strategies, my students and I became familiar with the routine. Eventually we were completing the process on a daily basis.

When I first started using the Model, I was also worried about the amount of time it might take away from students' reading. I used to divide reading into two periods: whole-group novel sharing and small-group guided reading or Literature Circles. My students also used a great deal of time answering comprehension questions. After using Guided Comprehension, I realized that my students spent very little time actually reading in my former organizational plan. Now, as I look around my room, I see my students spending that time reading, engaged with text and in conversations about text while applying higher level thinking.

Another time-related issue is planning. My planning took more time when the Model was new to me. When truly considering all students' strengths, needs, interests, and range of levels, reading does require plenty of planning time. Using the Model kept me well organized and well aware of all of my students' needs, responsibilities, and progress.

I am very pleased with this framework for teaching about comprehension. My students are benefiting from learning comprehension strategies, collaborating, reflecting, and setting new goals. They are participating in activities that are appropriate for their ability levels and using lots of different types of texts.

I have also benefited as a teacher by using this model. I now have a very good understanding of each child's capabilities and needs. I also have the flexibility to modify the plan in order to meet those needs.

Although I feel this is the best approach for me, I also I asked my students which approach to reading works best for them. Most of the class preferred Guided Comprehension because "we really dig into books and understand what we're reading" and "it makes us want to read more."

Other Teachers' Reactions

The following excerpts were taken from Grade 3–8 teachers' reflections on Guided Comprehension:

Guided Comprehension is realistic. The structure is easy to follow and, although I expected it to benefit my students, I was surprised and pleased that it helped me to develop better teaching habits. The constant use of assessment has helped me to understand my students in more in-depth ways.

I appreciate the focus on comprehension strategies. My students are in seventh grade and many of them were still unaware of how to use the strategies effectively.

The Model gives direction to teaching and learning. I knew that many of the components of the Model were important, but I always felt there was something missing. The Model and assessment system have given me a framework for teaching and that's what I needed.

Everyone in my class is well informed—we are always aware of our goals and we know that setting new ones is part of our learning experience. My students feel that they're part of the classroom community and motivation is built into the process.

I never thought my eighth graders would be interested in the comprehension centers, but I was wrong! They are really into this Model and seem to have special appreciation for the frequent opportunities to apply what they've learned with their peers and on their own.

All my students are reading and learning using multiple levels and different types of text. My students have a renewed interest in reading. I am no longer teaching to the middle; I'm teaching everyone. I think it's especially important that my students have plenty of opportunities to engage with more challenging text with my full support. My students are in eighth grade. Having access to the higher level text is important to them.

I used to teach Guided Reading in second grade. I think this Model goes further and gives us a framework for teaching reading in grades 3–8—not just in guided small groups, but in several different settings where comprehension and different types of text are a greater focus. It's a more comprehensive approach.

The Model and profile are perfect for differentiating instruction. I know I am meeting my students' individual needs now.

What I especially like is that everyone in my class—including me—has become so proficient in engaging in the Model as a routine.

It uses discussion, writing, drawing, drama, music, and authentic tasks to enhance students' reading comprehension. This helps maintain my students' interest and motivation. I think this contributes to the effectiveness of Guided Comprehension because even though we know responding in multiple modes benefits students, we have a tendency not to provide these opportunities for upper grade students.

When I first started using the Model I was concerned about the amount of time all the direct instruction took, but as my students and I became more familiar with the Model, the timing aspect worked itself out.

In addition to the classroom reading teachers' reactions, special education teachers particularly valued the incorporation of multiple modes of response; reading specialists appreciated the teacher-guided small groups as settings in which they could teach their students—either in push-in or pull-out programs; and reading supervisors valued the teaching framework, student access to a variety of levels of text, and the multiple instructional settings.

Teachers' comments about Guided Comprehension were generally quite positive. Time was the only element identified as a tension. But, as Kim and others noted in their reflections, the time required lessens as the initial organization is completed and as students and teachers gain experience with the Model and come to view it as a teaching and learning routine.

STUDENTS' REACTIONS TO GUIDED COMPREHENSION

The students shared some wonderfully insightful reactions, as only students can. We have featured some of their comments in our chapter openings throughout the book, and the following are additional excerpts from their reflections:

I like Guided Comprehension because before we did this I thought I knew about reading but now I know that if I really think while I'm reading, reading is more than I used to think it was. I can do more than I could do before. We always make goals and then we work to get them. It's kind of like having a reading road map.

When you're comprehending, your brain is like a vacuum cleaner pulling the dirt from the rugs. It takes a lot to get it all, but when you picture what you're reading in your head, the picture is all there. I like my book basket because it has a lot of books I want to read and I can read.

Now reading makes me think. I used to just do it and didn't like it very much, but now I think it's all about me: what I like to read, books I can read, talking with the other kids and my teacher, how I use the strategies, what I do at the centers, what I think.

Last year in fifth grade all we did every day was silent reading. I didn't think that was fun and I didn't think I learned much, but this is fun and I think I'm learning a lot. We're reading and writing and talking all the time.

I think my favorite thing is making pictures in my head and asking myself does this make sense when I'm reading. I don't remember doing this before. It helps me figure out what I'm reading.

I like that we're all together sometimes and sometimes we're not and then we're all together again. It's like we're in the same class, then we're not, then we are. I like when we set our goals and then we do different stuff to show how we got to them.

For me comprehension is figuring out the mysteries about a book that you like. The strategies and working together help me do that.

OUR REFLECTIONS

While working with teachers to implement the Model, the following ideas repeatedly emerged as significant:

- Reading is a meaning-making process.
- Reading is a thinking process.
- Reading is social.
- Student choice is vital.
- Knowledgeable teachers are key.
- Accessible texts are critical.
- Direct instruction is important.
- A viable framework for teaching comprehension strategies is essential.

These thoughts were supported by the following components of the Guided Comprehension Model:

- A variety of instructional settings
- Integration of numerous genres

- Knowledge of text structures
- Dynamic grouping
- Multiple opportunities for practice, guided to independent: students with teachers, with peers, on their own
- Engaging settings for independent practice—centers and routines
- Opportunities to respond in a variety of modes
- Students and teachers as active participants
- Dynamic assessment, multiple measures, reflection, sharing, and goal setting

In summary, all elements of the context work together to promote reading comprehension. We also note that effective teachers need time to

- develop comprehension centers and routines;
- level texts;
- gather, compile, and synthesize information about individual students; and
- plan and teach.

FINAL THOUGHTS

Throughout the book we have responded to the questions most frequently raised about comprehension that are shared in the Preface. We have explained what comprehension is, what current beliefs about best practice are, how comprehension strategies can be taught, what role context plays, how classrooms can be organized and managed effectively, and how reading comprehension can be assessed.

At the start of the book we also noted that as literacy professionals we are all seeking greater conceptual and practical understanding of comprehension—how it functions and how it can be integrated into our teaching. We hope that after learning about Guided Comprehension you feel that your knowledge has increased on both levels.

Teaching Ideas and Blackline Masters

TEACHING IDEAS AT A GLANCE

Teaching Idea	When to Use	Comprehension Strategy	Text
Previewing			
Anticipation/Reaction Guide	Before After	Previewing Monitoring	Narrative Expository
Predict-o-Gram	Before After	Previewing Summarizing	Narrative
Prereading Plan (PreP)	Before After	Previewing Making Connections	Expository
Probable Passages	Before	Previewing Making Connections	Narrative
Questioning the Text	Before During	Previewing Making Connections Summarizing	Narrative Expository
Semantic Map	Before After	Previewing Knowing How Words Work	Narrative Expository
Storybook Introductions	Before	Previewing Knowing How Words Work Making Connections	Narrative Expository
Story Impressions	Before	Previewing Making Connections	Narrative
Self-Questioning			
"I Wonder" Statements	Before During After	Self-Questioning Previewing Making Connections	Narrative Expository
K-W-L and K-W-L-S	Before During After	Self-Questioning Previewing Making Connections	Expository
Paired Questioning	During After	Self-Questioning Making Connections Monitoring	Narrative Expository
Question-Answer Relationship (QAR)	After	Self-Questioning Making Connections Monitoring	Narrative Expository
Thick and Thin Questions	Before During After	Self-Questioning Making Connections	Narrative Expository
Making Connections			
Coding the Text	During	Making Connections	Narrative Expository
Connection Stems	After	Making Connections	Narrative Expository
Double-Entry Journal	Before During After	Making Connections Monitoring Summarizing	Narrative Expository
Drawing Connections	During After	Making Connections Visualizing	Narrative Expository
Save the Last Word for Me	After	Making Connections Evaluating	Narrative Expository

(continued)

TEACHING IDEAS AT A GLANCE (continued)

Teaching Idea	When to Use	Comprehension Strategy	Text
Visualizing			
Gallery Images	After	Visualizing Making Connections	Expository
Graphic Organizers/ Visual Organizers	Before During After	Visualizing Making Connections Summarizing	Narrative Expository
Guided Imagery	Before After	Visualizing Making Connections	Narrative Expository
Open-Mind Portrait	After	Visualizing Making Connections	Narrative Expository
Sketch to Stretch	After	Visualizing Making Connections	Narrative Expository
Knowing How Words Work			
Concept of Definition Map	Before	Knowing How Words Work	Narrative Expository
Context Clues	During	Knowing How Words Work	Narrative Expository
Decoding by Analogy	During	Knowing How Words Work	Narrative Expository
List-Group-Label	Before After	Knowing How Words Work Previewing Making Connections	Expository
Possible Sentences	Before After	Knowing How Words Work Previewing Monitoring Summarizing	Expository
RIVET	Before	Knowing How Words Work Previewing	Expository
Semantic Feature Analysis	Before	Knowing How Words Work Making Connections	Narrative Expository
Vocabulary by Analogy	During	Knowing How Words Work	Narrative Expository
Vocabulary Self-Collection	After	Knowing How Words Work Making Connections	Narrative Expository
Monitoring			
Bookmark Technique	During After	Monitoring Knowing How Words Work Making Connections Evaluating	Narrative Expository
INSERT	During	Monitoring Making Connections	Expository
Patterned Partner Reading	During	Monitoring Making Connections Evaluating	Narrative Expository
Say Something	During	Monitoring Making Connections	Narrative Expository
Think-Alouds	Before During After	All	Narrative Expository

(continued)

Teaching Idea	When to Use	Comprehension Strategy	Text
Summarizing			
Bio-Pyramid	After	Summarizing Making Connections Monitoring	Expository
Lyric Summaries	After	Summarizing	Narrative Expository
Narrative Pyramid	After	Summarizing Making Connections Monitoring	Narrative
Paired Summarizing	After	Summarizing Making Connections Monitoring	Narrative Expository
QuIP (Questions Into Paragraphs)	Before During After	Summarizing Self-Questioning	Expository
Retelling	After	Summarizing	Narrative
Summary Cubes	Before During After	Summarizing	Narrative Expository
Evaluating			
Discussion Web	After	Evaluating Making Connections	Narrative Expository
Evaluative Questioning	During After	Evaluating Self-Questioning	Narrative Expository
Journal Responses	During After	Evaluating Making Connections Summarizing	Narrative Expository
Meeting of the Minds	After	Evaluating	Narrative Expository
Persuasive Writing	Before During After	Evaluating	Narrative Expository
Comprehension Routines			
Directed Reading-Thinking Activity	Before During After	Previewing Making Connections Monitoring	Narrative Expository
Literature Circles	After	Making Connections Knowing How Words Work Monitoring Summarizing Evaluating	Narrative Expository
Questioning the Author (QtA)	During	Making Connections Self-Questioning Monitoring	Narrative Expository
Reciprocal Teaching	Before During After	Previewing Self-Questioning Monitoring Summarizing	Narrative Expository

TEACHING IDEAS

Anticipation/Reaction Guide

Purposes: To set purposes for reading texts; to activate prior knowledge and help make connections with the text.

Comprehension Strategies: Previewing, Monitoring

Text: Narrative, Expository   **Use:** Before and After Reading

Procedure: (Begin by explaining and modeling Anticipation/Reaction Guides.)

1. Select a text for the students to read.

2. Create three to five general statements for the students to respond to with agree or disagree. Create statements that are intuitively sound but may be disconfirmed by reading the text or that appear intuitively incorrect but may be proven true by reading the text. Have students indicate agreement or disagreement by placing a check in the appropriate column.

3. Have students read the text to confirm or disconfirm their original responses.

4. After reading, have students revisit their predictions and modify, if necessary.

Example: (*Animal Fact/Animal Fable* [1979] by Seymour Simon)

Agree   Disagree

_____ _____ 1. Bats use their eyes and ears to help them see at night.
_____ _____ 2. The mudskipper is a fish that can climb a tree.
_____ _____ 3. The speed of a cricket's chirp changes with the temperature.

Source: Readence, J.E., Bean, T.W., & Baldwin, R. (2000). *Content area reading: An integrated approach* (7th ed.). Dubuque, IA: Kendall/Hunt.

Predict-o-Gram

(See blackline, page 142.)

Purposes: To make predictions about a story using narrative elements; to introduce vocabulary.

Comprehension Strategies: Previewing, Summarizing

Text: Narrative   **Use:** Before and After Reading (revisit)

Procedure: (Begin by explaining and modeling Predict-o-Grams.)

1. Select vocabulary from the story to stimulate predictions. Vocabulary should represent the story elements: characters, setting, problem, action, and solution.

2. Have students decide which story element the word tells about and write each word on the Predict-o-Gram in the appropriate place.

3. Have students read the story.

4. Revisit the original predictions with students and make changes as necessary. Use the resulting information to summarize or retell the story.

Source: Blachowicz, C.L. (1986). Making connections: Alternatives to the vocabulary notebook. *Journal of Reading, 29,* 643–649.

Prereading Plan (PreP)

Purposes: To activate prior knowledge about a topic; to introduce new vocabulary and make connections.

Comprehension Strategies: Previewing, Making Connections

Text: Expository   **Use:** Before and After Reading

Procedure: (Begin by explaining and modeling PreP.)

1. Provide students with a cue word or idea to stimulate thinking about the topic.

2. Have students brainstorm words or concepts related to the topic. Write all ideas.

3. After all the words and ideas are listed, go back to each word and ask the contributor why he or she suggested that word. Clarify ideas or elaborate on concepts.

4. Read the text.

5. After reading, revisit the original list of words and revise as necessary.

Source: Langer, J. (1981). From theory to practice: A prereading plan. *Journal of Reading, 25,* 152–156.

Probable Passages

(See blackline, page 143.)

Purposes: To make predictions using story elements; to introduce vocabulary; to use story vocabulary to make connections with story structure.

Comprehension Strategies: Previewing, Making Connections

Text: Narrative   **Use:** Before Reading

Procedure: (Begin by explaining and modeling Probable Passages.)

1. Introduce key vocabulary from the story to students. (Choose vocabulary that represents various elements of the story.)

2. Have students use the key vocabulary to create probable sentences to predict each element in the story. (Providing a story frame/story map facilitates this process.)

3. Encourage students to share their predictions with the class.

4. Read the story to confirm or modify original predictions.

Example: (*Chrysanthemum* [1991] by Kevin Henkes)
Key Vocabulary: *Chrysanthemum, dreadful, school, perfect, Victoria, wilted, bloomed, Mrs. Twinkle, name*
Story Map: Using the words above, create a probable sentence to predict each story element.

Setting:	I think the story takes place in school.
Characters:	The characters' names are Chrysanthemum, Victoria, and Mrs. Twinkle.
Problem:	The flowers were perfect when they bloomed, but then they wilted and looked dreadful.
Solution:	The students decided to buy new flowers for their school.

Source: Adapted from Wood, K. (1984). Probable passages: A writing strategy. *The Reading Teacher, 37,* 496–499.

Questioning the Text

(See blackline, page 144.)

Purposes: To use knowledge of text structures and text supports to facilitate comprehension; to make connections and summarize information.

Comprehension Strategies: Previewing, Making Connections, Summarizing

Text: Narrative, Expository **Use:** Before and During Reading

Procedure: (Begin by explaining and modeling Questioning the Text.)

1. Think aloud by asking some or all the following questions before reading the text:

What is the text structure? Narrative? Expository? What clues help me know this?

What questions will this text answer?

What questions do I have for this text?

What clues does the front cover (title, cover art, author) offer? The contents page?

What do the physical aspects (size, length, print size) of the book tell me?

Is the author familiar? What do I know about the author? What connections can I make?

Is the topic familiar? What do I know about the topic? What connections can I make?

What clues do the genre and writing style provide for me?

Is there a summary? What does it help me know?

What does the information on the back cover tell me?

2. Provide small groups of students with a text and the questions. Guide students to question the text.

3. Discuss the information students compile.

4. Summarize the information. Have students add to this information during reading.

Note: Encourage students to question the text before and during reading to enhance their comprehension.

Source: McLaughlin, M., & Allen, M.B. (2002). *Guided Comprehension: A teaching model for grades 3–8.* Newark, DE: International Reading Association.

Semantic Map

Purposes: To activate and organize knowledge about a specific topic.

Comprehension Strategies: Previewing, Knowing How Words Work

Text: Narrative, Expository **Use:** Before and After Reading

Procedure: (Begin by explaining and modeling Semantic Maps.)

1. Select the main idea or topic of the passage; write it on a chart, overhead, or chalkboard; and put a circle around it.

2. Have students brainstorm subtopics related to the topic. Use lines to connect these to the main topic.

3. Have students brainstorm specific vocabulary or ideas related to each subtopic. Record these ideas beneath each subtopic.

4. Read the text and revise the Semantic Map to reflect new knowledge.

Example:

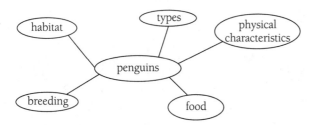

Source: Johnson, D.D., & Pearson, P.D. (1984). *Teaching reading vocabulary* (2nd ed.). New York: Holt, Rinehart and Winston.

Storybook Introductions

Purposes: To introduce story, characters, vocabulary, and style of a book prior to reading; to promote prediction and anticipation of a story; to make new texts accessible to readers.

Comprehension Strategies: Previewing, Knowing How Words Work, Making Connections

Text: Narrative, Expository   **Use:** Before Reading

Procedure: (Begin by explaining and modeling Storybook Introductions.)

1. Preview the text and prepare the introduction. Focus on those points that will help make the text accessible to students. These may include text structure, specific vocabulary, language patterns, plot, or difficult parts.

2. Introduce the topic, title, and characters.

3. Encourage students to respond to the cover and text illustrations by relating to personal experiences or other texts.

4. While browsing through the illustrations, introduce the plot up to the climax (if possible, not giving the ending away). Throughout this process, encourage students to make connections to personal experiences or other texts, and make predictions about what will happen next.

5. Choose to introduce some literary language, book syntax, specialized vocabulary, or repetitive sentence patterns that will be helpful to the readers.

6. Have students read the text. Then engage in discussion and other activities.

Note: It is important to make decisions about the introduction based on the text and the students' competency and familiarity with the text type. Introductions may range from teacher involvement in a rich introduction to a shorter, more focused introduction, to a brief introduction.

Source: Clay, M.M. (1991). Introducing a new storybook to young readers. *The Reading Teacher, 45,* 264–273.

Story Impressions

Purposes: To provide a framework for narrative writing; to encourage predictions about the story; to make connections between story vocabulary and story structure.

Comprehension Strategies: Previewing, Making Connections

Text: Narrative   **Use:** Before Reading

Procedure: (Begin by explaining and modeling Story Impressions.)

1. Provide students with a list of words that provide clues about the story. Choose words that relate to the narrative elements—characters, setting, problem, events, and solution.

2. List words in sequential order as they appear in the story. Connect them with downward arrows. Share the list of clues with the students.

3. In small groups, students then create stories using the clues in the order presented.

4. Have students share their stories with the class and discuss them.

5. Read the original story to the class and have students compare and contrast their story with the original.

Example: (*Stone Fox* [1988] by John Reynolds Gardiner)

Little Willy
↓
Grandfather
↓
sick
↓
potatoes
↓
taxes
↓
dogsled race
↓
Stone Fox
↓
win

Source: McGinley, W., & Denner, P. (1987). Story impressions: A prereading/prewriting activity. *Journal of Reading, 31,* 248–253.

"I Wonder" Statements

Purposes: To encourage self-questioning; to provide a model for active thinking during the reading process.

Comprehension Strategies: Self-Questioning, Previewing, Making Connections

Text: Narrative, Expository   **Use:** Before, During, and After Reading

Procedure: (Begin by explaining and modeling "I Wonder" Statements.)

1. Model for the students how to wonder. Do this orally and in writing, beginning your thoughts with "I wonder." Wonder about life experiences or the world, as well as events in stories or facts presented in texts.

2. Guide students to wonder about world or life things, story events, and ideas presented in texts.

3. Provide students with a format for sharing their wonderings orally or in writing. This may include an "I Wonder" book or a Think-Pair-Share session.

4. Share wonders and discuss them with text support, if possible.

5. Encourage students to wonder throughout the reading of a story or content area text. Use students' "I Wonder" Statements to provide structure for further reading or research.

Source: Harvey, S., & Goudvis, A. (2000). *Strategies that work: Teaching comprehension to enhance understanding*. York, ME: Stenhouse.

Know–Want to Know–Learn (K-W-L)

(See blacklines, pages 145–146.)

Purposes: To activate students' prior knowledge about a topic; to set purposes for reading; to confirm, revise, or expand original understandings related to a topic.

Comprehension Strategies: Self-Questioning, Previewing, Making Connections

Text: Expository   **Use:** Before, During, and After Reading

Procedure: (Begin by explaining and modeling K-W-L.)

1. Have students brainstorm everything they know, or think they know, about a specific topic. Write, or have students write, these ideas in the *K* column.

2. Next, have students write or tell some things they want to know about the topic. List these in the *W* column.

3. Have students read the text. (As they read, they can jot down new ideas, facts, or concepts they learn in the *L* column.)

4. List or have students list what they learned in the *L* column.

5. Revisit the *K* column to modify or confirm original understandings.

6. Revisit the *W* column to check if all questions have been answered.

7. Discuss the completed K-W-L.

Source: Ogle, D. (1986). K-W-L: A teaching model that develops active reading of expository text. *The Reading Teacher*, *39*, 564–570.

Adaptation: Know–Want to Know–Learned–Still Want to Know (K-W-L-S)

Extend K-W-L by having students list what they still want to know in a fourth column. Develop a plan to help them find answers to these questions.

Source: Sippola, A.E. (1995). K-W-L-S. *The Reading Teacher*, *48*, 542–543.

Paired Questioning

Purpose: To engage in questioning and active decision making during the reading of a narrative or expository text.

Comprehension Strategies: Self-Questioning, Making Connections, Monitoring

Text: Narrative, Expository   **Use:** During and After Reading

Procedure: (Begin by explaining and modeling Paired Questioning.)

1. In pairs each student reads the title or subtitle of a manageable section of text.

2. Students put the reading materials aside. Each student asks a question that comes to mind related to the title or subtitle. The partner tries to give a reasonable answer to the question.

3. Students silently read a predetermined (by teacher or students) section of text.

4. After reading, the students take turns asking a question about the reading. One student asks a question first; the partner answers, using the text if needed. Then they reverse roles. Students continue this process until the text is finished.

5. After they have completed reading the text, one partner tells what he or she believes to be the important and unimportant ideas in the text and explains why. The partner agrees or disagrees with the choices and offers support for his or her thinking.

Source: Vaughn, J., & Estes, T. (1986). *Reading and reasoning beyond the primary grades*. Boston: Allyn & Bacon.

Question-Answer Relationship (QAR)

(See blackline, page 147.)

Purposes: To promote self-questioning; to answer comprehension questions by focusing on the information source needed to answer the question.

Comprehension Strategies: Self-Questioning, Making Connections, Monitoring

Text: Narrative, Expository   **Use:** After Reading

Procedure: (Begin by explaining and modeling QAR.)

1. Introduce the QAR concept and terminology. Explain that there are two kinds of information:

 In the book—The answer is found in the text.

 In my head—The answer requires input from the student's understandings and background knowledge.

 Explain that there are two kinds of QARs for each kind of information:

 In the book:
     Right There—The answer is stated in the passage.
     Think and Search—The answer is derived from more than one sentence or paragraph but is stated in the text.
 In my head:
     On My Own—The answer is contingent on information the reader already possesses in his or her background
         knowledge.
     Author and Me—The answer is inferred in the text, but the reader must make the connections with his or her
         own prior knowledge.

2. Use a Think-Aloud to practice using QAR with a text. Model choosing the appropriate QAR, giving the answer from the source, and writing or telling the answer.

3. Introduce a short passage and related questions. Have groups or individuals work through the passages and the questions. Students answer the questions and tell the QAR strategy they used. Any justifiable answer should be accepted.

4. Practice QAR with additional texts.

Principles of Teaching QAR: Give immediate feedback; progress from shorter to longer texts; guide students from group to independent activities; provide transitions from easier to more difficult tasks.

Source: Raphael, T. (1986). Teaching children Question-Answer Relationships, revisited. *The Reading Teacher, 39,* 516–522.

Thick and Thin Questions

Purposes: To create questions pertaining to a text; to help students discern the depth of the questions they ask and are asked; to use questions to facilitate understanding a text.

Comprehension Strategies: Self-Questioning, Making Connections

Text: Narrative, Expository   **Use:** Before, During, and After Reading

Procedure: (Begin by explaining and modeling Thick and Thin Questions.)

1. Teach the students the difference between thick questions and thin questions. Thick questions deal with the big picture and large concepts. Answers to thick questions are involved, complex, and open ended. Thin questions deal with specific content or words. Answers to thin questions are short and close ended.

2. Guide students to create Thick and Thin Questions. Read a portion of text and prompt students with stems, such as "Why…" or "What if…" for thick questions and "How far…" and "When…" for thin questions.

3. Have students create Thick and Thin Questions for the texts they are reading. They can write the questions in their Guided Comprehension Journals, or write their thick questions on larger sticky notes and their thin questions on smaller sticky notes.

4. Share questions and answers in small and large groups.

Sources: Lewin, L. (1998). *Great performances: Creating classroom-based assessment tasks.* Alexandria, VA: Association for Supervision and Curriculum Development.

Harvey, S., & Goudvis, A. (2000). *Strategies that work: Teaching comprehension to enhance understanding.* York, ME: Stenhouse.

Coding the Text

Purposes: To make connections while reading; to actively engage in reading.

Comprehension Strategy: Making Connections

Text: Narrative, Expository   **Use:** During Reading

Procedure: (Begin by explaining and modeling Coding the Text.)

1. Using a read-aloud and thinking aloud, model for the students examples of making connections. These may include text-self, text-text, or text-world connections.

2. While reading out loud, demonstrate how to code a section of the text that elicits a connection by using a sticky note, a code (T-S = text-self, T-T = text-text, T-W = text-world), and a few words to describe the connection.

3. Have the students work in small groups to read a short text and code the text. Have them share their ideas with the class.

4. Encourage students to code the text using sticky notes to record their ideas and use these as the basis of small and large group discussions.

Example: ("On the Pulse of Morning" [1994] by Maya Angelou)

Text-Self	Text-Text	Text-World
When we read this poem, it reminded us that all of our ancestors had come here from other countries.	This poem reminded us of "The Road Not Taken" because in both poems, the poets describe situations that encourage us to make choices.	We made connections to the world because the poem talks about many nationalities and suggests that all should be hopeful and dream again.

Source: Harvey, S., & Goudvis, A. (2000). *Strategies that work: Teaching comprehension to enhance understanding.* York, ME: Stenhouse.

Connection Stems

Purposes: To provide a structure to make connections while reading; to encourage reflection during reading.

Comprehension Strategy: Making Connections

Text: Narrative, Expository   **Use:** After Reading

Procedure: (Begin by explaining and modeling Connection Stems.)

1. After reading a text aloud, show students a sentence stem and think aloud about the process you use for completing it. Use text support and personal experiences to explain the connection.

2. Read another text aloud and guide the students to complete the stem orally with a partner.

3. Have students read a short text in pairs and work together to complete a stem.

4. Share the completed stems through discussion or journal responses.

Sentence Stems:

- That reminds me of…
- I remember when…
- I have a connection…
- An experience I have had like that…
- I felt like that character when…
- If I were that character, I would…

Example: (*The View from Saturday* [1998] by E.L. Konigsburg)

- Julian going to a new school reminds me of when I transferred to a new school. I think I felt a lot like Julian did his first day.
- I remember when I went to visit my grandfather in Florida just like Nadia did.
- I have a connection because I have a dog that is as smart as Ginger.
- An experience I have had like Julian's tea party was when I went to an afternoon party given by people who used to live in England.
- I felt like Nadia when she was writing her report about sea turtles because I wrote a report about them last year and I got to see some when we were on vacation.
- If I were Mrs. Olinski, I would have felt sad that someone had called me a cripple.

Source: Adapted from Harvey, S., & Goudvis, A. (2000). *Strategies that work: Teaching comprehension to enhance understanding*. York, ME: Stenhouse.

Double-Entry Journal

(See blacklines, pages 148–149.)

Purposes: To provide a structure for reading response; to make decisions about significant aspects of text and reflect on personal connections to the text.

Comprehension Strategies: Making Connections, Monitoring, Summarizing

Text: Narrative, Expository   **Use:** Before, During, and After Reading

Procedure: (Begin by explaining and modeling Double-Entry Journals.)

1. Provide students with a Double-Entry Journal or have them make one.

2. Explain how to use the journal. Model procedure and provide examples of reflective comments. (Encourage text-self, text-text, or text-world connections.)

3. Have students read (or listen to) a text or part of a text.

4. Have students select a key event, idea, word, quote, or concept from the text and write it in the left column of the paper.

5. In the right column, have students write their response or connection to the item in the left column.

6. Use journals as a springboard for discussion of text.

Source: Tompkins, G.E. (1997). *Literacy for the 21st century: A balanced approach*. Upper Saddle River, NJ: Merrill.

Drawing Connections

(See blackline, page 150.)

Purposes: To provide a structure to make connections while reading; to use visual representations to express connections.

Comprehension Strategies: Making Connections, Visualizing

Text: Narrative, Expository   **Use:** During and After Reading

Procedure: (Begin by explaining and modeling Drawing Connections.)

1. Demonstrate how to draw visual representations (pictures, shapes, lines) to communicate connections with text.

2. Read a section of text and think aloud about a connection you can make. Model creating a visual representation of your thoughts. Then think aloud as you write a sentence or paragraph explaining the connection you made.

3. Read another section of text to the students and ask them to create visual representations of their connections to the text. Next, have them write a sentence or paragraph explaining their connection. Finally, have them share their drawings and explain their connections in small groups.

4. Encourage students to create visual representations of texts they are reading on their own and write a sentence or paragraph explaining their connection.

Adaptation: Instead of connections, have students sketch their visualizations.

Source: McLaughlin, M., & Allen, M.B. (2002). *Guided Comprehension: A teaching model for grades 3–8.* Newark, DE: International Reading Association.

Save the Last Word for Me

Purposes: To provide a structure to discuss the information and ideas in the text; to make connections to and evaluations of the information presented in the text.

Comprehension Strategies: Making Connections, Evaluating

Text: Narrative, Expository   **Use:** After Reading

Procedure: (Begin by explaining and modeling Save the Last Word for Me.)

1. Have students read a designated text.

2. After reading, have them complete an index card with the following information:

   Side 1: Students select an idea, phrase, quote, concept, fact, etc. from the text that evokes a response. It can be something new, something that confirms previous ideas, something they disagree with, etc. Students write their selection on side 1 and indicate the page number where it can be found in the text.

   Side 2: Students write their reaction to what they wrote on side 1.

3. Students gather in small groups to discuss their information.

4. Students discuss using the following procedure: A student reads side 1 of his card; each student in the group responds to the information shared. The student who authored the card gets the last word by sharing side 2 of his card. The process is repeated until everyone in the group has shared.

Example: (*Hatchet* [1987] by G. Paulsen)

Quote from *Hatchet*:	Reaction:
Not hope that he would be rescued—that was gone. But hope in his knowledge. Hope in the fact that he could learn and survive and take care of himself. Tough hope, he thought to himself. I am full of tough hope. (p. 127)	I chose this part of the book because when I read it, it reminded me of my own life. I thought about how sometimes I think I know everything I need to know and then something happens and I realize I need some new kind of knowledge to survive. Like when my grandfather died or when my parents were in a car accident, I think those are times I needed tough hope.

Source: Short, K.G., Harste, J.C., & Burke, C. (1996). *Creating classrooms for authors and inquirers.* Portsmouth, NH: Heinemann.

Gallery Images

Purposes: To create mental images while reading; to provide a format for sharing visualizations.

Comprehension Strategies: Visualizing, Making Connections

Text: Expository   **Use:** After Reading

Procedure: (Begin by explaining and modeling Gallery Images.)

1. Explain the concept of using images to represent information. Show two to four examples of different images representing content area concepts.

2. In small groups, have students read a section of expository text and create two to four images on poster size paper to represent the content. Share with the class. Start a gallery on a classroom or hallway wall to display images.

3. Have students create images for various content areas they study.

Source: Ogle, D.M. (2000). Make it visual: A picture is worth a thousand words. In M. McLaughlin & M.E. Vogt (Eds.), *Creativity and innovation in content area teaching* (pp. 55–71). Norwood, MA: Christopher-Gordon.

Graphic Organizers/Visual Organizers

(See blacklines, pages 151–155.)

Purposes: To provide a visual model of the structure of text; to provide a format for organizing information and concepts.

Comprehension Strategies: Visualizing, Making Connections, Summarizing

Text: Narrative, Expository   **Use:** Before, During, and After Reading

Procedure: (Begin by explaining and modeling Graphic Organizers/Visual Organizers.)

1. Introduce the Graphic Organizer to the students. Demonstrate how it works by reading a piece of text and noting key concepts and ideas on the organizer.

2. Have groups of students practice using the Graphic Organizers with ideas from an independently read text. Share ideas with the class.

3. Choose organizers that match text structures and thinking processes.

Examples:

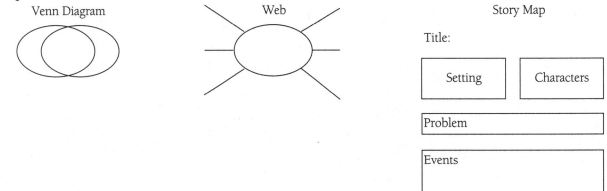

Guided Imagery

Purposes: To create mental images; to provide occasions to discuss visualizations.

Comprehension Strategies: Visualizing, Making Connections

Text: Narrative, Expository   **Use:** Before and After Reading

Procedure: (Begin by explaining and modeling Guided Imagery.)

1. Have students close their eyes and create pictures in their minds. Have them work in partners, and describe to each other what they "see" when you provide a verbal stimulus of things with which the students are familiar—a baseball game, a birthday party, a favorite pet, or a fireworks display. Provide time for students to elaborate on their mental picture.

2. Have students preview the text they will be reading next. Focus their preview on illustrations, charts, or any other graphics.

3. Tell the students to close their eyes, breathe deeply, and relax. Guide the students to think more deeply about the topic they will read about. Provide a detailed description of the setting, the action, sensory images, emotions, etc.

4. Have students open their eyes and in small groups share the pictures they made in their minds. Clarify any confusions and answer questions.

5. Then have students write or draw information gleaned from Guided Imagery.

6. Finally, have students read the text to add to or modify their writing or drawing. Share ideas with other small groups.

Source: Lasear, D. (1991). *Seven ways of teaching: The artistry of teaching with multiple intelligences*. Palatine, IL: Skylight.

Open-Mind Portrait

Purposes: To create and represent personal meanings for a story; to understand a character's perspective or point of view.

Comprehension Strategies: Visualizing, Making Connections

Text: Narrative, Expository   **Use:** After Reading

Procedure: (Begin by explaining and modeling Open-Mind Portraits.)

1. Students draw and color a portrait of a character from a story or a famous person from a biography.

2. Students cut out the portrait and use it to trace on one or several sheets of paper to create one or more blank head shapes.

3. Staple the color portrait and the blank sheets together.

4. On the blank pages, students draw or write about the person's thoughts and feelings throughout the text.

5. Share Open-Mind Portraits in book clubs, Literature Circles, or class meeting time.

Adaptation: Students fold a large sheet of paper (11" × 16") in half. On one half, they draw a portrait of a character from the book. On the other half, they draw the same shape of the portrait but do not fill in facial features. Instead, they fill the head with words and pictures to represent the thoughts and feelings of the character.

Source: Tompkins, G.E. (2001). *Literacy for the 21st century: A balanced approach* (2nd ed.). Upper Saddle River, NJ: Prentice Hall.

Sketch to Stretch

Purposes: To create, represent, and share personal meanings for a narrative or expository text; to summarize understandings through sketches.

Comprehension Strategies: Visualizing, Making Connections

Text: Narrative, Expository   **Use:** After Reading

Procedure: (Begin by explaining and modeling Sketch to Stretch.)

1. After reading or listening to text, have students sketch what the text means to them.

2. Encourage students to experiment and assure them there are many ways to represent personal meanings.

3. Have students gather in groups of three to five.

4. Each person in the group shares his or her sketch. As the sketch is shared, all other group members give their interpretation of the sketch. Once everyone has shared, the artist tells his or her interpretation.

5. Repeat Step 4 until everyone in the group has had a chance to share.

Source: Short, K.G., Harste, J.C., & Burke, C. (1996). *Creating classrooms for authors and inquirers*. Portsmouth, NH: Heinemann.

Concept of Definition Map

(See blackline, page 156.)

Purposes: To make connections with new words and topics and build personal meanings by connecting the new information with prior knowledge.

Comprehension Strategy: Knowing How Words Work

Text: Narrative, Expository   **Use:** Before Reading

Procedure: (Begin by explaining and modeling a Concept of Definition Map.)

1. Select or have student(s) select a word to be explored and place the word in the center of the map. (Example: *city*)

2. Ask students to determine a broad category that best describes the word and write it in the *What is it?* section. (Example: *A city is a place.*)

3. Have student(s) provide some words that describe the focus word in the *What is it like?* section. (Examples: *noisy, crowded, fast-paced*)

4. Have students provide some specific examples of the word in the *What are some examples?* section. (Examples: New York, Chicago, Los Angeles)

5. Have students determine a comparison. (Example: *a town*)

6. Discuss the Concept of Definition Map.

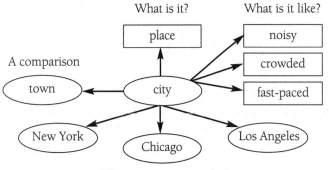

What are some examples?

7. Read the text. Revisit the map. Make modifications or additions.

Source: Schwartz, R., & Raphael, T. (1985). Concept of definition: A key to improving students' vocabulary. *The Reading Teacher, 39*, 198–205.

Context Clues

Purposes: To use semantics and syntax to figure out unknown words; to use a variety of cueing systems to make sense of text.

Comprehension Strategy: Knowing How Words Work

Text: Narrative, Expository   **Use:** During Reading

Procedure: (Begin by modeling how to use Context Clues to figure out word meanings.)

1. Explain to students the eight types of Context Clues and give examples of each:

   Definition—provides a definition that often connects the unknown word to a known word

   Example-Illustration—provides an example or illustration to describe the word

   Compare-Contrast—provides a comparison or contrast to the word

   Logic—provides a connection (such as a simile) to the word

   Root Words and Affixes—provides meaningful roots and affixes that the reader uses to determine meaning

   Grammar—provides syntactical cues that allow for reader interpretation

   Cause and Effect—cause and effect example allows the reader to hypothesize meaning

   Mood and Tone—description of mood related to the word allows readers to hypothesize meaning

2. Using a read-aloud and Think-Aloud, demonstrate using one or more of the clues to determine the meaning of a difficult or unfamiliar word in the text. (The Think-Aloud demonstrates the most effective clue based on the context of the sentence.) Readers use several of the clues to figure out unknown words.

3. If the context does not provide enough information, demonstrate other strategies for figuring out the meaning of the word.

Sources: Tompkins, G.E. (2001). *Literacy for the 21st century: A balanced approach* (2nd ed.). Upper Saddle River, NJ: Prentice Hall.
Vacca, R.T., & Vacca, J.L. (1999). *Content area reading: Literacy and learning across the curriculum* (6th ed.). New York: Longman.

Decoding by Analogy

Purpose: To use graphic cues in rime to decode unfamiliar words.

Comprehension Strategy: Knowing How Words Work

Text: Narrative, Expository   **Use:** During Reading

Procedure: (Begin by explaining and modeling Decoding by Analogy.)

1. Teach students high frequency words that have common spelling patterns.

2. Keep a word wall of these example words.

3. Model for students, using Think-Aloud, how to use these patterns to decode unfamiliar words.

4. Provide opportunities for students to practice decoding new words by analogy in context. Prompt students with verbal cues if necessary.

5. Encourage students to use this strategy as a way to decode new words and spell conventionally.

Example: new word = *attentive*

"I don't know this word, but I recognize some parts of it from our word wall. I see the same patterns in the words *at*, *ten*, and *give*. When I use those patterns to decode the word in my story, I can read *at* + *ten* + *tive*. That says *attentive*. Now I need to read the sentence and make sure *attentive* makes sense there."

Source: Gaskins, I.W., Ehri, L.C., Cress, C., O'Hara, C., & Donnelly, K. (1996). Procedures for word learning: Making discoveries about words. *The Reading Teacher, 50*, 2–18.

List-Group-Label

Purposes: To activate prior knowledge about a topic; to develop clearer understandings about concepts.

Comprehension Strategies: Knowing How Words Work, Previewing, Making Connections

Text: Expository   **Use:** Before and After Reading

Procedure: (Begin by explaining and modeling List-Group-Label.)

1. Write a cue word on the board or overhead.

2. Have students brainstorm words or concepts related to the topic. Write down all ideas.

3. Lead a discussion about whether any words should be eliminated, and if so, why?

4. Divide the class into groups of three or four. Have groups cluster the words and give each cluster a descriptive term.

5. Have groups share their clusters and give reasons for their choices. (There are no wrong answers if clusters and labels can be justified.)

6. Have students read the text. Afterward, have students revisit their clusters and modify, if necessary.

Source: Maring, G., Furman, G., & Blum-Anderson, J. (1985). Five cooperative learning strategies for mainstreamed youngsters in content area classrooms. *The Reading Teacher, 39,* 310–313.

Possible Sentences

Purposes: To improve understanding of text and key concepts presented in the text; to use vocabulary to make predictions about the content.

Comprehension Strategies: Knowing How Words Work, Previewing, Monitoring, Summarizing

Text: Expository   **Use:** Before and After Reading

Procedure: (Begin by explaining and modeling Possible Sentences.)

1. Choose six to eight words from the text that may be difficult and list them on the board or overhead.

2. Choose another four to six words from the text that may be more familiar to the students and list them on the board or overhead.

3. Define the words. If possible, let the students do this by using their background knowledge.

4. Have the students (individuals or groups) develop sentences using at least two of the words in each sentence. Write all contributed sentences on the board.

5. Have students read the text to confirm, modify, or extend the information from the board.

6. After reading, revisit the original sentences and revise as needed. Add any new information to the list. Use the revised list as the basis for creating summaries.

Source: Stahl, S. & Kapinus, B. (1991). Possible sentences: Predicting word meaning to teach content area vocabulary. *The Reading Teacher, 45,* 36–43.

RIVET

Purposes: To activate prior knowledge of a topic; to make predictions; to introduce vocabulary; to model spelling of specific vocabulary words.

Comprehension Strategies: Knowing How Words Work, Previewing

Text: Expository   **Use:** Before Reading

Procedure: (Begin by explaining and modeling RIVET.)

1. Choose six to eight interesting and important words from the selection to be read.

2. Create a visual representation of the words in a numbered list, leaving lines for each letter in the words. (You may want to provide students with a copy of this.)

3. Fill in the letters of the first word, one by one. Have students fill in their sheets or copy the words along with you. Ask students to predict what the word might be.

4. Continue this process for each word on the list.

5. Make sure students understand word meanings. Encourage them to share.

6. Using the list of words, have students make predictions about the text. Record them.

7. Encourage students to ask questions prompted from the list of words. Record them.

8. Read the text. Revisit predictions to confirm or modify. Answer questions on the list.

Examples: (*Stargazers* [1992] by Gail Gibbons)

1.   ___ ___ ___ ___   (STAR)
       S   T

2.   ___ ___ ___ ___ ___ ___   (GALAXY)
       G   A   L

Source: Cunningham, P. (1995). *Phonics they use*. New York: HarperCollins.

Semantic Feature Analysis

(See blackline, page 157.)

Purposes: To make predictions about attributes related to specific vocabulary words or concepts; to set a purpose for reading or researching; to confirm predictions.

Comprehension Strategies: Knowing How Words Work, Making Connections

Text: Narrative, Expository   **Use:** Before Reading

Procedure: (Begin by explaining and modeling Semantic Feature Analysis.)

1. Select a topic and some words or categories that relate to that topic. List the words in the left-hand column of the Semantic Feature Analysis chart.

2. Choose characteristics that relate to one or more of the related words. List those across the top row of the chart.

3. Have students make predictions about which characteristics relate to each word by placing a + if it is a characteristic, a – if it is not, and a ? if they are not sure.

4. Discuss students' predictions. Have them explain why they chose the characteristics.

5. Have students read about the topic and modify their charts as necessary.

6. Have students share completed charts in small groups and then discuss as a class.

Example:

+ = yes
– = no
? = don't know

Categories / Characteristics	hair/fur	lay eggs	warm-blooded	care for young	live in water	breathe air	have gills
Fish							
Birds							
Mammals							
Amphibians							

Source: Johnson, D.D., & Pearson, P.D. (1984). *Teaching reading vocabulary* (2nd ed.). New York: Holt, Rinehart and Winston.

Vocabulary by Analogy

Purposes: To help students make connections between words they know and new words; to help students use morphemes to figure out the meaning of unknown words.

Comprehension Strategy: Knowing How Words Work

Text: Narrative, Expository   **Use:** During Reading

Procedure: (Begin by explaining and modeling Vocabulary by Analogy.)

1. Teach students the meanings of common roots, prefixes, and suffixes, and provide examples of each:

   Roots—graph, psych, scope, script

   Prefixes—tele, pre, trans, un

   Suffixes—ology, ship, ment, hood

2. Keep a word wall or individual word charts of these examples.

3. Model for students, using Think-Aloud, how to use these parts of words to figure out the meaning of unfamiliar words.

4. Provide opportunities for students to practice figuring out new vocabulary by analogy in context. Prompt students with verbal cues if necessary. Refer them to use the class word wall as a resource.

5. Encourage students to use this strategy to figure out the meaning of new words they meet while reading.

Example: new word = *autobiography*

"I don't know this word, but I recognize some parts of it from our word wall. I see the chunk *auto* and that means *self*, *bio* means *life*, and *graph* means *write*. If I put these together, I think it means something written about a person's own life."

Source: McLaughlin, M., & Allen, M.B. (2002). *Guided Comprehension: A teaching model for grades 3–8*. Newark, DE: International Reading Association.

Vocabulary Self-Collection Strategy (VSS)

Purposes: To motivate students to engage in vocabulary study; to expand vocabulary.

Comprehension Strategies: Knowing How Words Work, Making Connections

Text: Narrative, Expository   **Use:** After Reading

Procedure: (Begin by explaining and modeling VSS.)

1. Have student groups or individuals select words from a previously read text that they would like to study or learn more about. The teacher also chooses a word.

2. Have students share the word, the context, where it was found, what they think it means, and why the class should study it.

3. Accept all nominations and record them. Encourage more discussion about the words.

4. Narrow the list to a predetermined number for study and refine definitions.

5. Have students record final word lists and definitions in their vocabulary journals.

6. Plan lessons to reinforce the words' meanings and uses.

7. Use the words in follow-up assignments, other learning experiences, or tests.

Source: Haggard, M.R. (1986). The vocabulary self-collection strategy: Using student interest and world knowledge to enhance vocabulary growth. *Journal of Reading, 29*, 634–642.

Bookmark Technique

Purposes: To monitor comprehension while reading; to make evaluative judgments about aspects of text.

Comprehension Strategies: Monitoring, Knowing How Words Work, Making Connections, Evaluating

Text: Narrative, Expository   **Use:** During and After Reading

Procedure: (Begin by explaining and modeling the Bookmark Technique.)

1. Have students create four bookmarks by folding and cutting 8.5" × 11" sheets of paper into four equal parts. (These can be prepared in advance.)

2. As students read, have them make decisions and record specific information on each bookmark, including the page and paragraph where their choice is located.

   Bookmark 1—write and/or sketch about the part of the text that they found most interesting.

   Bookmark 2—write and/or sketch something they found confusing.

   Bookmark 3—write a word they think the whole class needs to discuss.

   Bookmark 4—student choice (e.g., Note a favorite illustration, graph, another focus word, etc.).

3. Use the completed bookmarks to promote discussion about the text.

Source: McLaughlin, M., & Allen, M.B. (2002). *Guided Comprehension: A teaching model for grades 3–8.* Newark, DE: International Reading Association.

INSERT (Interactive Notation System to Effective Reading and Thinking)

Purposes: To provide opportunities for reflection; to make connections between prior knowledge and text content.

Comprehension Strategies: Monitoring, Making Connections

Text: Expository   **Use:** During Reading

Procedure: (Begin by explaining and modeling INSERT.)

1. Engage in direct instruction and think aloud to teach the INSERT method.

2. Introduce a topic and ask students to brainstorm lists of what they already know about it.

3. Teach students the following modified notation system:

If an idea:	Put this notation in the margin:
• confirms what you thought (makes you say "I knew that.")	✓ Insert a checkmark
• contradicts what you thought (makes you say "I thought differently.")	– Insert a minus sign
• is new to you (makes you say "I didn't know that!")	+ Insert a plus sign
• confuses you (makes you question, "What does this mean?")	? Insert a question mark

4. Encourage students to use the notation system in the margins of an informational article or on sticky notes, as they read various parts of the text. For example, students place a checkmark (✓) in the margin if the information they're reading verifies what is on their brainstormed list; they place a plus sign (+) if the information is new to them—not on their list; they place a minus sign (–) if the information contradicts or disproves information on the brainstormed list; they place a question mark (?) if the information is confusing.

5. After the students finish reading and inserting the symbols, use that information as the basis of discussion, to seek more information, to answer questions, or to raise new questions.

Source: Vaughn, J., & Estes, T. (1986). *Reading and reasoning beyond the primary grades.* Boston: Allyn & Bacon.

Patterned Partner Reading

Purposes: To provide a structure for reading interactively with another; to promote strategic reading.

Comprehension Strategies: Monitoring, Making Connections, Evaluating

Text: Narrative, Expository   **Use:** During Reading

Procedure: (Begin by explaining and modeling Patterned Partner Reading.)

1. Students select a text and a partner with whom they will read.

2. Partners determine the amount of text to be read and which of the following patterns they will use to engage in the reading:

   - "Take Turn" days—partners take turns reading the text out loud

   - "Ask Question" days—partners read a page silently and then ask each other a question about that page before moving on

   - "Sticky Note" days—partners decide together where to put a predetermined number of sticky notes to mark what is most interesting, most important, and most confusing

   - "Predict-Read-Discuss" days—partners make predictions about material, read to confirm or disconfirm their predictions, discuss the outcome, and renew the cycle

   - "Read-Pause-Retell" days—partners read, stop to think, and take turns retelling what they have read to a given point; repeat

   - "Making Connections" days—partners read a predetermined amount and then tell the text-self, text-text, or text-world connections they have made

   - "Visualizing" days—partners read a portion of the text and describe the pictures they have created in their minds; repeat

   - "You Choose" days—partners select which pattern to use

Source: Adapted from Cunningham, P., & Allington, R. (1999). *Classrooms that work: They can all read and write* (2nd ed.). New York: Addison-Wesley.

Say Something

Purposes: To make connections with texts during reading; to enhance comprehension of written material through short readings and oral discussion.

Comprehension Strategies: Monitoring, Making Connections

Text: Narrative, Expository   **Use:** During Reading

Procedure: (Begin by explaining and modeling Say Something.)

1. Choose a text for the students to read and have them work in pairs.

2. Designate a stopping point for reading.

3. Have students read to the stopping point and then "say something" about the text to their partner.

4. Allow pairs to choose the next stopping point. (If the text has subheadings, these make good stopping points). Students repeat Steps 3 and 4 until they have finished reading the text.

Source: Adapted from Short, K.G., Harste, J.C., & Burke, C. (1996). *Creating classrooms for authors and inquirers*. Portsmouth, NH: Heinemann.

Think-Alouds

Purpose: To provide a model for active thinking during the reading process.

Comprehension Strategies: Previewing, Visualizing, Monitoring, Self-Questioning, Making Connections, Knowing How Words Work, Summarizing, Evaluating

Text: Narrative, Expository   **Use:** Before, During, and After Reading

Procedure: (Begin by explaining and modeling Think-Alouds.)

1. Select a passage to read aloud to the students. The passage should require some strategic thinking in order to clarify understandings.

2. Before reading, share your predictions for the story or chapter and explain your reasoning. (For example, "From the title [or cover], I predict…because….")

3. As you read, think aloud to demonstrate strategies such as

   - Making/confirming/modifying predictions ("I was thinking _____, but now I predict _____"; "I thought that was what was going to happen because _____.")
   - Visualizing—making pictures in your mind ("What I am seeing in my mind right now is _____.")
   - Making connections ("This reminds me of _____"; This is like a _____.")
   - Monitoring ("This is confusing; I need to reread (or read on or ask someone for help)"; "This is not what I expected.")
   - Figuring out unknown words ("I don't know that word, but it looks like _____"; "That word must mean _____ because _____.")

4. After modeling several times, guide students to practice with partners.

5. Eventually, encourage students to use this technique on their own.

Source: Davey, B. (1983). Think-aloud—modeling the cognitive processes of reading comprehension. *Journal of Reading,* 27, 44–47.

Bio-Pyramid

(See blackline, page 158.)

Purposes: To summarize a person's life; to provide a format for summary writing.

Comprehension Strategies: Summarizing, Making Connections, Monitoring

Text: Expository   **Use:** After Reading

Procedure: (Begin by explaining and modeling the Bio-Pyramid.)

1. After reading about a person's life, show students the format for writing Bio-Pyramids.

   Line 1 – person's name
   Line 2 – two words describing the person
   Line 3 – three words describing the person's childhood
   Line 4 – four words indicating a problem the person had to overcome
   Line 5 – five words stating one of his or her accomplishments
   Line 6 – six words stating a second accomplishment
   Line 7 – seven words stating a third accomplishment
   Line 8 – eight words stating how mankind benefited from the accomplishments

2. Create a Bio-Pyramid as a class.

3. In small groups or pairs have students create Bio-Pyramids.

4. Use the completed pyramids to promote discussion.

Source: Macon, J.M. (1991). *Literature response.* A paper presented at the Annual Literacy Workshop, Anaheim, CA.

Lyric Summaries

(See blackline, page 159.)

Purposes: To provide an alternative format for narrative or expository text summaries; to provide opportunities to use multiple modalities when creating summaries; to link content learning and the arts.

Comprehension Strategy: Summarizing

Text: Narrative and Expository   **Use:** After Reading

Procedure: (Begin by explaining and modeling Lyric Summary.)

1. Review summarizing with the students. Ask them to note the types of information that comprise narrative or expository summaries.

2. Introduce the musical aspect of the Lyric Summary by explaining to students that summaries can also be written as song lyrics to familiar tunes (popular, rock, jazz, disco, children's songs).

3. Choose a melody with which students are familiar and use it as the background for writing a Lyric Summary. Write the first line and then encourage pairs of students to suggest subsequent lines. When the Lyric Summary is completed, sing it with the class.

4. Have small groups of students choose a melody they know and a topic they have recently studied to create their own Lyric Summaries. The topic may be a story they have recently read or information from a content area.

5. Have the students sing their completed summaries for the class.

Source: McLaughlin, M., & Allen, M.B. (2002). *Guided Comprehension: A teaching model for grades 3–8.* Newark, DE: International Reading Association.

Narrative Pyramid

(See blackline, page 160.)

Purposes: To summarize a narrative text; to provide a format for summary writing.

Comprehension Strategies: Making Connections, Monitoring, Summarizing

Text: Narrative   **Use:** After Reading

Procedure:

1. After reading a story, show students the format for writing narrative pyramids.

> Line 1 – character's name
> Line 2 – two words describing the character
> Line 3 – three words describing the setting
> Line 4 – four words stating the problem
> Line 5 – five words describing one event
> Line 6 – six words describing another event
> Line 7 – seven words describing a third event
> Line 8 – eight words describing the solution to the problem

2. Create a Narrative Pyramid as a class.

3. Have students create Narrative Pyramids in small groups or pairs for a story they have read.

4. Use the completed pyramids as the basis for discussion.

Example: (*Thank You, Mr. Falker* [1998] by Patricia Polacco)

Trisha
artistic sensitive
Michigan and California
Trisha struggled to read
She learned to fake reading
A boy named Eric taunted her
Her teacher noticed she didn't read well
With Mr. Falker's help she learned to read

Source: Waldo, B. (1991). Story pyramid. In J.M. Macon, D. Bewell, & M.E.Vogt (Eds.), *Responses to literature: Grades K–8* (pp. 23–24). Newark, DE: International Reading Association.

Paired Summarizing

Purposes: To provide a format for pairs to summarize narrative or expository text and articulate understandings and confusions.

Comprehension Strategies: Summarizing, Making Connections, Monitoring

Text: Narrative, Expository   **Use:** After Reading

Procedure: (Begin by explaining and modeling Paired Summarizing.)

1. Pairs of students read a selection and then each writes a Retelling. They may refer back to the text to help cue their memory, but they should not write while they are looking back.

2. When the Retellings are completed, the partners trade papers and read each other's work. Then each writes a summary of the other partner's paper.

3. The pairs of students compare or contrast their summaries. The discussion should focus on

   • articulating what each reader understands,
   • identifying what they collectively cannot come to understand, and
   • formulating clarification questions for classmates and the teacher.

4. Share understandings and questions in a whole-class or large-group discussion.

Source: Vaughn, J., & Estes, T. (1986). *Reading and reasoning beyond the primary grades*. Boston: Allyn & Bacon.

QuIP (Questions Into Paragraphs)

(See blackline, page 161.)

Purpose: To provide a framework for initiating research and structuring writing.

Comprehension Strategies: Summarizing, Self-Questioning

Text: Expository   **Use:** Before, During, and After Reading

Procedure: (Begin by explaining and modeling QuIP.)

1. Students choose a topic to explore and write the topic at the top of the QuIP grid.

2. Students generate three broad questions related to the topic.

3. Students locate and read two sources to find the answers to their questions. They write the titles of the sources in spaces provided on the grid.

4. Students record answers to the questions in the spaces provided on the grid.

5. Students synthesize information into a paragraph. (Modeling synthesizing and paragraph writing facilitates this process.)

6. Students share their paragraphs in pairs or small groups.

Source: McLaughlin, E.M. (1987). QuIP: A writing strategy to improve comprehension of expository structure. *The Reading Teacher, 40*, 650–654.

Retelling

(See blackline, page 162.)

Purposes: To promote reflection about narrative text; to provide a format for summarizing narrative text structure.

Comprehension Strategy: Summarizing

Text: Narrative   **Use:** After Reading

Procedure: (Begin by explaining and modeling Retelling.)

1. Explain to the students the purpose of retelling a story and the major ideas that are included (characters, setting, problem, attempts to resolve, resolution).

2. Demonstrate a Retelling after reading a story aloud. Discuss the components you included. (A story map or other Graphic Organizer may help.)

3. Read another story to the students and in small groups, have them retell the story. (You may want to give each student in the group a card listing a specific story element; i.e., characters, setting, problem, attempts to resolve, resolution.)

4. Share information with the class and record it on a chart or overhead. Review the Retellings to assure all elements are addressed.

5. Encourage students to do Retellings using oral presentation, writing, visual representation, or dramatization to demonstrate understanding of a narrative text.

Source: Morrow, L.M. (1985). Retelling stories: A strategy for improving children's comprehension, concept of story, and oral language complexity. *The Elementary School Journal, 85*(5), 647–661.

Summary Cubes

(See blackline, page 163.)

Purpose: To provide a structure for summarizing factual information or retelling key points of a story.

Comprehension Strategy: Summarizing

Text: Narrative, Expository   **Use:** Before, During, and After Reading

Procedure: (Begin by explaining and modeling Summary Cubes.)

1. Explain the idea of cubing to the students. Describe the information that goes on each side of the cube.

2. Demonstrate through read-aloud and Think-Aloud the process of determining key ideas about either narrative or expository text to write on the cube. Show the students how to assemble the cube.

3. In small groups, guide the students to read a text and create Summary Cubes.

4. Share ideas with the class. Display Summary Cubes.

5. Encourage students to create their own cubes as follow-ups to reading narrative and expository texts.

Information for cubes:

	Option 1	Option 2	Option 3	Option 4
Side 1	Who?	Title	Animal	Topic
Side 2	What?	Characters	Habitat	Subtopic 1 and details
Side 3	Where?	Setting	Food	Subtopic 2 and details
Side 4	When?	Problem	Physical description	Subtopic 3 and details
Side 5	Why?	Solution	Classification	Summary
Side 6	How?	Theme	Illustration	Illustration

Source: McLaughlin, M., & Allen, M.B. (2002). *Guided Comprehension: A teaching model for grades 3–8.* Newark, DE: International Reading Association.

Discussion Web

(See blackline, page 164.)

Purposes: To provide a structure for conversing about a topic; to provide opportunities for critical thinking.

Comprehension Strategies: Evaluating, Making Connections

Text: Narrative, Expository   **Use:** After Reading

Procedure: (Begin by explaining and modeling Discussion Webs.)

1. After reading a text, think of a two-sided question supported by the text. Write the question in the middle of the Discussion Web.

2. Have students work in groups to find support in the text for the pro and con positions about the question.

3. Encourage the students to discuss the question and answers, and then come to consensus, as a group, in pairs, or individually. Students will justify their thinking.

4. Write the conclusion at the bottom of the web.

5. Write the reasoning students used to come to their conclusion in the space provided.

6. Discuss conclusions and reasoning as a whole class.

Source: Alvermann, D. (1991). The discussion web: A graphic aid for learning across the curriculum. *The Reading Teacher, 45*, 92–99.

Evaluative Questioning

Purpose: To promote self-questioning and evaluative thinking.

Comprehension Strategy: Evaluating, Self-Questioning

Text: Narrative, Expository   **Use:** During and After Reading

Procedure: (Begin by explaining and modeling Evaluative Questioning.)

1. Explain the importance of multiple levels of questioning, focusing on evaluative questions. (See Chapter 2.)

2. Model creating and responding to evaluative questions using a read-aloud and Think-Aloud. Explain the signal words and cognitive operations used to form and respond to evaluative questions.

   Signal words: *defend, judge, justify*

   Cognitive operations: valuing, judging, defending, justifying

3. Using a common text, guide small groups of students to read the text and create an evaluative question. One at a time, have groups share their question and allow the rest of the class to respond. Discuss the cognitive processes they used to answer each question.

4. Provide opportunities for students to use evaluative questions to engage in reflection and conversations about the texts they read.

Source: Chiardello, A.V. (1998). Did you ask a good question today? Alternative cognitive and metacognitive strategies. *Journal of Adolescent & Adult Literacy, 42*, 210–219.

Journal Responses

Purposes: To respond in writing to the texts they are reading; to provide opportunities for reflection and critical thinking.

Comprehension Strategies: Evaluating, Making Connections, Summarizing

Text: Narrative, Expository   **Use:** During and After Reading

Procedure: (Begin by explaining and modeling Journal Responses.)

1. Provide students with a journal or a system for keeping their responses.

2. Show students examples of good responses to texts. Help students identify aspects of thoughtful reading responses.

3. Read a portion of text out loud and think aloud through a thoughtful response. Discuss with students why it was thoughtful and not shallow.

4. Read another portion of text aloud and have students write a thoughtful response. Share in groups.

5. For independent reading, have students write the date and the title of the text or chapter at the top of the page or in the left margin.

6. After reading a text, or listening to one, use Journal Responses as one of many methods students use to respond to what they read. Journal Responses can include reactions, questions, wonderings, predictions, connections, or feelings.

7. Encourage students to share responses in groups or with the whole class.

Example:

Journal Response prompts:

- What was your favorite part? Explain.

- How did this make you feel? Explain.

- What was important in the chapter? How do you know?

- What is something new you learned? Explain.

- What connection(s) did you make? Explain.

Meeting of the Minds

Purposes: To support a point of view with facts from reading; to promote debate and evaluative thinking.

Comprehension Strategy: Evaluating

Text: Narrative, Expository   **Use:** After Reading

Procedure: (Begin by explaining and modeling Meeting of the Minds.)

1. Teach students how to participate in Meeting of the Minds, a debate format between two characters that have differing viewpoints on a topic.

2. Choose a few students to help you model the procedure. Give each one a role—moderator, characters (at least two), and summarizer. The moderator poses questions to which the characters respond. The characters must support their points of view with references from the text. The summarizer recaps the information presented. Prepare the students to use a debate format to respond to predetermined questions. Model Meeting of the Minds for the whole class with these students. Discuss the process with the students, seeking questions, generating reflections, and summarizing benefits.

3. Divide the class into groups of 8 to 10. Have four or five students participate in Meeting of the Minds while the other students act as audience members. Then have the students reverse the roles. Have students participate in Meeting of the Minds with various narrative and expository topics occasionally throughout the year.

Source: Adapted from Richard-Amato, P.A. (1988). *Making it happen: Interaction in the second language classroom.* New York: Longman.

Persuasive Writing

Purposes: To express points of view with supporting ideas; to foster understanding of multiple perspectives on a topic.

Comprehension Strategy: Evaluating

Text: Narrative, Expository   **Use:** Before, During, and After Reading

Procedure: (Begin by explaining and modeling Persuasive Writing.)

1. Introduce a topic by reading an article that contains two points of view about the same issue.

2. Use a Think-Aloud to share the different perspectives about the topic.

3. Then choose a side and write persuasively to defend your choice. Think aloud throughout this process. Be certain to support your argument with facts.

4. Discuss your writing with the students and encourage them to express their ideas about the topic.

5. Then guide the students to engage in Persuasive Writing by sharing a different article and scaffolding their ability to write persuasively.

6. Provide additional opportunities for students to engage in practice by using current events, character choices, and historical events in other instructional settings.

Source: McLaughlin, M., & Allen, M.B. (2002). *Guided Comprehension: A teaching model for grades 3–8*. Newark, DE: International Reading Association.

COMPREHENSION ROUTINES

Directed Reading–Thinking Activity/ Directed Listening–Thinking Activity

Purposes: To encourage students to make predictions about a story or text; to use the author's clues to make meaningful connections and predictions; to foster active reading or listening of a text.

Comprehension Strategies: Previewing, Making Connections, Monitoring

Text: Narrative, Expository   **Use:** Before, During, and After Reading

Procedure: (Begin by explaining and modeling DR-TA or DL-TA.)

1. Students look at title and/or cover of a book. Teacher asks, "What do you think this story (or book) is about? Explain." Students respond with predictions and reasons for their thinking. This helps build background and activate prior knowledge.

2. Students read to a designated stopping point in the text. Teacher asks students to review their predictions, make new predictions, and explain the reasons for the new predictions.

3. Repeat Step 3 until the text is finished.

4. Students reflect on their predictions, stating what was helpful, what was surprising, and what was confusing.

Other ideas for using DR-TA:
- Students can predict orally, in writing, or by illustrating.
- For DL-TA, students listen to the story. The reader stops at various preselected places and asks students to review predictions, make new ones, and explain their reasoning.

Source: Stauffer, R. (1975). *Directing the reading-thinking process*. New York: Harper & Row.

Literature Circles

(See Chapter 2.)

Purposes: To provide a structure for student talk about texts from a variety of perspectives; to provide opportunities for social learning.

Comprehension Strategies: Making Connections, Knowing How Words Work, Monitoring, Summarizing, Evaluating

Text: Narrative, Expository   **Use:** After Reading

Procedure: (Begin by explaining and modeling Literature Circles.)

1. Students select books to read and form groups based on their text selections.

2. Groups meet to develop a schedule—how much they will read, when they will meet, etc.

3. Students read the predetermined amount of text independently, taking notes as they read. Students keep their notes in their Guided Comprehension Journals. The notes can reflect the student's role in the Literature Circle or their personal connections to the text. Roles within the Literature Circles should vary from meeting to meeting.

4. Students meet according to the group schedule to discuss ideas about the text until the book is completed.

5. Provide opportunities for students to participate in Literature Circles in Stage Two of Guided Comprehension.

Source: Daniels, H. (1994). *Literature circles: Voice and choice in the student-centered classroom.* York, ME: Stenhouse.

Questioning the Author (QtA)

(See Chapter 2.)

Purposes: To facilitate understanding of text; to use questions to promote discussion for the purpose of collaboratively constructing meaning from text.

Comprehension Strategies: Making Connections, Self-Questioning, Monitoring

Text: Narrative, Expository   **Use:** During Reading

Procedure: (Begin by explaining and modeling QtA.)

1. Read the text to determine major understandings and potential problems.

2. Determine segments within the text to use for discussion. These segments should be chosen because of their importance in helping students to construct meaning related to the major understandings that have been determined in Step 1.

3. Create queries that will lead the students to the major understandings. Develop initiating queries to start the discussion. Anticipate student responses to these queries to determine follow-up queries. Use these to focus and move the discussion.

4. Guide the students to read the text, using the queries to facilitate discussion during reading.

5. When students become proficient at QtA, have them use it in Stage Two of Guided Comprehension as an independent comprehension routine.

Sample Queries:

Initiating
- What is the author trying to say here?
- What is the author's message?
- What is the author talking about?

Follow-up
- What does the author mean here?
- Did the author explain this clearly?
- Does this make sense with what the author told us before?
- How does this connect with what the author had told us here?
- Does the author tell us why?
- Why do you think the author tells us this now?

Narrative
- How do things look for this character now?
- How has the author let you know that something has changed?
- How has the author settled this for us?
- Given what the author has already told us about the character, what do you think he's up to?

Source: Beck, I.L., McKeown, M.G., Hamilton, R.L., & Kucan, L. (1997). *Questioning the author: An approach to enhancing student engagement with text.* Newark, DE: International Reading Association.

Reciprocal Teaching

(See Chapter 2.)

Purposes: To provide a format for using comprehension strategies—predicting, questioning, monitoring, and summarizing—in a small-group setting; to facilitate a group effort to bring meaning to a text; to monitor thinking and learning.

Comprehension Strategies: Previewing, Self-Questioning, Monitoring, Summarizing

Text: Narrative, Expository   **Use:** Before, During, and After Reading

Procedure: (Begin by explaining and modeling Reciprocal Teaching.)

1. Explain the procedure and each of the four reading comprehension strategies: predicting, questioning, monitoring, summarizing.

2. Model thinking related to each of the four strategies using an authentic text and thinking aloud.

3. With the whole class, guide students to engage in similar types of thinking by providing responses for each of the strategies. Sentence stems, such as the following, facilitate this:

    Predicting:

    > I think…
    > I bet…
    > I wonder…
    > I imagine…
    > I suppose…

    Questioning:

    > What connections can I make?
    > How does this support my thinking?

    Clarifying:

    > I did not understand the part where…
    >
    > I need to know more about…

    Summarizing:

    > The important ideas in what I read are…

4. Place students in groups of four and provide each group with copies of the same text to use as the basis for Reciprocal Teaching.

5. Assign each student one of the four strategies and the suggested prompts.

6. Have students engage in Reciprocal Teaching using the process that was modeled.

7. Have students reflect on the process and their comprehension of the text.

8. Provide opportunities for the students to engage in Reciprocal Teaching in Stage Two of Guided Comprehension as an independent comprehension routine.

Source: Palincsar, A.S., & Brown, A.L. (1986). Interactive teaching to promote independent learning from text. *The Reading Teacher, 39,* 771–777.

PREDICT-O-GRAM

Vocabulary Words

Characters

Setting

Problem

Action

Solution

PROBABLE PASSAGES

Setting:

Characters:

Problem:

Events:

Solution:

QUESTIONING THE TEXT

What is the text structure (e.g., narrative, expository)? What clues help me know this?

_____

What questions will this text answer?

_____

What questions do I have for this text?

_____

What clues does the cover (title, cover art, author) offer? What does the contents page tell me?

_____

What do the physical aspects (size, length, print size) of the book tell me?

_____

Is the author familiar? What do I know about the author? What connections can I make?

_____

Is the topic familiar? What do I know about the topic? What connections can I make?

_____

What clues do the genre and writing style provide for me?

_____

Is there a summary? What does it help me know?

_____

What does the information on the book jacket tell me?

_____

Summary of what I now know about the text:

_____

_____

_____

Guided Comprehension: A Teaching Model for Grades 3–8 by Maureen McLaughlin and Mary Beth Allen ©2002.
Newark, DE: International Reading Association. May be copied for classroom use.

K-W-L

Topic: _____

K (What I know or think I know)	W (What I want to know)	L (What I learned)

K-W-L-S

Topic: _____

K (What I know or think I know)	W (What I want to know)	L (What I learned)	S (What I still want to know)

QUESTION-ANSWER RELATIONSHIP (QAR)

- In the text

  - Right There—the answer is within one sentence in the text.

  - Think and Search—the answer is contained in more than one sentence from the text.

- In my head

  - Author and You—the answer needs information from the reader's background knowledge and the text.

  - On Your Own—the answer needs information from only the reader's background knowledge.

DOUBLE-ENTRY JOURNAL

Idea	Reflection/Reaction

DOUBLE-ENTRY JOURNAL

Idea/Text From Story	My Connection

DRAWING CONNECTIONS

Draw a picture to represent a connection you made while reading the story.

Write one or more sentences to explain your drawing.

SEQUENCE CHAIN

Title

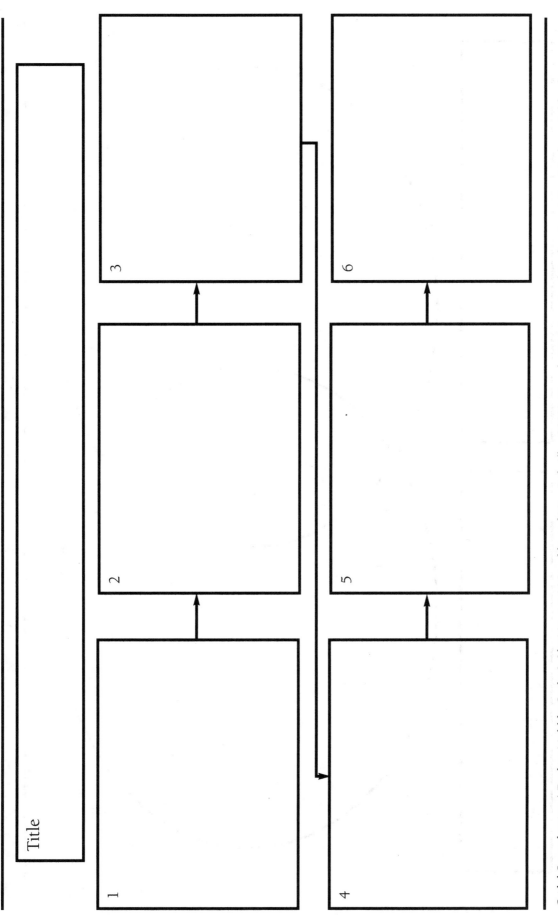

VENN DIAGRAM

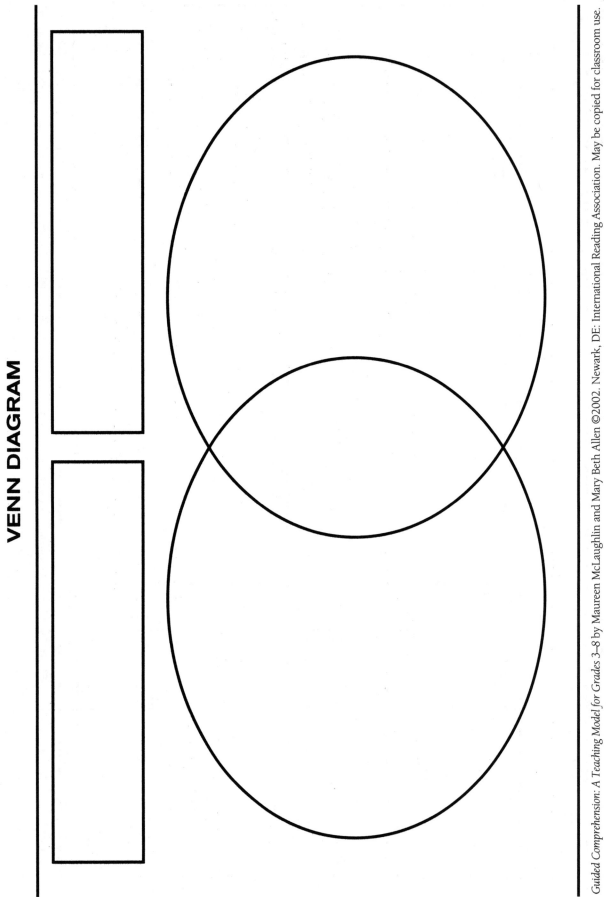

STORY MAP

Title/Chapter: _____

Setting	Characters

Problem

Event 1

Event 2

Event 3

Event 4

Event 5

Solution

Theme

MAIN IDEA TABLE

Main Idea

Supporting Details

COMPARE/CONTRAST MATRIX

Story Elements

Title	Characters	Setting	Problem	Solution

CONCEPT OF DEFINITION MAP

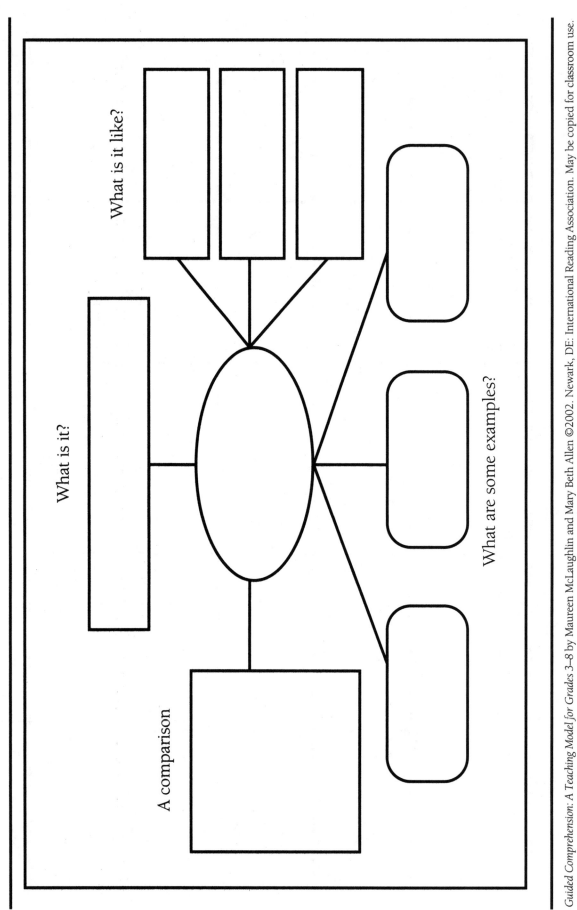

What is it?

What is it like?

A comparison

What are some examples?

Guided Comprehension: A Teaching Model for Grades 3–8 by Maureen McLaughlin and Mary Beth Allen ©2002. Newark, DE: International Reading Association. May be copied for classroom use.

SEMANTIC FEATURE ANALYSIS

Characteristics

Categories											

Guided Comprehension: A Teaching Model for Grades 3–8 by Maureen McLaughlin and Mary Beth Allen ©2002. Newark, DE: International Reading Association. May be copied for classroom use.

BIO-PYRAMID

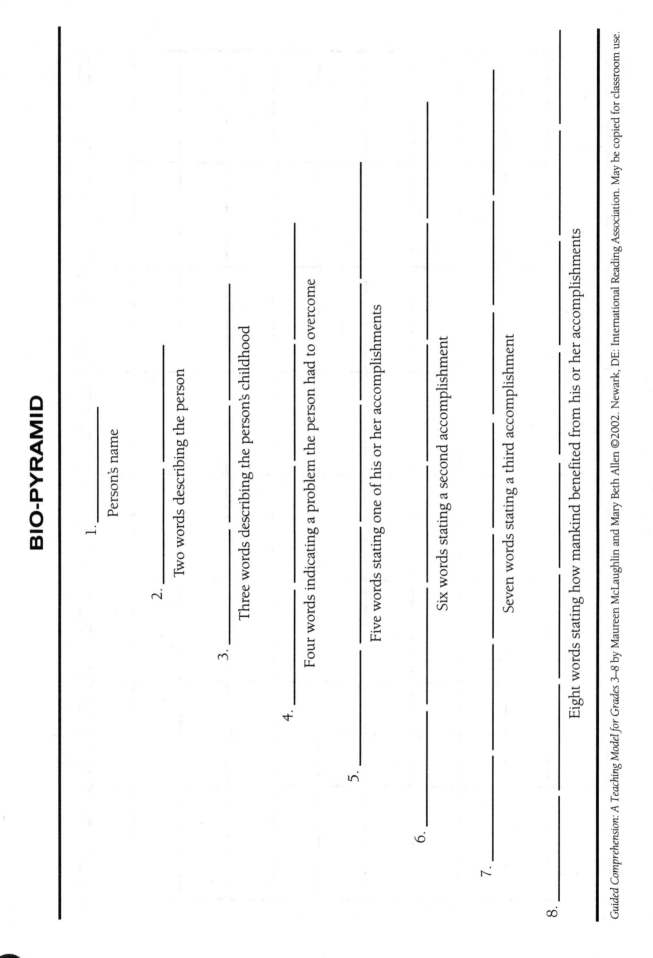

1. _____
   Person's name

2. _____
   Two words describing the person

3. _____
   Three words describing the person's childhood

4. _____
   Four words indicating a problem the person had to overcome

5. _____
   Five words stating one of his or her accomplishments

6. _____
   Six words stating a second accomplishment

7. _____
   Seven words stating a third accomplishment

8. _____
   Eight words stating how mankind benefited from his or her accomplishments

Guided Comprehension: A Teaching Model for Grades 3–8 by Maureen McLaughlin and Mary Beth Allen ©2002. Newark, DE: International Reading Association. May be copied for classroom use.

LYRIC SUMMARY

Text: _____

Tune: _____

Verse 1:

_____

_____

_____

_____

Verse 2:

_____

_____

_____

_____

Refrain (or Verse 3):

_____

_____

_____

_____

_____

_____

NARRATIVE PYRAMID

1. _____
   Character's name

2. _____
   Two words describing the character

3. _____
   Three words describing the setting

4. _____
   Four words stating the problem

5. _____
   Five words describing one event

6. _____
   Six words describing another event

7. _____
   Seven words describing a third event

8. _____
   Eight words describing a solution to the problem

Guided Comprehension: A Teaching Model for Grades 3–8 by Maureen McLaughlin and Mary Beth Allen ©2002. Newark, DE: International Reading Association. May be copied for classroom use.

QuIP RESEARCH GRID

Topic: _____

Questions	Answers	
	Source:	Source:
1.		
2.		
3.		

RETELLING FOR _____

Who?	Where?
Draw:	Draw:
Label:	Label:

What happened?	How did it end?
Draw:	Draw:
Label:	Label:

SUMMARY CUBE

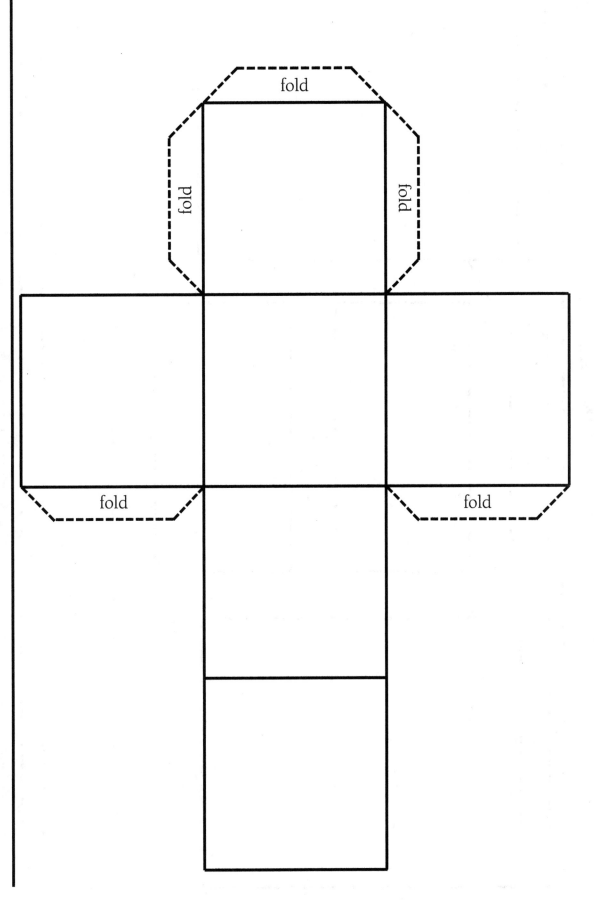

Guided Comprehension: A Teaching Model for Grades 3–8 by Maureen McLaughlin and Mary Beth Allen ©2002. Newark, DE: International Reading Association. May be copied for classroom use.

DISCUSSION WEB

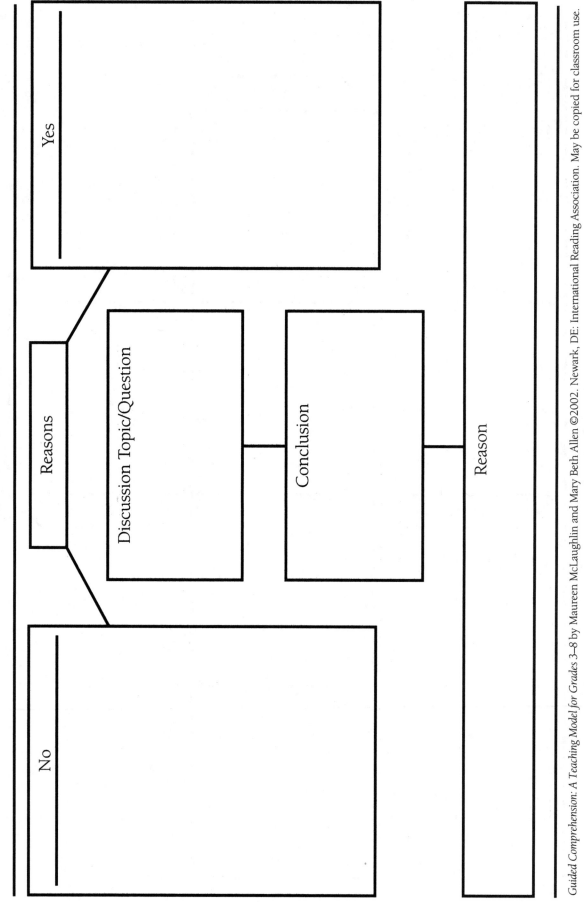

Reasons

Yes	No

Discussion Topic/Question

Conclusion

Reason

APPENDIX B

Forms for Organizing and Managing Comprehension Centers and Routines

CENTER REFLECTIONS

Name:_____ Date: _____

Center: _____

While I was working at this center, I was able to

_____

_____

_____

_____

I learned

_____

_____

_____

_____

The next time I plan to

_____

_____

_____

_____

_____

_____

CENTER STUDENT SELF-EVALUATION

Name:_____ Date:_____

Center: _____

My goal was

_____

_____

_____

What I did well

_____

_____

_____

I think I achieved my goal because

_____

_____

My new goal is

_____

_____

_____

_____

_____

CENTER RUBRIC

Center: _____

Directions: Think about what you did at the center today. Then use this rubric to describe your performance.

	Minimal	**Satisfactory**	**Good**	**Excellent**
	1	2	3	4
My work is complete.	1	2	3	4
I followed the directions.	1	2	3	4
I made personal interpretations.	1	2	3	4
My presentation is appealing.	1	2	3	4
I made connections that are supported by the text.	1	2	3	4
I used multiple modes of response.	1	2	3	4

Comments:

_____

_____

_____

_____

_____

_____

_____

_____

_____

_____

_____

Name: _____   Date: _____

MANAGING STAGE TWO

OPTION 1: Participation Chart

Student	Session 1	Session 2
_____	_____	_____
_____	_____	_____
_____	_____	_____
_____	_____	_____
_____	_____	_____
_____	_____	_____
_____	_____	_____
_____	_____	_____
_____	_____	_____
_____	_____	_____
_____	_____	_____
_____	_____	_____
_____	_____	_____
_____	_____	_____
_____	_____	_____
_____	_____	_____
_____	_____	_____
_____	_____	_____
_____	_____	_____
_____	_____	_____
_____	_____	_____
_____	_____	_____

OPTION 2: Center Rotation Chart

Center _____ _____ _____ _____				
Group				
Blue	1	2	3	4
Green	2	3	4	1
Red	3	4	1	2
Yellow	4	1	2	3

CENTER CHART FOR STUDENTS

Center: _____ Week: _____

Directions: If you used this center, sign your name and place a check mark underneath the day you visited.

Students	Monday	Tuesday	Wednesday	Thursday	Friday

CLASS CENTER CHART FOR TEACHERS

Centers					
Students					

CHOOSE YOUR OWN PROJECT CHART

Choose one idea from each column to create the project you will complete to demonstrate your knowledge of the topic.

For example:

Verb	Topic/Theme	Products/Performance
	Desert	
Retell	characteristics	acrostic
Explain	climate to survive	fact/fable book
Summarize	uses and benefits	drawing
Describe	environment	diamante
Construct	life span/process	report
Illustrate	protection	newspaper article
Show		slide show presentation
Demonstrate		song
Compare		dramatic interpretation
Classify		collage
Organize		three-dimensional model
Predict		
Imagine		
Design		
Evaluate		
Support		
Rate		

Example Project: Compare the environment where a cactus lives to that of the ocean using a diamante.

- -

Verb	Topic/Theme	Products/Performance
	_____	
	Subtopics	
Retell	_____	acrostic
Explain		fact/fable book
Summarize	_____	drawing
Describe		diamante
Construct	_____	report
Illustrate		newspaper article
Show	_____	slide show presentation
Demonstrate		song
Compare	_____	dramatic interpretation
Classify		collage
Organize		three-dimensional model
Predict		_____
Imagine		_____
Design		
Evaluate		
Support		
Rate		

My Project: _____

_____

Name: _____ Date: _____

DIRECTIONS FOR MAKING BOOKS

Slotted Book

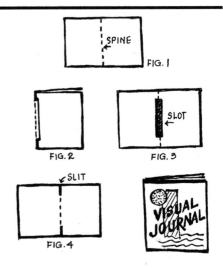

STEP 1

Take at least two pieces of paper and hold them in a landscape (horizontal) position (Fig. 1). You can use more than two pages to create books with more than four pages.

STEP 2—MAKING THE SLOT

Separate one page from the pack of papers. Make sure the fold or SPINE is nice and flat. Measure 1 1/2 inches from the top of the spine and make a mark and the same at the bottom of the page of the spine.

Cut into the spine and carefully cut away the spine between the marks you have made. Only cut into the spine about 1/16 of an inch (Fig. 2). Open your page and you should see a SLOT (Fig. 3).

STEP 3—MAKING THE SLITS

Take the other page(s) and make sure the spine is nice and flat. Measure the same 1 1/2 inches from the top and bottom of the spine.

This time cut from the bottom of the page up to the mark to create a SLIT. Repeat the process at the top of the page. You should have a SLIT at the top and bottom of the page (Fig. 4).

STEP 4—SLIPPING THE BOOK TOGETHER

Open the slotted page. Take the other page(s) with slits and bend them in half horizontally. SLIP them through the slot until you have reached the center of the book. Carefully slip the slit and slot together and roll the pages open and fold it like a book.

Dos à Dos Dialogue Journals

Dos à dos is a French expression meaning a couch or a carriage that holds two people sitting back to back. When two people sit back to back they see different things or they see the same thing from different points of view. This book is really two books in one (or three or more—you decide). There is room for each person's point of view or story. Dos à dos can be a wonderful way to structure a dialogue journal where you and another person write back and forth to each other. Each person has their own book and in turn responds to the others ideas, questions, and feelings. Turn them around and read each others response!

STEP 1

For a two part dos à dos take a piece of 11 × 17 paper and cut it lengthwise in half (5 1/2 inches). Take one strip and fold into three equal parts. It should look like a Z (Fig. 1).

STEP 2

Cut all the text pages so they are 8 × 5 1/2 inches. Fold them in half and divide them to create two booklets or signatures with equal pages.

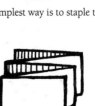

STEP 3

Slip a signature into the first fold. The crease of the signature or booklet should be nested inside the crease of the cover. You can either staple the signature into the cover or sew the signature into the cover. The simplest way is to staple the booklet in by using a book arm stapler that lets you staple deep into the center of the signature.

STEP 4

Repeat step 3 for other signature nesting it in the other crease.

STEP 5

Fold the book back and forth so that you can open one signature from the front and one from the back.

STEP 6—DECORATE THE COVERS.

Consider these wild variations! As with any book, you can change the shape, size, and materials of this book. Make a dos à dos dialogue journal for three or four people (Fig. 2). Just make an extra long cover or paste together two of them. What an interesting conversation you could have!

Try different types of text pages. If you need some extra long pages, cut some text pages longer than the others, and make fold outs. Cut some pages taller than others and make fold downs. Add some pop-ups.

Basic Origami Book

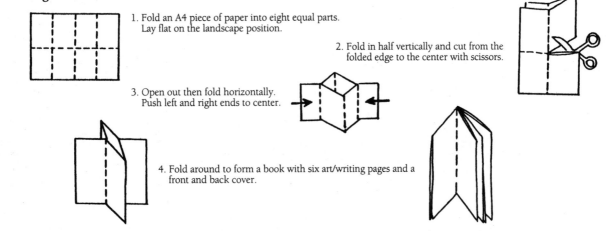

1. Fold an A4 piece of paper into eight equal parts. Lay flat on the landscape position.

2. Fold in half vertically and cut from the folded edge to the center with scissors.

3. Open out then fold horizontally. Push left and right ends to center.

4. Fold around to form a book with six art/writing pages and a front and back cover.

Source: Pinciotti, P. (2001b). *Book arts: The creation of beautiful books.* East Stroudsburg, PA: East Stroudsburg University of Pennsylvania.

GUIDED COMPREHENSION JOURNAL

"IF I WERE IN CHARGE OF THE WORLD"

If I Were in Charge of _____

by _____

If I were in charge of _____, I'd cancel

_____,

_____,

_____, and also

_____.

If I were in charge of _____,

There'd be _____,

_____, and

_____.

If I were in charge of _____,

You wouldn't have _____

You wouldn't have _____

You wouldn't have _____

Or _____

You wouldn't even have _____

If I were in charge of _____,

_____

_____

And a person _____

And _____

Would still be allowed to be in charge of the world.

Source: Adapted from Viorst, J. (1981). *If I were in charge of the world and other worries*. New York: Atheneum.

LITERATURE CIRCLE SELF-EVALUATION

Name: _____   Date: _____

Text: _____

1. How would you rate your participation in the discussion?

   just right   too much   too little   not at all

2. What did you do to prepare for the Literature Circle that was helpful?

   _____

   _____

   _____

3. What is something you learned in your Literature Circle?

   _____

   _____

   _____

4. How would you rate your group's discussion?

   lively   average   boring

5. How helpful was today's discussion?

   very helpful   somewhat helpful   not helpful

6. What worked well today? What will you do to improve next time?

   _____

   _____

   _____

   _____

   _____

   _____

   _____

   _____

MAKING AND WRITING WORDS CENTER

How many words can you make from the word _____ ?

Two-letter words:

_____ _____   _____ _____   _____ _____   _____ _____   _____ _____

Three-letter words:

_____ _____ _____   _____ _____ _____   _____ _____ _____   _____ _____ _____

_____ _____ _____   _____ _____ _____   _____ _____ _____   _____ _____ _____

_____ _____ _____   _____ _____ _____   _____ _____ _____   _____ _____ _____

Four-letter words:

_____ _____ _____ _____   _____ _____ _____ _____   _____ _____ _____ _____

_____ _____ _____ _____   _____ _____ _____ _____   _____ _____ _____ _____

_____ _____ _____ _____   _____ _____ _____ _____   _____ _____ _____ _____

Larger words:

_____   _____

_____   _____

Making and Writing Words

Directions: Use the vowels and consonants provided to make words based on the clues given by the teacher.

Vowels	Consonants

Directions: Listen carefully as your teacher or classmate provides clues to words that you will write in each box.

1	7	13
2	8	14
3	9	15
4	10	16
5	11	17
6	12	18

Source: Adapted from Rasinski, T.V. (1999). Making and writing words using letter patterns. *Reading Online* [Online]. Available: http://www.readingonline.org/articles/words/rasinski_index.html.

MYSTERY PYRAMID

1. _____
(one word—detective's name)

2. _____
(two words—describe the detective)

3. _____
(three words—describe the victim)

4. _____
(four words—describe the crime/crime scene)

5. _____
(five words—explain the motive)

6. _____
(six words—clues that distract you from discovering the culprit)

7. _____
(seven words—clues that help you discover the culprit)

8. _____
(eight words—how the case was solved)

MYSTERY SUSPECT ORGANIZER

Name:_____ Date: _____

Prediction
(Who do you think the culprit is?)

_____

_____

_____

Suspect

_____

Clues:

_____

_____

_____

_____

_____

_____

Suspect

_____

Clues:

_____

_____

_____

_____

_____

_____

Suspect

_____

Clues:

_____

_____

_____

_____

_____

_____

Conclusion
(Who is the culprit? Why do you think so?)

_____

_____

_____

_____

_____

_____

_____

_____

PATTERN BOOK ORGANIZER

Title:

Fortunately _____

Unfortunately _____

Fortunately _____

Unfortunately _____

Fortunately _____

Unfortunately _____

Fortunately _____

Unfortunately _____

Fortunately _____

Unfortunately _____

Fortunately _____

Unfortunately _____

Fortunately _____

Unfortunately _____

Fortunately _____

Unfortunately _____

Fortunately _____

Unfortunately _____

Source: Charlip, R. (1993). *Fortunately*. New York: Aladdin.

PATTERN BOOK ORGANIZER

Fact or Fable?

Fact or Fable

_____

_____

_____

Answer _____

Support

_____

_____

_____

_____

Fact or Fable

_____

_____

_____

Answer _____

Support

_____

_____

_____

_____

PATTERN BOOK ORGANIZER

The Important Book

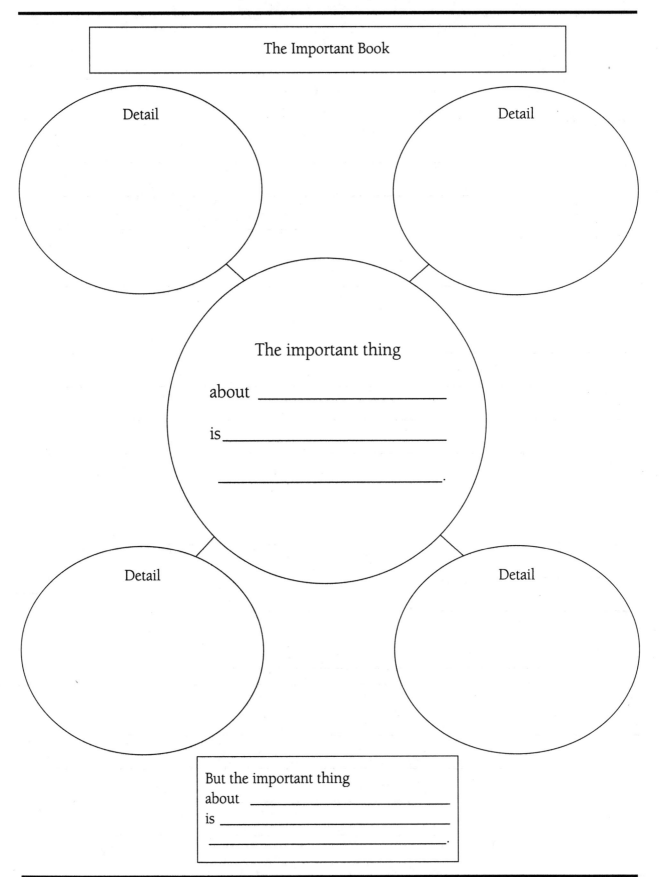

Detail

Detail

The important thing

about _____

is _____

_____.

Detail

Detail

But the important thing
about _____
is _____
_____.

POETRY FORM

Cinquain

_____

one word—noun

_____ _____

two adjectives describing line one

_____ _____ _____

three -ing words telling actions of line 1

_____ _____ _____ _____

four word phrase describing a feeling related to line 1

_____

one word—synonym or reference to line 1

Diamante

_____

subject—one noun

_____ _____

two adjectives describing the subject

_____ _____ _____

three participles (-ing) telling about the subject

_____ _____ _____ _____

four nouns—first two relate to the subject; last two relate to the opposite

_____ _____ _____

three participles (-ing) telling about the opposite

_____ _____

two adjectives describing the opposite

_____

opposite of subject—one noun

POETRY FORM

Bio-Poem

Line 1 — First name _____

Line 2 — Four traits that describe #1 _____

Line 3 — Related to/sibling of _____

Line 4 — Cares about/likes _____

Line 5 — Who feels _____

Line 6 — Who needs _____

Line 7 — Who gives _____

Line 8 — Who fears _____

Line 9 — Who would like to see _____

Line 10 — Resident of _____

Line 11 — Last name _____

Definition Poem

What is _____? (topic)

_____
Description of topic

_____
Description of topic

_____
Description of topic

_____
Description of topic

_____
Description of topic

_____
Description of topic

_____
Description of topic

That is _____! (topic)

QUESTIONING THE AUTHOR SELF-EVALUATION

Name: _____   Date: _____

Text: _____

1. How would you rate your participation in the discussion?

    just right   too much   too little   not at all

2. What did you figure out about the text from Questioning the Author? What new insights did you gain?

    _____

    _____

    _____

3. What is the main message or theme of the text? What makes you think this?

    _____

    _____

    _____

4. How would you rate your group's discussion?

    lively   average   boring

5. How helpful was today's discussion?

    very helpful   somewhat helpful   not helpful

6. What worked well today? What will you do to improve next time?

    _____

    _____

    _____

    _____

    _____

    _____

    _____

REQUIRED AND OPTIONAL CENTER AND ACTIVITY FORM

Name: _____   Date: _____

Centers	Monday	Tuesday	Wednesday	Thursday	Friday
D					
D					
W					
W					
W					
W					
W My Choice:_____					
W My Choice:_____					

Mark the day with an X when you visit that center.
D = visit center daily; W = visit center weekly

RECIPROCAL TEACHING SELF-EVALUATION

Name: _____   Date: _____

Text: _____

1. How would you rate your participation in the discussion?

   just right   too much   too little   not at all

2. What did you figure out about the text from Reciprocal Teaching? What new insights did you gain?

   _____

   _____

   _____

3. What is the main message or theme of the text? What makes you think this?

   _____

   _____

   _____

4. How would you rate your group's discussion?

   lively   average   boring

5. How helpful was today's discussion?

   very helpful   somewhat helpful   not helpful

6. What worked well today? What will you do to improve next time?

   _____

   _____

   _____

   _____

   _____

   _____

WORD DETECTIVE—
SEQUENTIAL ROUNDTABLE ORGANIZER

A	J	S
B	K	T
C	L	U
D	M	V
E	N	W
F	O	X
G	P	Y
H	Q	Z
I	R	

WRITE YOUR OWN MYSTERY

Draw, describe, or explain the crime scene.

Choose the detective, a suspect, or a victim and write four words to describe that character.

Write four clues. Two of the clues should lead the reader to the culprit. Two other clues should distract the reader's attention from the culprit.

_____

_____

_____

_____

Write a brief description of how the mystery was or will be solved.

Guided Comprehension: A Teaching Model for Grades 3–8 by Maureen McLaughlin and Mary Beth Allen ©2002. Newark, DE: International Reading Association. May be copied for classroom use.

Literature Response Prompts

Students may select the prompt to which they will respond. To accommodate personal strengths, offer students choices based on a variety of modalities.

Prompts That Focus on Writing

1. Write yourself into the story. Explain your reasoning.
2. Pretend that you are one of the characters and keep a journal as that person.
3. Use persuasive letter writing techniques to write to the author to convince him or her to write a prequel or sequel.
4. Write newspaper articles appropriate for the time in which the novel took place.
5. What would happen next? Sketch the next chapter.
6. Write a letter of advice to the main character from your perspective.
7. Write a eulogy for one of the characters from the perspective of another character.
8. Rewrite the ending. Explain why you chose to end it the way you did.
9. Write a personal recommendation for the book for future readers.
10. Research the time period in which the novel takes place and choose an activity from the research center to report significant changes that have taken place over time.
11. Rewrite the story from another point of view and discuss how this changes the story.
12. Use a "Dear Abby" format to describe the problem or conflict in the story and assume the "Abby" role to write a response.
13. Write a letter to a character in the story relating the experiences of the character to experiences you have had.
14. Write a short story or poem addressing the theme of the novel.
15. Write the next chapter of the novel and publish it for the classroom library.
16. Assume the identity of the head of a publishing company and write a letter to the author and/or illustrator detailing why you have accepted or rejected the manuscript.
17. Explain how changing the setting would affect the story. (Example: If *To Kill a Mockingbird* had been set in New York, how would the story change?)
18. Create a Venn diagram to illustrate similarities and differences between the novel and its film version.
19. Create a storyboard of major elements in the novel.
20. Create a chapter chart and record information about characters, plot, theme, and symbolism.
21. Rewrite the novel (or a chapter) in a different genre. (Example: Take a story and rewrite it into a play. Organize a group to assume roles such as director, program designer, costume designer, actors, etc.)

---

22. Imagine that you are one of the characters and a poem or note that you wrote about another character fell out of your pocket. What would it say?

23. Write a persuasive essay to convince someone why the book should or should not be read. Be specific when supporting your argument.

24. Write a letter to your friend, your parents, or your teacher to tell them about the book.

25. Compare or contrast this novel with others you have read or viewed from the same time period. What novel-related issues do you think tie into current events?

26. Write and perform a theme song for the book.

27. Compare or contrast segments of the film or video with various episodes of the novel.

28. E-mail the author and/or visit the author's Web site. Summarize what you learned in a Press Conference (see Chapter 3).

Prompts That Focus on Researching and Creating Projects

1. Create a museum exhibit for the novel as a whole-group or small-group project. (Example: Research clothing, music, sports, or transportation of the time in which the book was written.)

2. Create an illustrated time line for the story. Be creative in your design.

3. Design a creative response to the novel. (Example: a dramatization, song, painting, or project.)

4. Create a memorabilia bag or book report in a bag (a collection of concrete items that represent various facets of the story).

5. Create a Readers Theatre for a chapter of the book.

6. Create a "wanted" poster for a character in the book.

7. Create a comic strip based on a scene or chapter from the book.

8. Complete "I Prompts" based on the story. (Example: I think.... I feel.... I was surprised.... I do not understand....) Or, complete character prompts based on the novel. (Example: In *To Kill a Mockingbird*, Scout thinks.... Scout feels....)

9. Create a travel brochure for the setting of the story.

10. Create a book jacket to use in a book sell—a commercial to convince others to read the book. It may be as simple as introducing the book and telling part of the story without revealing the ending, or as elaborate as dressing up as a character and acting out part of the story.

11. Create an artistic rendering of a scene in the story and explain why you chose that scene.

12. Create audiotapes of excerpts from novels, short stories, plays, or poetry and include your critique of the work.

13. Decorate a section of the classroom in the time period of the book you are reading.

14. Create a scrapbook from the perspective of one of the characters in the novel. Explain why the artifacts are important to that character.

15. Create an alphabet quilt based on the novel.

16. Create a Web page about the book.

17. Create a cookbook or a menu of the favorite foods of characters in the book.

18. Create a time capsule from the perspective of one of the characters in the novel. Describe the significance of items to be included. Write a newspaper article about opening the time capsule in present day.

19. Create a children's book—narrative or alphabet—telling the essential story of the novel.
20. Create a newspaper based on the place and time of the book.
21. Create advertisements—audio, video, print—depicting characters or events in the book to persuade others to read the novel. (Examples: photography, paint, collage.)
22. Videotape a "trailer" (film clip for advertising purposes) for the novel as it is being released as a film.
23. Develop background music for a particular scene or chapter in a novel. Explain how the music you chose relates to that section of the book.
24. Develop and market a product that would solve the major conflict in the novel.
25. Create a video or dramatization demonstrating a conflict between two characters and a resolution that could be achieved if more effective communication skills were used. Show the conflict segment to the class and follow this with discussion. Then show the resolution segment that features the more effective communication and follow this with discussion.
26. Use a memorable quote from the novel to create a picture book, repeated phrase poem, or other project.
27. Research the author's life and share what you learn through a creative presentation.

Prompts That Involve Talk Shows or Game Shows

1. If a character were a guest on a talk show that you were hosting, what are four questions you would ask? Use your knowledge of the character and the novel to predict and support the character's responses. Choose your mode of response: audio, video, dramatization.
2. Create a game or game show that uses the literary elements (characters, setting, etc.) of the novel as its premise.
3. Formulate questions for Jeopardy, Wheel of Fortune, or Who Wants to Be a Millionaire based on the novel.
4. Create a game show atmosphere by developing questions related to the novel. Fold the questions and place them in a container. Have other students participate in the game show by choosing a question and responding to it.

Prompts That Focus on Characters

1. If you (from the perspective of another character) could have said one thing to the principal character, what would it have been? At what point in the story would you have said it? How do you think it would have influenced the outcome of the story?
2. How do you think it would change the story if the character was a different gender? Support your thinking with examples from the story and your experience. (Example: How would *The View from Saturday* have changed if all four members of the group had been girls? Boys?)
3. If you could add or remove a character from the story, explain who it would be. Explain why you made this choice and how it would affect the story.
4. Select the character you admire the most and explain why.
5. Explain which character in the book you would trust or not trust. Support your thinking with examples from the text.

6. Become a particular character and deliver a monologue. Explain your choice.

7. Choose a character, note character traits from the text, and describe a gift you think the character would appreciate receiving. Make connections between your choice and the text.

8. Have a character from one book solve a problem or offer insights to a character in another book.

9. Develop character traits for major characters in a novel and then create a new story by placing the characters in a contemporary setting.

10. Choose a theme from a novel you have read and use it as the basis for writing a scene that includes a character from a young adult novel and a character from a classic novel.

11. Combine characters from various books and situate them in a new story.

12. Choose a character from the novel and describe how he or she changed as a result of the story. Predict what you think this character's next life experience will be.

13. Design a postcard illustrating your favorite scene and write the postcard to a character either from yourself or another character.

14. Create a short survey (four or five questions) about the characters and/or their actions. Survey class members about their opinions. Report your findings and discuss them with the class.

15. Write to the author as a character in the novel and question aspects of story and character development. (Example: In *To Kill a Mockingbird*, take on the identity of Tom Robinson and ask Harper Lee why she didn't have the jury acquit him instead of finding him guilty.) Another student who has read the same novel may reply as the author.

16. Create an acrostic poem about a character. Then create an artistic interpretation of the acrostic. (Example: Design a mobile made of the letters of the name and write the descriptors on the letters.)

17. Imagine that you are a character in the story. Use that person's "voice" to explain your role in the story (orally or in diary entry format).

18. Explain why you or one of your friends would be especially good at playing a particular character in the movie version of the book.

19. Create a character collage of pictures and words by cutting out faces that represent the characters and words to describe them.

20. Explain what you think would happen in a sequel to the novel that takes place 20 years after the original story. (Example: Include where you think the main characters will be located, what they will be doing, what their accomplishments have been, what joys and tragedies they have experienced, and what their future goals are.)

21. Create a dialogue journal between two characters.

22. Create a mural (wall-sized) character map.

23. Visualize and sketch a character from the story.

24. Create an emotion map indicating high and low points in the character's life. Support your thinking with examples from the story.

25. Use a Venn diagram to compare or contrast a character in the book and you. (Example: Identify the character you like the least in the novel. Use a Venn diagram to compare or contrast yourself with this character. Which traits, especially undesirable ones, do you share? What advice would you offer to eliminate such undesirable traits?)

26. Show how two minor characters felt and reacted to each other in the book. Explain how you think these characters contribute to the overall story.

27. Choose another novel in which you think a character from the book you are reading could play. Explain which role the character would play and why you think he or she would be effective in this role.

28. Create a two-sided mask showing a character at the beginning of the book and at the conclusion. Explain why you think the character changed.

29. Invite a guest speaker from the community to visit your class to share his or her expertise about novel-related topics (adventure, survival, World War II, etc.).

Prompts That Require Assuming the Identity of the Author

1. Explain why you wrote the book. Reflect on what you have written. What might you do differently now? Consider how author style impacts the reader.

2. If you could change one event in the story, what would it be? Explain your reasoning. What effect would this have on the story as a whole?

3. Explain your thoughts about having your novel turned into a movie. If you respond positively, explain whom you would cast to play the major characters.

4. Explain how you could change your writing to accommodate a different audience. (Example: If you were sharing this story with a primary class, how would you do it?)

5. Explain why you chose the title for the book. Offer an alternative title that you think would have also worked well.

6. Extend the study of your novel by teaching a narrative element literary device. (Example: Use traditional fairy tales versus transformational fairy tales to illustrate point of view, or use *The View from Saturday* to teach similes.)

7. Tell about something you learned, realized, or felt while you were writing the book that influenced your thinking.

Leveled Book Resources

This appendix features resources for leveled books created by teachers, school districts, and publishers. It is important to remember that all levels are approximate and that students' abilities to read text are influenced by multiple factors, including background knowledge and motivation.

Web Sites Maintained by Individual Teachers

Children's Literature Research Resource Page by Bruce Ellis

Teacher Resource Center
440 Titles Sorted By Reading Level
Reading Level Range: 1.0 to 8.9
http://www.tamu-commerce.edu/coe/shed/espinoza/s/ellis-b-rdlevl.html

Sample Anchor Books:

Level	Title	Author
1.0	*Goodnight Moon*	M.W. Brown
1.6	*Polar Bear, Polar Bear, What Do You Hear?*	B. Martin Jr.
2.0	*Freckle Juice*	J. Blume
2.6	*The Very Hungry Caterpillar*	E. Carle
3.0	*The Mitten*	J. Brett
3.6	*The Emperor and the Nightingale*	H.C. Anderson
4.0	*Dear Mr. Henshaw*	B. Clearly
4.6	*Fudge-a-mania*	J. Blume
5.0	*Where the Red Fern Grows*	W. Rawls
5.6	*The Mouse and the Motorcycle*	B. Clearly
6.0	*Charlotte's Web*	E.B. White
6.7	*Charlie and the Chocolate Factory*	R. Dahl
7.0	*Treasure Island*	R.L. Stevenson
7.9	*Little Women*	L.M. Alcott
8.1	*Grimm's Fairy Tales*	Grimm
8.5	*Adventures of Tom Sawyer*	M. Twain
8.9	*Rip Van Winkle*	W. Irving

Web Sites Maintained by School Districts

Oster Elementary School, San Jose, California

http://www.unionsd.org/oster/artestsbylevel.html

Sample Anchor Books:

Level	Title	Author
1.0	*Goodnight Moon*	M.W. Brown
1.5	*Henry and Mudge and the Wild Wind*	C. Rylant
2.0	*Nate the Great and the Pillowcase*	M. Sharmat & R. Weinman
2.5	*Two Bad Ants*	C. Van Allsburg
3.0	*Cam Jansen and the Mystery of the Dinosaur Bones*	D. Adler
3.5	*Encyclopedia Brown Takes the Case*	D. Sobol
4.0	*Dear Mr. Henshaw*	B. Cleary
4.5	*Chocolate Fever*	R. Smith
5.0	*Maniac Magee*	J. Spinelli
5.5	*A Wrinkle in Time*	M. L'Engle
6.0	*Charlotte's Web*	E.B. White
6.5	*The Black Pearl*	S. O'Dell
7.0	*Bridge to Terabithia*	K. Paterson
7.5	*The Secret Garden*	F. Burnett
8.3	*Jacob Have I Loved*	K. Paterson
8.5	*The Incredible Journey*	S. Burnford
9.0	*Frederick Douglass*	P. McKissack
9.8	*Journey to the Center of the Earth*	J. Verne

Portland Public Schools, Portland, Oregon

http://www.pps.k12.or.us/instruction-c/literacy/leveled_books

Sample Anchor Books:

Level	Title	Author
1.0	*Are You My Mother?*	P.D. Eastman
1.5	*The Carrot Seed*	R. Krauss
2.0	*The Doorbell Rang*	P. Hutchins
2.5	*Madeline's Rescue*	L. Bemelmans
3.0	*Grandfather's Journey*	A. Say
3.5	*Alexander and the Terrible, Horrible, No Good Very Bad Day*	J. Viorst
4.0	*Ice Magic*	M. Christopher
4.5	*Beezus and Ramona*	B. Cleary
5.0	*Where the Red Fern Grows*	W. Rawls
5.5	*The Fighting Ground*	Avi
6.0	*The Flunking of Joshua T. Bates*	S. Shreve

6.3	*Tuck Everlasting*	N. Babbitt
7.1	*James and the Giant Peach*	R. Dahl
7.6	*Anne of Green Gables*	L.M. Montgomery
8.5	*The Incredible Journey*	S. Burnford

Leveled Materials Available From Publishers

Houghton Mifflin Reading Cumulative Listing of Leveled Books

More than 600 titles, grades K–6
Wordless picture books to full-length young adult novels.

Levels A–B   The books in these first levels are for the emergent reader. This reader is just learning reading behaviors.

Examples: *See What We Can Do*
Nat at Bat
Cat on the Mat
Once Upon a Dig
The Bug Hut

Levels C–G   The books in the second group of levels are for the early reader. These readers range in their abilities and needs. Some are just beginning to decode words, some can read simple sentences, and others can read several lines of text.

Examples: *Curious George Rides a Bike*
Benny's Pennies
One Hundred Hungry Ants
Ira Sleeps Over
Sheep in a Jeep

Levels H–M   The books in the third group are for the transitional reader. These readers have early reading behaviors well under control. They are beginning to be fluent readers.

Examples: *Curious George Flies a Kite*
What Do Authors Do?
The Wednesday Surprise
The Dive
Mufaro's Beautiful Daughters

Levels N–R   The books in the fourth group are for the self-extending reader. These are fluent readers who are able to apply many reading strategies to the task of reading texts. These books are more complex and lengthy.

Examples: *I Am Rosa Parks*
Sarah, Plain and Tall
Jumanji
The Boy Who Loved to Draw
Mark McGwire: Home Run Hero

Levels S–Z   The books in the fifth group are for the advanced reader. The advanced readers have moved well into literacy learning. They are having varied reading experiences and are using literature for many different purposes. Readers at this level see that language has meaning, purpose, and function. They use sophisticated word-solving strategies, read and reread critically and for meaning, and understand and identify nuances in literature. Advanced readers continually build their fluency and the length of text that they can read and understand.

Examples: *Anastasia at Your Service*
Pyramid
Growing Up in Coal Country
Number the Stars
Eileen Collins: First Woman Commander in Space

Great Source Education Group

Next Steps: High-interest chapter books for guided instruction

Beginning: Grades K–2

Grades 1–2   *Norma Jean, Jumping Bean*
Parakeet Girl
R is for Radish
Dragon's Scales
Dinosaur Babies

Intermediate: Grades 2–4

Grade 3   *Brave Maddie Egg*
Silver
Little Swan
Slam Dunk Saturday
Soccer Mania!

Grade 4   *The Stories Huey Tells*
Adventure in Alaska
Harriet's Hare
Harry's Mad
Babe: The Gallant Pig

Advanced: Grades 4–6

Grade 5   *The Night Crossing*
The Secret of the Seal
Black-Eyed Susan
Dear Levi
Toliver's Secret

Grade 6   *Crash*
Dog Years
Some Friends
There's a Boy in the Girl's Bathroom
Dogs Don't Tell Jokes

National Geographic School Publishing

Reading Expeditions—Content Area Readers—Grades 3–6
Reading Level Range—Upper Grade 2 to Grade 5

American Communities Across Time

A Whaling Community of the 1840s
A Homesteading Community of the 1880s
An Immigrant Community of the 1900s
A Suburban Community of the 1950s
Communities Across America Today

Kids Make a Difference

Kids Care for the Earth
Kids Are Citizens
Kids Communicate
Kids Manage Money
Kids Are Consumers

Civilizations Past to Present:

	Voices From America's Past
Egypt	*Colonial Life*
Greece	*The Spirit of a New Nation*
Rome	*Our Journey West*
China	*Blue or Gray? A Family Divided*
Mexico	*Our New Life in America*

Travels Across America:

	Seeds of Change in America's History
The Northeast	*Two Cultures Meet: Native American and European*
The Southeast	*The Industrial Revolution*
The Midwest	*Building the Transcontinental Railroad*
The Southwest	*The Age of Inventions*
The West	*The Great Migration*

APPENDIX E

Assessment Forms

ATTITUDE SURVEY 1

1. I think reading is _____

   because _____

   _____.

2. I think I am a _____ reader because _____

   _____

   _____.

3. I think _____ is a good reader because

   _____

   _____.

4. I think writing is _____

   because _____

   _____.

5. I think I am a _____ writer because _____

   _____

   _____.

6. I think _____ is a good writer because

   _____

   _____.

Name: _____ Date: _____

ATTITUDE SURVEY 2

Directions: Please place a check under the category that best describes your response.

SA = Strongly Agree
A = Agree
D = Disagree
SD = Strongly Disagree

	SA	A	D	SD
1. I read in my free time.	____	____	____	____
2. I like to receive books as gifts.	____	____	____	____
3. I like to choose what I read.	____	____	____	____
4. Reading is a rainy-day activity I enjoy.	____	____	____	____
5. I would rather read than watch television.	____	____	____	____
6. I keep a journal.	____	____	____	____
7. I like to write to my friends.	____	____	____	____
8. I like to write in school.	____	____	____	____
9. I use my computer to write.	____	____	____	____
10. I often revise my writing to make it better.	____	____	____	____

Name: _____ Date: _____

GUIDED COMPREHENSION PROFILE SUMMARY SHEET

Name: _____ Grade:_____ School Year:_____

<table>
<tr><td colspan="4">Summary of Background Information:
Interests:

Reader Perceptions (September):

Reader Perceptions (June):

Writer Perceptions (September):

Writer Perceptions (June):</td></tr>
<tr><td>Reading Levels:</td><td>September</td><td>January</td><td>June</td></tr>
<tr><td>Independent</td><td></td><td></td><td></td></tr>
<tr><td>Guided</td><td></td><td></td><td></td></tr>
<tr><td>Strategy Use:</td><td></td><td></td><td></td></tr>
<tr><td>Previewing</td><td></td><td></td><td></td></tr>
<tr><td>Self-Questioning</td><td></td><td></td><td></td></tr>
<tr><td>Making Connections</td><td></td><td></td><td></td></tr>
<tr><td>Visualizing</td><td></td><td></td><td></td></tr>
<tr><td>Knowing How Words Work</td><td></td><td></td><td></td></tr>
<tr><td>Monitoring</td><td></td><td></td><td></td></tr>
<tr><td>Summarizing</td><td></td><td></td><td></td></tr>
<tr><td>Evaluating</td><td></td><td></td><td></td></tr>
</table>

Not Observed (NO) – Student does not use the strategy.
Emerging (E) – Student attempts to use the strategy.
Developing (D) – Student is using the strategy on some occasions.
Consistent (C) – Student effectively uses the strategy to make meaning from text.

Comments:

INTEREST INVENTORY

1. What was your favorite subject last year? What do you think it will be this year? Why?

   _____

   _____

2. What is your favorite book? Why do you like it?

   _____

   _____

3. Do you have a library card? How often do you visit the library?

   _____

   _____

4. If someone were giving you a book as a gift, what would you want the book to be about?

   _____

   _____

5. What is a dream or wish you have?

   _____

6. What do you like to do after school?

   _____

   _____

7. If you had a day off from school, how would you spend the day?

   _____

   _____

8. If someone wanted to give you a magazine subscription for a gift, what magazine would you choose? Why?

   _____

   _____

9. If you won a contest and your grand prize was to meet and get to know any famous person in the world today, whom would you choose? What would you like to talk about?

   _____

10. If you could go into a bookstore and get any three books free, what kinds of books would you choose? _____

   _____

Name: _____ Date: _____

LITERACY HISTORY PROMPTS

The following are not questions to be answered, but rather ideas to prompt students' thinking as they are creating their literacy histories. Depending on the grade level, students may reflect on the entire list or the teacher may provide selected prompts.

1. What are your earliest memories of reading and writing?
2. Before you were able to read, did you pretend to read books? Can you remember the first time you read a book?
3. Do you read and/or write with your siblings or friends?
4. Can you recall your early writing attempts (scribbling, labeling drawings, etc.)?
5. Is a newspaper delivered to your home? Do you recall seeing others read the newspaper? Do you read the newspaper?
6. Do you subscribe to magazines? Do your parents/siblings have magazine subscriptions?
7. Do your parents belong to a book club? Do they maintain a personal library? Do they read for pleasure?
8. Do you receive or send mail (e.g., birthday cards, thank-you notes, letters)?
9. Can you detail your first memories of reading and/or writing instruction? Materials used? Methods of teaching? Content?
10. Can you recall reading for pleasure in elementary school?
11. Can you remember writing for pleasure in elementary school?
12. Can you recall the first book you chose to read in elementary school?
13. Can you recall your first writing assignment in elementary school?
14. Did you write a report in elementary school? What do you remember about this experience?
15. Do you remember the purposes for your reading and writing in elementary school? Do you recall any particular type of instruction you received? Can you describe any instructional materials that were used?
16. Can you recall the first book you loved (couldn't put down)?
17. Do you feel that you've ever read a book that has made a difference in your life?
18. Can you recall sharing books with friends?
19. Did you read a certain type of book (i.e., mysteries, biographies) at a particular age? Why do you think you made such choices?
20. When did you first visit a bookstore? What was it like?
21. What is your all-time favorite book?
22. Have you ever seen a book you've read turned into a film? Explain which you preferred.
23. What contributions have your reading and writing abilities made to your life?
24. Are you a reader now? What are you currently reading?
25. Are you a writer now? What are you currently writing?

Source: Adapted from McLaughlin, M., & Vogt, M.E. (1996). *Portfolios in teacher education*. Newark, DE: International Reading Association.

METACOMPREHENSION STRATEGY INDEX

Directions: Think about what kinds of things you can do to understand a story better before, during, and after you read it. Read each of the lists of four statements and decide which one of them would help *you* the most. *There are no right answers.* It is just what *you* think would help the most. Circle the letter of the statement you choose.

I. In each set of four, choose the one statement which tells a good thing to do to help you understand a story better *before* you read it.

1. Before I begin reading, it's a good idea to
   A. See how many pages are in the story.
   B. Look up all of the big words in the dictionary.
   C. Make some guesses about what I think will happen in the story.
   D. Think about what has happened so far in the story.

2. Before I begin reading, it's a good idea to
   A. Look at the pictures to see what the story is about.
   B. Decide how long it will take me to read the story.
   C. Sound out the words I don't know.
   D. Check to see if the story is making sense.

3. Before I begin reading, it's a good idea to
   A. Ask someone to read the story to me.
   B. Read the title to see what the story is about.
   C. Check to see if most of the words have long or short vowels in them.
   D. Check to see if the pictures are in order and make sense.

4. Before I begin reading, it's a good idea to
   A. Check to see that no pages are missing.
   B. Make a list of words I'm not sure about.
   C. Use the title and pictures to help me make guesses about what will happen in the story.
   D. Read the last sentence so I will know how the story ends.

5. Before I begin reading, it's a good idea to
   A. Decide on why I am going to read the story.
   B. Use the difficult words to help me make guesses about what will happen in the story.
   C. Reread some parts to see if I can figure out what is happening if things aren't making sense.
   D. Ask for help with the difficult words.

6. Before I begin reading, it's a good idea to
   A. Retell all of the main points that have happened so far.
   B. Ask myself questions that I would like to have answered in the story.
   C. Think about the meanings of the words which have more than one meaning.
   D. Look through the story to find all of the words with three or more syllables.

7. Before I begin reading, it's a good idea to
   A. Check to see if I have read this story before.
   B. Use my questions and guesses as a reason for reading the story.
   C. Make sure I can pronounce all of the words before I start.
   D. Think of a better title for the story.

8. Before I begin reading, it's a good idea to
   A. Think of what I already know about the things I see in the pictures.
   B. See how many pages are in the story.
   C. Choose the best part of the story to read again.
   D. Read the story aloud to someone.

Source: Schmitt, M.C. (1990). A questionnaire to measure children's awareness of strategic reading processes. *The Reading Teacher, 43,* 454–461.

(continued)

9. Before I begin reading, it's a good idea to
   A. Practice reading the story aloud.
   B. Retell all of the main points to make sure I can remember the story.
   C. Think of what the people in the story might be like.
   D. Decide if I have enough time to read the story.

10. Before I begin reading, it's a good idea to
    A. Check to see if I am understanding the story so far.
    B. Check to see if the words have more than one meaning.
    C. Think about where the story might be taking place.
    D. List all of the important details.

II. In each set of four, choose the one statement which tells a good thing to do to help you understand a story better *while* you are reading it.

11. While I'm reading, it's a good idea to
    A. Read the story very slowly so that I will not miss any important parts.
    B. Read the title to see what the story is about.
    C. Check to see if the pictures have anything missing.
    D. Check to see if the story is making sense by seeing if I can tell what's happened so far.

12. While I'm reading, it's a good idea to
    A. Stop to retell the main points to see if I am understanding what has happened so far.
    B. Read the story quickly so that I can find out what happened.
    C. Read only the beginning and the end of the story to find out what it is about.
    D. Skip the parts that are too difficult for me.

13. While I'm reading, it's a good idea to
    A. Look all of the big words up in the dictionary.
    B. Put the book away and find another one if things aren't making sense.
    C. Keep thinking about the title and the pictures to help me decide what is going to happen next.
    D. Keep track of how many pages I have left to read.

14. While I'm reading, it's a good idea to
    A. Keep track of how long it is taking me to read the story.
    B. Check to see if I can answer any of the questions I asked before I started reading.
    C. Read the title to see what the story is going to be about.
    D. Add the missing details to the pictures.

15. While I'm reading, it's a good idea to
    A. Have someone read the story aloud to me.
    B. Keep track of how many pages I have read.
    C. List the story's main character.
    D. Check to see if my guesses are right or wrong.

16. While I'm reading, it's a good idea to
    A. Check to see that the characters are real.
    B. Make a lot of guesses about what is going to happen next.
    C. Not look at the pictures because they might confuse me.
    D. Read the story aloud to someone.

17. While I'm reading, it's a good idea to
    A. Try to answer the questions I asked myself.
    B. Try not to confuse what I already know with what I'm reading about.
    C. Read the story silently.
    D. Check to see if I am saying the new vocabulary words correctly.

Source: Schmitt, M.C. (1990). A questionnaire to measure children's awareness of strategic reading processes. *The Reading Teacher, 43,* 454–461.

(continued)

18. While I'm reading, it's a good idea to
    A. Try to see if my guesses are going to be right or wrong.
    B. Reread to be sure I haven't missed any of the words.
    C. Decide on why I am reading the story.
    D. List what happened first, second, third, and so on.

19. While I'm reading, it's a good idea to
    A. See if I can recognize the new vocabulary words.
    B. Be careful not to skip any parts of the story.
    C. Check to see how many of the words I already know.
    D. Keep thinking of what I already know about the things and ideas in the story to help me decide what is going to happen.

20. While I'm reading, it's a good idea to
    A. Reread some parts or read ahead to see if I can figure out what is happening if things aren't making sense.
    B. Take my time reading so that I can be sure I understand what is happening.
    C. Change the ending so that it makes sense.
    D. Check to see if there are enough pictures to help make the story ideas clear.

III. **In each set of four, choose the one statement which tells a good thing to do to help you understand a story better *after* you have read it.**

21. After I've read a story it's a good idea to
    A. Count how many pages I read with no mistakes.
    B. Check to see if there were enough pictures to go with the story to make it interesting.
    C. Check to see if I met my purpose for reading the story.
    D. Underline the causes and effects.

22. After I've read a story it's a good idea to
    A. Underline the main idea.
    B. Retell the main points of the whole story so that I can check to see if I understood it.
    C. Read the story again to be sure I said all of the words right.
    D. Practice reading the story aloud.

23. After I've read a story it's a good idea to
    A. Read the title and look over the story to see what it is about.
    B. Check to see if I skipped any of the vocabulary words.
    C. Think about what made me make good or bad predictions.
    D. Make a guess about what will happen next in the story.

24. After I've read a story it's a good idea to
    A. Look up all of the big words in the dictionary.
    B. Read the best parts aloud.
    C. Have someone read the story aloud to me.
    D. Think about how the story was like things I already knew about before I started reading.

25. After I've read a story it's a good idea to
    A. Think about how I would have acted if I were the main character in the story.
    B. Practice reading the story silently for practice of good reading.
    C. Look over the story title and pictures to see what will happen.
    D. Make a list of the things I understood the most.

Source: Schmitt, M.C. (1990). A questionnaire to measure children's awareness of strategic reading processes. *The Reading Teacher, 43,* 454–461.

DIRECTIONS FOR SCORING

Part One: Responses that indicate metacomprehension strategy awareness.

I Before Reading:	II During Reading:	III After Reading:
1. C	11. D	21. C
2. A	12. A	22. B
3. B	13. C	23. C
4. C	14. B	24. D
5. A	15. D	25. A
6. B	16. B	
7. B	17. A	
8. A	18. A	
9. C	19. D	
10. C	20. A	

Part Two: Insights about the student's metacomprehension strategy use:

Name: _____ Date: _____

METACOGNITIVE READING AWARENESS INVENTORY

There's more than one way to cope when you run into difficulties in your reading. Which ways are best? Under each question here, put a checkmark beside all the responses you think are effective.

1. What do you do if you encounter a word and you don't know what it means?
    a. Use the words around it to figure it out.
    b. Use an outside source, such as a dictionary or expert.
    c. Temporarily ignore it and wait for clarification.
    d. Sound it out.

2. What do you do if you don't know what an entire sentence means?
    a. Read it again.
    b. Sound out all the difficult words.
    c. Think about the other sentences in the paragraph.
    d. Disregard it completely.

3. If you are reading science or social studies material, what would you do to remember the important information you've read?
    a. Skip parts you don't understand.
    b. Ask yourself questions about the important ideas.
    c. Realize you need to remember one point rather than another.
    d. Relate it to something you already know.

4. Before you start to read, what kind of plans do you make to help you read better?
    a. No specific plan is needed; just start reading toward completion of the assignment.
    b. Think about what you know about the subject.
    c. Think about why you are reading.
    d. Make sure the entire reading can be finished in as short a period of time as possible.

5. Why would you go back and read an entire passage over again?
    a. You didn't understand it.
    b. To clarify a specific or supporting idea.
    c. It seemed important to remember.
    d. To underline or summarize for study.

Source: Miholic, V. (1994). An inventory to pique students' metacognitive awareness of reading strategies. *The Journal of Reading, 38,* 84–86.

(continued)

6. Knowing that you don't understand a particular sentence while reading involves understanding that
   a. the reader may not have developed adequate links or associations for new words or concepts introduced in the sentence.
   b. the writer may not have conveyed the ideas clearly.
   c. two sentences may purposely contradict each other.
   d. finding meaning for the sentence needlessly slows down the reader.

7. As you read a textbook, which of these do you do?
   a. Adjust your pace depending on the difficulty of the material.
   b. Generally, read at a constant, steady pace.
   c. Skip the parts you don't understand.
   d. Continually make predictions about what you are reading.

8. While you read, which of these are important?
   a. Know when you know and when you don't know key ideas.
   b. Know what it is that you know in relation to what is being read.
   c. Know that confusing text is common and usually can be ignored.
   d. Know that different strategies can be used to aid understanding.

9. When you come across a part of the text that is confusing, what do you do?
   a. Keep on reading until the text is clarified.
   b. Read ahead and then look back if the text is still unclear.
   c. Skip those sections completely; they are usually not important.
   d. Check to see if the ideas expressed are consistent with one another.

10. Which sentences are the most important in the chapter?
    a. Almost all of the sentences are important; otherwise, they wouldn't be there.
    b. The sentences that contain the important details or facts.
    c. The sentences that are directly related to the main idea.
    d. The ones that contain the most details.

Source: Miholic, V. (1994). An inventory to pique students' metacognitive awareness of reading strategies. *The Journal of Reading, 38*, 84–86.

DIRECTIONS FOR SCORING

Part One: Responses that indicate metacognitive reading awareness.

1. a, b, c
2. a, c
3. b, c, d
4. b, c
5. a, c, d
6. a, b, c
7. a, d
8. a, b, d
9. a, b, d
10. b, c

Part Two: Insights about the student's metacognitive reading awareness:

Name: _____ Date: _____

MOTIVATION TO READ PROFILE
CONVERSATIONAL INTERVIEW

Name: _____ Date: _____

A. Emphasis: Narrative text

Suggested prompt (designed to engage student in a natural conversation): I have been reading a good book...I was talking with...about it last night. I enjoy talking about good stories and books that I've been reading. Today I'd like to hear about what you have been reading.

1. Tell me about the most interesting story or book you have read this week (or even last week). Take a few minutes to think about it. (Wait time.) Now, tell me about the book or story.

Probes: What else can you tell me? Is there anything else? _____

_____

_____

_____

_____

2. How did you know or find out about this story? _____

_____

_____

☐ assigned   ☐ in school

☐ chosen   ☐ out of school

3. Why was this story interesting to you? _____

_____

_____

_____

_____

Source: Gambrell, L.B., Palmer, B.M., Codling, R.M., & Mazzoni, S.A. (1996). Assessing motivation to read. *The Reading Teacher, 49*, 518–533.
(continued)

B. Emphasis: Informational text

Suggested prompt (designed to engage student in a natural conversation): Often we read to find out about something or to learn about something. We read for information. For example, I remember a student of mine…who read a lot of books about…to find out as much as he/she could about…. Now, I'd like to hear about some of the informational reading you have been doing.

1. Think about something important that you learned recently, not from your teacher and not from television, but from a book or some other reading material. What did you read about? (Wait time.) Tell me about what you learned.

   Probes: What else could you tell me? Is there anything else? _____

   _____

   _____

   _____

   _____

2. How did you know or find out about this book/article?_____

   _____

   _____

   ☐ assigned   ☐ in school

   ☐ chosen   ☐ out of school

3. Why was this book (or article) important to you? _____

   _____

   _____

   _____

   _____

Source: Gambrell, L.B., Palmer, B.M., Codling, R.M., & Mazzoni, S.A. (1996). Assessing motivation to read. *The Reading Teacher, 49*, 518–533.

(continued)

C. Emphasis: General reading

1. Did you read anything at home yesterday? _____ What?

_____

_____

2. Do you have any books at school (in your desk/storage area/locker/book bag) today that you are reading? _____ Tell me about them.

_____

_____

3. Tell me about your favorite author.

_____

_____

4. What do you think you have to learn to be a better reader?

_____

_____

5. Do you know about any books right now that you'd like to read? Tell me about them.

_____

_____

6. How did you find out about these books?

_____

_____

7. What are some things that get you really excited about reading books?

_____

_____

8. Tell me about…

_____

_____

9. Who gets you really interested and excited about reading books?

_____

_____

10. Tell me more about what they do.

_____

_____

Source: Gambrell, L.B., Palmer, B.M., Codling, R.M., & Mazzoni, S.A. (1996). Assessing motivation to read. *The Reading Teacher, 49*, 518–533.

LITERATURE CIRCLE OBSERVATION

Directions: Place a check if the behavior is observed.
Observation:

Student is prepared for the Literature Circle. _____

Student is focused on the group task. _____

Student engages in discussion. _____

    Talk focuses on the content of the book. _____

    Talk focuses on the reading process. _____

    Talk focuses on personal connections. _____

    Talk focuses on the group process. _____

Student is competent in his or her discussion role. _____

Student's contributions demonstrate
depth of understanding. _____

Student respects ideas of other group members. _____

Student's self-evaluation indicates _____

_____

_____

_____

_____

Notes: _____

_____

_____

_____

_____

Name:_____ Date: _____

QUESTIONING THE AUTHOR (QtA) OBSERVATION

Directions: Place a check if the behavior is observed.

Observation:

Student is prepared for Questioning the Author. _____

Student is focused on the group task. _____

Student is actively engaged in QtA. _____

Student uses a reviser's eye. _____

Student generates meaningful queries. _____

Student contributes meaningful responses. _____

Student draws meaningful conclusions. _____

Student is a competent participant in QtA. _____

Student's contributions demonstrate depth of understanding. _____

Student respects ideas of other group members. _____

Student's self-evaluation indicates _____

_____

_____

_____

_____

Notes: _____

_____

_____

_____

_____

Name:_____ Date: _____

RECIPROCAL TEACHING OBSERVATION

Directions: Place a check if the behavior is observed.
Observation:

Student is prepared for Reciprocal Teaching.   _____

Student is focused on the group task.   _____

Student is actively engaged in Reciprocal Teaching.   _____

Student successfully engages in prediction.   _____

Student successfully generates meaningful questions.   _____

Student successfully clarifies meaning.   _____

Student successfully summarizes text.   _____

Student uses strategy prompts.   _____

Student's contributions demonstrate depth of understanding.   _____

Student respects ideas of other group members.   _____

Student's self-evaluation indicates _____

_____

_____

_____

_____

Notes: _____

_____

_____

_____

_____

Name:_____ Date: _____

READER SELF-PERCEPTION SCALE

Listed below are statements about reading. Please read each statement carefully. Then circle the letters that show how much you agree or disagree with the statement. Use the following scale:

SA = Strongly Agree   A = Agree   U = Undecided   D = Disagree   SD = Strongly Disagree

Example: **I think pizza with pepperoni is the best.**   SA   A   U   D   SD

If you are *really positive* that pepperoni pizza is best, circle SA (Strongly Agree).

If you *think* that it is good but maybe not great, circle A (Agree).

If you *can't decide* whether or not it is best, circle U (Undecided).

If you *think* that pepperoni pizza is not all that good, circle D (Disagree).

If you are *really positive* that pepperoni pizza is not very good, circle SD (Strongly Disagree).

	1.	I think I am a good reader.	SA	A	U	D	SD
[SF]	2.	I can tell that my teacher likes to listen to me read.	SA	A	U	D	SD
[SF]	3.	My teacher thinks that my reading is fine.	SA	A	U	D	SD
[OC]	4.	I read faster than other kids.	SA	A	U	D	SD
[PS]	5.	I like to read aloud.	SA	A	U	D	SD
[OC]	6.	When I read, I can figure out words better than other kids.	SA	A	U	D	SD
[SF]	7.	My classmates like to listen to me read.	SA	A	U	D	SD
[PS]	8.	I feel good inside when I read.	SA	A	U	D	SD
[SF]	9.	My classmates think that I read pretty well.	SA	A	U	D	SD
[PR]	10.	When I read, I don't have to try as hard as I used to.	SA	A	U	D	SD
[OC]	11.	I seem to know more words than other kids when I read.	SA	A	U	D	SD
[SF]	12.	People in my family think I am a good reader.	SA	A	U	D	SD
[PR]	13.	I am getting better at reading.	SA	A	U	D	SD
[OC]	14.	I understand what I read as well as other kids do.	SA	A	U	D	SD
[PR]	15.	When I read, I need less help than I used to.	SA	A	U	D	SD
[PS]	16.	Reading makes me feel happy inside.	SA	A	U	D	SD
[SF]	17.	My teacher thinks I am a good reader.	SA	A	U	D	SD
[PR]	18.	Reading is easier for me than it used to be.	SA	A	U	D	SD
[PR]	19.	I read faster than I could before.	SA	A	U	D	SD
[OC]	20.	I read better than other kids in my class.	SA	A	U	D	SD
[PS]	21.	I feel calm when I read.	SA	A	U	D	SD
[OC]	22.	I read more than other kids.	SA	A	U	D	SD
[PR]	23.	I understand what I read better than I could before.	SA	A	U	D	SD
[PR]	24.	I can figure out words better than I could before.	SA	A	U	D	SD
[PS]	25.	I feel comfortable when I read.	SA	A	U	D	SD
[PS]	26.	I think reading is relaxing.	SA	A	U	D	SD
[PR]	27.	I read better now than I could before.	SA	A	U	D	SD
[PR]	28.	When I read, I recognize more words than I used to.	SA	A	U	D	SD
[PS]	29.	Reading makes me feel good.	SA	A	U	D	SD
[SF]	30.	Other kids think I'm a good reader.	SA	A	U	D	SD
[SF]	31.	People in my family think I read pretty well.	SA	A	U	D	SD
[PS]	32.	I enjoy reading.	SA	A	U	D	SD
[SF]	33.	People in my family like to listen to me read.	SA	A	U	D	SD

Source: Henk, W.A., & Melnick, S.A. (1995). The Reader Self-Perception Scale (RSPS): A new tool for measuring how children feel about themselves as readers. *The Reading Teacher, 48*, 470–482.

(continued)

DIRECTIONS FOR ADMINISTRATION, SCORING, AND INTERPRETATION

The Reader Self-Perception Scale (RSPS) is intended to provide an assessment of how children feel about themselves as readers. The scale consists of 33 items that assess self-perceptions along four dimensions of self-efficacy (Progress, Observational Comparison, Social Feedback, and Physiological States). Children are asked to indicate how strongly they agree or disagree with each statement on a 5-point scale (5 = Strongly Agree, 1 = Strongly Disagree). The information gained from this scale can be used to devise ways to enhance children's self-esteem in reading and, ideally, to increase their motivation to read. The following directions explain specifically what you are to do.

Administration

For the results to be of any use, the children must: (a) understand exactly what they are to do, (b) have sufficient time to complete all items, and (c) respond honestly and thoughtfully. Briefly explain to the children that they are being asked to complete a questionnaire about reading. Emphasize that this is not a *test* and that there are no *right* answers. Tell them that they should be as honest as possible because their responses will be confidential. Ask the children to fill in their names, grade levels, and classrooms as appropriate. Read the directions aloud and work through the example with the students as a group. Discuss the response options and make sure that all children understand the rating scale before moving on. It is important that children know that they may raise their hands to ask questions about any words or ideas they do not understand.

The children should then read each item and circle their response for the item. They should work at their own pace. Remind the children that they should be sure to respond to all items. When all items are completed, the children should stop, put their pencils down, and wait for further instructions. Care should be taken that children who work more slowly are not disturbed by children who have already finished.

Scoring

To score the RSPS, enter the following point values for each response on the RSPS scoring sheet (Strongly Agree = 5, Agree = 4, Undecided = 3, Disagree = 2, Strongly Disagree = 1) for each item number under the appropriate scale. Sum each column to obtain a raw score for each of the four specific scales.

Interpretation

Each scale is interpreted in relation to its total possible score. For example, because the RSPS uses a 5-point scale and the Progress scale consists of 9 items, the highest total score for Progress is 45 ($9 \times 5 = 45$). Therefore, a score that would fall approximately in the middle of the range (22–23) would indicate a child's somewhat indifferent perception of her or himself as a reader with respect to Progress. Note that each scale has a different possible total raw score (Progress = 45, Observational Comparison = 30, Social Feedback = 45, and Physiological States = 40) and should be interpreted accordingly.

Source: Henk, W.A., & Melnick, S.A. (1995). The Reader Self-Perception Scale (RSPS): A new tool for measuring how children feel about themselves as readers. *The Reading Teacher, 48,* 470–482. (continued)

SCORING SHEET

Student name _____

Teacher _____

Grade _____ Date _____

Scoring key: 5 = Strongly Agree (SA)
4 = Agree (A)
3 = Undecided (U)
2 = Disagree (D)
1 = Strongly Disagree (SD)

Scales

General Perception	Progress	Observational Comparison	Social Feedback	Physiological States
1. ____	10. ____	4. ____	2. ____	5. ____
	13. ____	6. ____	3. ____	8. ____
	15. ____	11. ____	7. ____	16. ____
	18. ____	14. ____	9. ____	21. ____
	19. ____	20. ____	12. ____	25. ____
	23. ____	22. ____	17. ____	26. ____
	24. ____		30. ____	29. ____
	27. ____		31. ____	32. ____
	28. ____		33. ____	

Raw score	____ of 45	____ of 30	____ of 45	____ of 40

Score interpretation				
High	44+	26+	38+	37+
Average	39	21	33	31
Low	34	16	27	25

Source: Henk, W.A., & Melnick, S.A. (1995). The Reader Self-Perception Scale (RSPS): A new tool for measuring how children feel about themselves as readers. *The Reading Teacher, 48*, 470–482.

STUDENT SELF-REFLECTION AND GOAL SETTING

Hobby or Special Interest

This activity is designed to help you reflect on one of your hobbies or special interests. Remember that self-reflection involves thinking about what you did, how well you did it, and what you can do to make it better next time. To begin your reflection, focus on your hobby or special interest. Then think about the last time you did it. How well did it go? What is one thing you can do to improve it next time? What is your new goal?

My hobby or special interest is

Something I learned to do in my hobby or special interest is

The last time I did it

One thing I can do to improve it next time is

My new goal for my hobby or special interest is

Source: Adapted from McLaughlin, M. (1995). *Performance assessment: A practical guide to implementation.* Boston: Houghton Mifflin.

STUDENT SELF-REFLECTION AND GOAL SETTING IN GUIDED COMPREHENSION

This activity is designed to help you create a self-reflection about your reading. Remember that self-reflection involves thinking about what you did, how well you did it, and what you can do to make it better next time. To begin your reflection focus on something you have learned during Guided Comprehension. Then think about the last time you did it. How well did it go? What is one thing you can do to improve it next time? What is your new goal?

What I read

What I learned

The last time I did it

One thing I can do to improve it next time is

My new goal is

SPECIAL QUESTION FROM YOUR TEACHER: What can I do to help you reach your new goal?

Source: Adapted from McLaughlin, M. (1995). *Performance assessment: A practical guide to implementation*. Boston: Houghton Mifflin.

REFLECTION AND GOAL SETTING

Today my goal was

What I did

What I learned

Questions I have

When I reflect on how well I achieved my goal, I think

Tomorrow my goal will be

Name:_____ Date: _____

TICKETS OUT

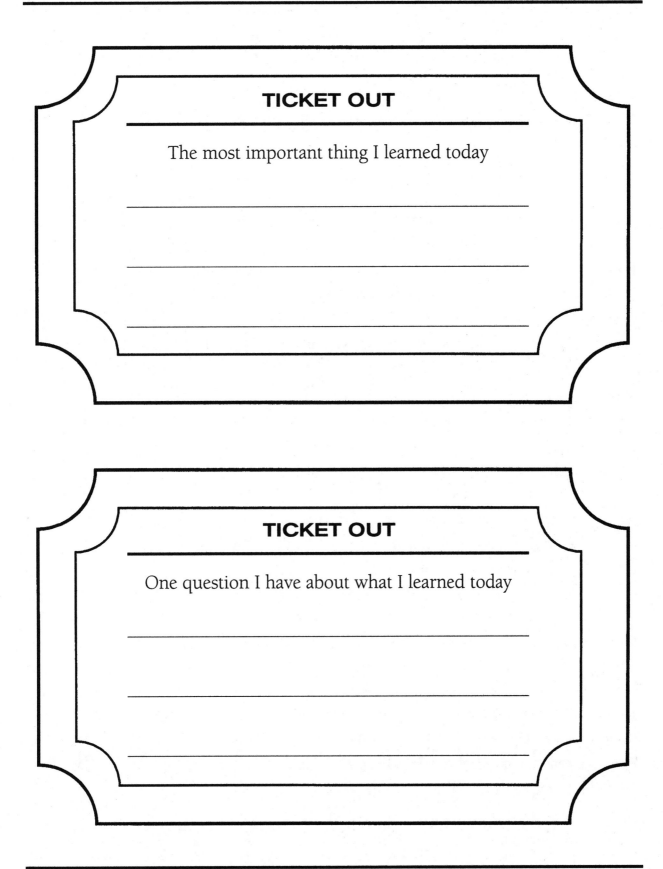

TICKET OUT

The most important thing I learned today

_____

_____

_____

TICKET OUT

One question I have about what I learned today

_____

_____

_____

WRITER SELF-PERCEPTION SCALE

Listed below are statements about writing. Please read each statement carefully. Then circle the letters that show how much you agree or disagree with the statement. Use the following scale:

SA = Strongly Agree
A = Agree
U = Undecided
D = Disagree
SD = Strongly Disagree

Example: **I think Batman is the greatest super hero.**   SA   A   U   D   SD

If you are *really positive* that Batman is the greatest, circle SA (Strongly Agree).

If you *think* that Batman is good but maybe not great, circle A (Agree).

If you *can't decide* whether or not Batman is the greatest, circle U (Undecided).

If you *think* that Batman is not all that great, circle D (Disagree).

If you are *really positive* that Batman is not the greatest, circle SD (Strongly Disagree).

(OC)	1. I write better than other kids in my class.	SA	A	U	D	SD
(PS)	2. I like how writing makes me feel inside.	SA	A	U	D	SD
(GPR)	3. Writing is easier for me than it used to be.	SA	A	U	D	SD
(OC)	4. When I write, my organization is better than the other kids in my class.	SA	A	U	D	SD
(SF)	5. People in my family think I am a good writer.	SA	A	U	D	SD
(GPR)	6. I am getting better at writing.	SA	A	U	D	SD
(PS)	7. When I write, I feel calm.	SA	A	U	D	SD
(OC)	8. My writing is more interesting than my classmates' writing.	SA	A	U	D	SD
(SF)	9. My teacher thinks my writing is fine.	SA	A	U	D	SD
(SF)	10. Other kids think I am a good writer.	SA	A	U	D	SD
(OC)	11. My sentences and paragraphs fit together as well as my classmates' sentences and paragraphs.	SA	A	U	D	SD
(GPR)	12. I need less help to write well than I used to.	SA	A	U	D	SD
(SF)	13. People in my family think I write pretty well.	SA	A	U	D	SD
(GPR)	14. I write better now than I could before.	SA	A	U	D	SD

Source: Bottomley, D.M., Henk, W.A., & Melnick, S.A. (1997/1998). Assessing children's views about themselves as writers using the Writer Self-Perception Scale. *The Reading Teacher, 51*, 286–296.   (continued)

(GEN) 15. I think I am a good writer.	SA	A	U	D	SD
(OC) 16. I put my sentences in a better order than the other kids.	SA	A	U	D	SD
(GPR) 17. My writing has improved.	SA	A	U	D	SD
(GPR) 18. My writing is better than before.	SA	A	U	D	SD
(GPR) 19. It's easier to write well now than it used to be.	SA	A	U	D	SD
(GPR) 20. The organization of my writing has really improved.	SA	A	U	D	SD
(OC) 21. The sentences I use in my writing stick to the topic more than the ones the other kids use.	SA	A	U	D	SD
(SPR) 22. The words I use in my writing are better than the ones I used before.	SA	A	U	D	SD
(OC) 23. I write more often than other kids.	SA	A	U	D	SD
(PS) 24. I am relaxed when I write.	SA	A	U	D	SD
(SPR) 25. My descriptions are more interesting than before.	SA	A	U	D	SD
(OC) 26. The words I use in my writing are better than the ones other kids use.	SA	A	U	D	SD
(PS) 27. I feel comfortable when I write.	SA	A	U	D	SD
(SF) 28. My teacher thinks I am a good writer.	SA	A	U	D	SD
(SPR) 29. My sentences stick to the topic better now.	SA	A	U	D	SD
(OC) 30. My writing seems to be more clear than my classmates' writing.	SA	A	U	D	SD
(SPR) 31. When I write, the sentences and paragraphs fit together better than they used to.	SA	A	U	D	SD
(PS) 32. Writing makes me feel good.	SA	A	U	D	SD
(SF) 33. I can tell that my teacher thinks my writing is fine.	SA	A	U	D	SD
(SPR) 34. The order of my sentences makes better sense now.	SA	A	U	D	SD
(PS) 35. I enjoy writing.	SA	A	U	D	SD
(SPR) 36. My writing is more clear than it used to be.	SA	A	U	D	SD
(SF) 37. My classmates would say I write well.	SA	A	U	D	SD
(SPR) 38. I choose the words I use in my writing more carefully now.	SA	A	U	D	SD

Source: Bottomley, D.M., Henk, W.A., & Melnick, S.A. (1997/1998). Assessing children's views about themselves as writers using the Writer Self-Perception Scale. *The Reading Teacher, 51,* 286–296.

(continued)

DIRECTIONS FOR ADMINISTRATION, SCORING, AND INTERPRETATION

The Writer Self-Perception Scale (WSPS) provides an estimate of how children feel about themselves as writers. The scale consists of 38 items that assess self-perception along five dimensions of self-efficacy (General Progress, Specific Progress, Observational Comparison, Social Feedback, and Physiological States). Children are asked to indicate how strongly they agree or disagree with each statement using a 5-point scale ranging from Strongly Agree (5) to Strongly Disagree (1). The information yielded by this scale can be used to devise ways of enhancing children's self-esteem in writing and, ideally, to increase their motivation for writing. The following directions explain specifically what you are to do.

Administration

To ensure useful results, the children must (a) understand exactly what they are to do, (b) have sufficient time to complete all items, and (c) respond honestly and thoughtfully. Briefly explain to the children that they are being asked to complete a questionnaire about writing. Emphasize that this is not a test and that there are no right or wrong answers. Tell them that they should be as honest as possible because their responses will be confidential. Ask the children to fill in their names, grade levels, and classrooms as appropriate. Read the directions aloud and work through the example with the students as a group. Discuss the response options and make sure that all children understand the rating scale before moving on. The children should be instructed to raise their hands to ask questions about any words or ideas that are unfamiliar.

The children should then read each item and circle their response to the statement. They should work at their own pace. Remind the children that they should be sure to respond to all items. When all items are completed, the children should stop, put their pencils down, and wait for further instructions. Care should be taken that children who work more slowly are not disturbed by classmates who have already finished.

Scoring

To score the WSPS, enter the following point values for each response on the WSPS scoring sheet (Strongly Agree = 5, Agree = 4, Undecided = 3, Disagree = 2, Strongly Disagree = 1) for each item number under the appropriate scale. Sum each column to obtain a raw score for each of the five specific scales.

Interpretation

Each scale is interpreted in relation to its total possible score. For example, because the WSPS uses a 5-point scale and the General Progress scale consists of 8 items, the highest total score is 40 (8 × 5 = 40). Therefore, a score that would fall approximately at the average or mean score (35) would indicate that the child's perception of her- or himself as a writer falls in the average range with respect to General Progress. Note that each remaining scale has a different possible maximum raw score (Specific Progress = 35, Observational Comparison = 45, Social Feedback = 35, and Physiological States = 30) and should be interpreted accordingly using the high, average, and low designations on the scoring sheet.

Source: Bottomley, D.M., Henk, W.A., & Melnick, S.A. (1997/1998). Assessing children's views about themselves as writers using the Writer Self-Perception Scale. *The Reading Teacher, 51*, 286–296.

(continued)

WRITER SELF-PERCEPTION SCALE (continued)

SCORING SHEET

Student name _____

Teacher _____

Grade _____ Date _____

Scoring key: 5 = Strongly Agree (SA)
4 = Agree (A)
3 = Undecided (U)
2 = Disagree (D)
1 = Strongly Disagree (SD)

Scales

General Progress (GPR)	Specific Progress (SPR)	Observational Comparison (OC)	Social Feedback (SF)	Physiological States (PS)
3. _____	22. _____	1. _____	5. _____	2. _____
6. _____	25. _____	4. _____	9. _____	7. _____
12. _____	29. _____	8. _____	10. _____	24. _____
14. _____	31. _____	11. _____	13. _____	27. _____
17. _____	34. _____	16. _____	28. _____	32. _____
18. _____	36. _____	21. _____	33. _____	35. _____
19. _____	38. _____	23. _____	37. _____	
20. _____		26. _____		
		30. _____		

Raw score

_____ of 40	_____ of 35	_____ of 45	_____ of 35	_____ of 30

Score interpretation	GPR	SPR	OC	SF	PS
High	39+	34+	37+	32+	28+
Average	35	29	30	27	22
Low	30	24	23	22	16

Source: Bottomley, D.M., Henk, W.A., & Melnick, S.A. (1997/1998). Assessing children's views about themselves as writers using the Writer Self-Perception Scale. *The Reading Teacher, 51*, 286–296.

Guided Comprehension Instructional Plans

* Guided Comprehension instructional plans for previewing and evaluating can be found in Chapter 7.

Self-Questioning: "I Wonder" Statements

Teacher-Directed Whole-Group Instruction

I began by reviewing the class goal about self-questioning, telling the students that using this strategy would help them to question and clarify what they are reading. I explained "I Wonder" Statements and modeled them through a Think-Aloud as I read *Armadillo Tattletale* aloud. I started with the cover and wondered out loud. I shared why I was wondering that. I continued this process for a few pages. The students were very eager to discuss answers for what I was wondering about. I told them that the author might provide us with those answers later in the text. If not we would have time to discuss them later. After I modeled, I read additional sections of text out loud, and I had the students wonder in small groups and share why they thought that. When we finished the book, we discussed which of our wonderings were clarified and which were not. We discussed which were more important and which were less important to understanding the story. Then we reflected on how the wonderings helped us comprehend. The following "I Wonder" Statements are examples the students and I used during this large-group direct instruction.

Book: Kettelman, H. (2000). *Armadillo Tattletale*. New York: Scholastic.

Summary: Armadillo once had very long ears, but he used them to eavesdrop and tell tales. Therefore, Alligator teaches him a lesson by trimming his long ears.

"I Wonder" Statements: I wonder...

...why he had short ears on the cover.

...if the other animals become angry with him.

...if Armadillo is going to tell Blue Jay what Egret said about him.

...why Armadillo lied about what Egret said.

...if he will keep his promise.

...why he keeps eavesdropping and telling tales.

...what he will tell Toad.

...if he learned his lesson.

...why the animals believe what Armadillo says.

Teacher-Guided Small-Group Instruction

Within this small group setting, I reviewed the importance of self-questioning when reading. I also reminded the students of all the strategies we use to comprehend. I then guided the students to wonder as they read *The Whipping Boy*. First, they wondered by looking at the cover and completing the sentence "I wonder..." and sharing why they wondered that. I prompted them to go beyond just the surface and to think about what information the title and cover art provide. I guided the students to read a portion of the text, stop to wonder, and provide support as to why they wondered that. Unfortunately, the students were a little apprehensive and offered little depth in their wonderings. Therefore, I felt the need to provide more guidance with this teaching idea. I continued to model for them by scaffolding their reading. I asked them to silently read a section of text and after they had finished, I dramatically announced, "I wonder...." The students were eager to discuss what I was wondering about and provide reasons for the responses with support from the text. I continued this process until students were wondering competently. I had them finish the chapter and share wonderings for the next chapter. We then reflected on the importance of self-questioning and how it helped us understand the story. We talked about ways we could think about questioning while we were reading and set new goals.

GUIDED COMPREHENSION: SELF-QUESTIONING—"I WONDER" STATEMENTS

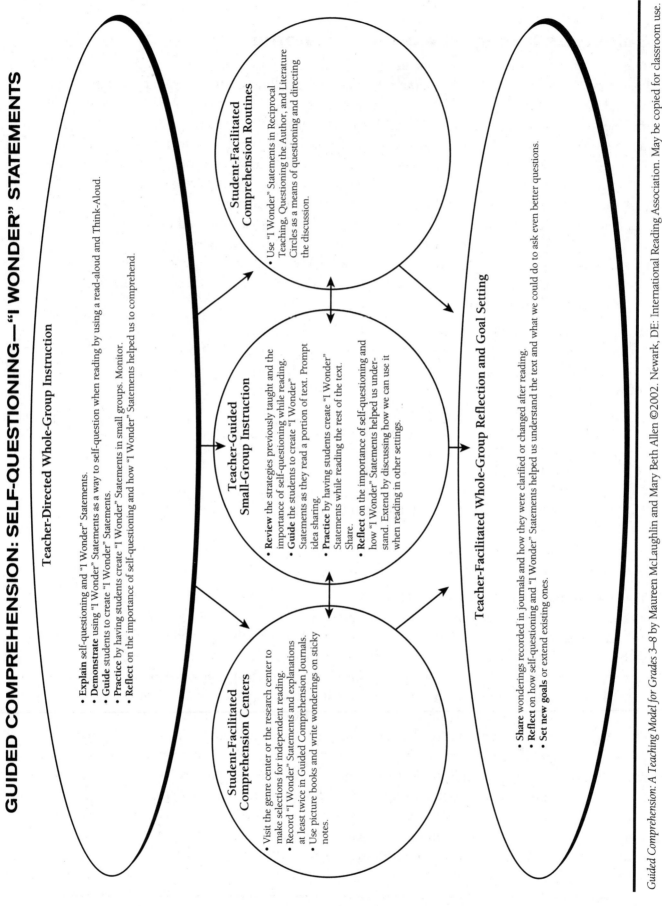

Teacher-Directed Whole-Group Instruction

- **Explain** self-questioning and "I Wonder" Statements.
- **Demonstrate** using "I Wonder" Statements as a way to self-question when reading by using a read-aloud and Think-Aloud.
- **Guide** students to create "I Wonder" Statements.
- **Practice** by having students create "I Wonder" Statements in small groups. Monitor.
- **Reflect** on the importance of self-questioning and how "I Wonder" Statements helped us to comprehend.

Student-Facilitated Comprehension Centers

- Visit the genre center or the research center to make selections for independent reading.
- Record "I Wonder" Statements and explanations at least twice in Guided Comprehension Journals.
- Use picture books and write wonderings on sticky notes.

Teacher-Guided Small-Group Instruction

- **Review** the strategies previously taught and the importance of self-questioning while reading.
- **Guide** the students to create "I Wonder" Statements as they read a portion of text. Prompt idea sharing.
- **Practice** by having students create "I Wonder" Statements while reading the rest of the text. Share.
- **Reflect** on the importance of self-questioning and how "I Wonder" Statements helped us understand. Extend by discussing how we can use it when reading in other settings.

Student-Facilitated Comprehension Routines

- Use "I Wonder" Statements in Reciprocal Teaching, Questioning the Author, and Literature Circles as a means of questioning and directing the discussion.

Teacher-Facilitated Whole-Group Reflection and Goal Setting

- **Share** wonderings recorded in journals and how they were clarified or changed after reading.
- **Reflect** on how self-questioning and "I Wonder" Statements helped us understand the text and what we could do to ask even better questions.
- **Set new goals** or extend existing ones.

Book: Fleischman, S. (1990). *The whipping boy*. New York: Troll.

Summary: Jemmy, a commoner, and Prince Brat run away and switch places to help them escape from the villains.

"I Wonder" Statements: I wonder...

...if the villains will whip Prince Brat.

...why the soldiers didn't check the wagon.

Student-Facilitated Comprehension Centers

Students used "I Wonder" Statements with their independent reading at a variety of centers by recording wonderings in their Guided Comprehension Journals. I was able to look at these and determine if they were using self-questioning in an effective way. Although most students were able to write thoughtful wonderings, some still need more modeling with this. I will provide additional direct instruction on this strategy.

Another group of students visited the genre and research centers and wrote "wonders" on sticky notes. The students were actively engaged with and conversing about these texts. Some of the students selected and read picture books. When they came to a section of text that made them wonder about something, they recorded it on a sticky note and placed it in that section of the text. If another student came to the sticky note they could write their thoughts on that "I Wonder" Statement. I was pleased with the discussion this activity prompted. A brief list of picture books placed in this station and some of the students' examples are provided below.

Book: Nickle, J. (1998). *The ant bully*. New York: Scholastic.

Summary: Lucas is bullied by the neighborhood meanie. Lucas takes out his frustrations on the ants. The ants decide to teach him a valuable lesson.

"I Wonder" Statement: I wonder...

...if the ants are going to treat Locus like he treated them.

Book: Kettelman, H. (2000). *Armadillo Tattletale*. New York: Scholastic.

Summary: Armadillo once had very long ears, but he used them to eavesdrop and tell tales. Therefore, Alligator teaches him a lesson by trimming his long ears.

"I Wonder" Statements: I wonder...

...why everyone believed him.

...why a vulture is in this picture.

...why the characters don't notice his big ears.

Book: Teague, M. (1994). *Pigsty*. New York: Scholastic.

Summary: Wendell's room is so messy that two pigs decide to live with him. When Wendell finally gets annoyed with the pigs, he cleans up his room.

"I Wonder" Statements: I wonder...

...if the pigs are going to be in Wendell's room.

...what is going to happen to him.

...if he will clean his room and if the pig will help.

...if his mother is going to check on him.

...if his mom knows the pig is in his room.

...if two more pigs will come.

...if Wendell will get rid of the pigs.

...if his mother believes him.

Note: Some of these questions were answered by reading further. However, some students asked these questions after reading the pertaining information. I made a note that these students would need further scaffolding with monitoring comprehension.

Student-Facilitated Comprehension Routines

A small group of students were participating in a reciprocal teaching session while reading *The Whipping Boy*. They recorded their wonderings in their Guided Comprehension Journals and discussed them with one another. The students used the text to support their responses and also discussed possible responses to the statements that were not clarified by the text.

Book: Fleischman, S. (1990). *The whipping boy.* New York: Troll.

Summary: Jemmy, a commoner, and Prince Brat run away and switch places to help them escape
　　　　　from the villains.

"I Wonder" Statements: I wonder...

　　...if Betsy will help them again.

　　...how Hold-Your-Nose-Billy can learn to swim instantly.

　　...if Jimmy is going to be punished.

Teacher-Facilitated Whole-Group Goal Setting and Reflection

We started with a review of why self-questioning is an important strategy for making sense of text. Then, students shared some of the wonderings they had and how they were clarified or changed after reading. We got into a discussion about how sometimes our questions are not answered and what to do if that happens. We then talked about the process of using "I Wonder" Statements as a way to guide self-questioning. The students agreed that it was an easy way to remind them to question and they enjoyed listening to one another's wonderings. I then encouraged students to reflect on how self-questioning helped them with understanding the text and what they could do to ask even better questions while they read. Finally, we assessed our ability to use "I Wonder" Statements and set new personal goals.

Assessment Options

I used informal assessments throughout this lesson. These included observing students practicing and applying, responding to their Guided Comprehension Journals, and reviewing their new personal goals.

Making Connections: Double-Entry Journals

A variety of mystery books were used in these Guided Comprehension plans.

Teacher-Directed Whole-Group Instruction

I began by reviewing our goal for making connections and explaining Double-Entry Journals. I was careful to note that Double-Entry Journals can be used for making connections in several different ways, including idea and response, quotation and response, and prediction and verification. Next, I asked students if they had ever predicted the outcome of anything—a sporting event, a television show, a book. As we engaged in discussion, I recorded a number of the ideas that the students shared.

GUIDED COMPREHENSION: MAKING CONNECTIONS—DOUBLE-ENTRY JOURNAL

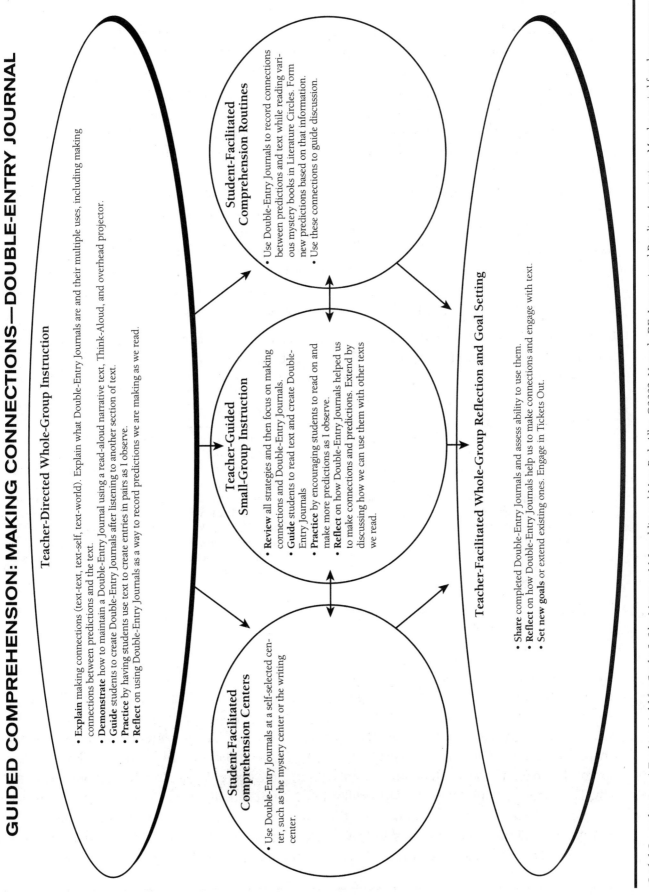

Teacher-Directed Whole-Group Instruction

- **Explain** making connections (text-text, text-self, text-world). Explain what Double-Entry Journals are and their multiple uses, including making connections between predictions and the text.
- **Demonstrate** how to maintain a Double-Entry Journal using a read-aloud narrative text, Think-Aloud, and overhead projector.
- **Guide** students to create Double-Entry Journals after listening to another section of text.
- **Practice** by having students use text to create entries in pairs as I observe.
- **Reflect** on using Double-Entry Journals as a way to record predictions we are making as we read.

Student-Facilitated Comprehension Centers

- Use Double-Entry Journals at a self-selected center, such as the mystery center or the writing center.

Teacher-Guided Small-Group Instruction

- **Review** all strategies and then focus on making connections and Double-Entry Journals.
- **Guide** students to read text and create Double-Entry Journals
- **Practice** by encouraging students to read on and make more predictions as I observe.
- **Reflect** on how Double-Entry Journals helped us to make connections and predictions. Extend by discussing how we can use them with other texts we read.

Student-Facilitated Comprehension Routines

- Use Double-Entry Journals to record connections between predictions and text while reading various mystery books in Literature Circles. Form new predictions based on that information.
- Use these connections to guide discussion.

Teacher-Facilitated Whole-Group Reflection and Goal Setting

- **Share** completed Double-Entry Journals and assess ability to use them.
- **Reflect** on how Double-Entry Journals help us to make connections and engage with text.
- **Set new goals** or extend existing ones. Engage in Tickets Out.

Many of them had made predictions about how a book would end. Realizing that a number of the students had background knowledge about predicting, I modified my teaching plan and reviewed predicting with them by modeling how to predict based on the cover and title of a book. I then modeled the verification process. Not as many students seemed familiar with this, so I was careful to explain how to verify predictions, using a Think-Aloud to model how it worked. I used the overhead and a transparency of a Double-Entry Journal page to record my prediction and verification. Then I introduced a new book by reading the title, showing selected pictures from the chapters, and reading the information on the back of the book. I asked pairs of students to write a prediction about what they thought the book might be about. Then students read the beginning of Chapter 1. I guided them to verify their predictions by thinking about whether their predictions had changed and if so, what information in the text had caused them to change their minds. After discussing responses, students recorded their verifications on the right side of their Double-Entry Journal pages. Then students wrote their new predictions on the left side of the journal page. Following discussion, we reiterated the class goal we had developed at the conclusion of the previous day's class and talked about how we would use Double-Entry Journals to help us make connections while reading.

Book: Adler, D.A. (1981). *Cam Jansen and the mystery of the dinosaur bones.* New York: Scholastic.
Summary: Cam tries to find out who took the missing bones and why.
Double-Entry Journal:

Prediction	Verification
Book Introduction: I think that the Milkman is going to ride his bicycle past the school and see the children getting on the bus. They are going to the museum in Paris to look at the Brachiosaurs skeleton. Eric will always remember what the Dinosaur looks like because he has a Photographic memory. The guards yell at Eric because he tries to take a lizard home.	Well it looks like most of my prediction is not confirmed. From the cover and the pictures inside the book, I can tell that the students do go a museum and look at dinosaur bones. But in the pictures the Milkman rides in a truck and one of the kids are on the bike. I was wrong about Eric's memory. On the back of the book it says that Cam has a photographic memory. I don't think the guards are going to yell at Eric for taking a lizard because I didn't see the guards or a lizard in the pictures.
Now, I think that Cam and Eric are going to help solve a mystery. Maybe some of the dinosaur bones are missing and they will help find them. They keep looking at postcards in the pictures; maybe someone is trying to leave them clues. I think the milkman will help them because I see his truck in a lot of the pictures.	

Teacher-Guided Small-Group Instruction

In one small group, I reviewed the strategies good readers use and then focused on predicting and Double-Entry Journals. I asked the students to revisit the predictions that they had made during whole-group instruction and we used those as models for making new predictions. Next we read Chapters 1 and 2 of *Cam Jansen and the Mystery of the Dinosaur Bones* together. After reading each section of the chapters, we discussed if students' predictions were verified by the text and explained why. They wrote that information in the verification column of their journal. Based on the information in Chapters 1 and 2 they made new predictions and wrote them in the prediction column. When they were using this process successfully, we talked about how Double-Entry Journals helped us comprehend a story. Finally we discussed how we could use Double-Entry Journals in other settings.

Student-Facilitated Comprehension Centers

Students used a comprehension center of their choice to transfer their knowledge of Double-Entry Journals to another setting. For example, some students visited the mystery center and, following the same procedure of recording their predictions and verifications, created new journal entries. They chose their books from a wide variety of mystery books including The Cam Jansen series, The Encyclopedia Brown series, The Bunnicula series, and The Bailey School House Kids series. Other students visited the writing center and wrote Story Impressions. In their Double-Entry Journals they recorded their predictions about the clues before they wrote their stories and then they recorded their verifications after they read the author's original story.

Student-Facilitated Comprehension Routines

In small groups students read other mystery books appropriate for their independent reading levels. Before reading each section they wrote a prediction, and after reading they verified it. The group members discussed their Double-Entry Journals as information sources in their Literature Circle.

Book: Howe, J. (1982). *Howliday Inn*. New York: Macmillan.

Summary: When the family goes on vacation they leave the pets at a boarding house. The pets watch as one boarder after another disappears. They rename this house Howliday Inn, because they hear plenty of howling throughout the night.

Double-Entry Journal:

Prediction	Verification
Chap. 2: Harold and Chester will be dropped off at the Howliday Inn. It turns out to be a very creepy place. The rooms they stay in are dark and scary. They hear noises at night. Maybe there are ghosts at this place. Maybe they will be lost there forever.	The Howliday Inn does not seem that bad after all. They have cages outside with toys and food dishes, but still the place does not seem perfect. The people that work there may be a bit strange.

Teacher-Facilitated Whole-Group Reflection and Goal Setting

We talked about how predicting and verifying helped us to make connections between the text and ourselves. A number of students commented that this technique also gave them a reason to read the next section of the text. Then I asked students if they could predict if we had achieved our goal of making connections by successfully using Double-Entry Journals. They responded positively. When I asked how we could verify their answers, they suggested we share our Double-Entry Journals. We did this in small groups and then some students shared with the whole class. Then we talked more about how Double-Entry Journals helped us make connections and how that helped us to comprehend a story. Finally we assessed our progress, set a new class goal, and engaged in Tickets Out.

Assessment Options

I observed students' abilities to use Double-Entry Journals to make connections and the depth of their comments during discussion. I also reviewed their Double-Entry Journals.

Visualization: Sketch to Stretch

Teacher-Directed Whole-Group Instruction

I began by reminding students that we are still working on our goal of using visualization to support our comprehension. I chose to use a poem from *Insectlopedia* (Florian, 1999) to demonstrate visualization because we are studying insects in science. Before reading "The Black Widow Spider" to the students, I reviewed Sketch to Stretch, which we had previously used with stories. I read the poem, without reading the title, and explained to the students that while I was reading I was going to create pictures in my head about what the poem was saying. I did a Think-Aloud with the students about what the poem brought to mind for me. I then drew a picture of a spider making sure it included details from the poem, and a picture of me looking scared. I explained that I created this image because I am afraid of spiders and the poem reminded me of that and made me feel scared. I made a point of saying that I didn't need to be a great artist to sketch my ideas, and I demonstrated how to draw some basic shapes that might help students to sketch their ideas. I discussed my visualizing and sketching with the class. Then I guided them through the Sketch to Stretch process about another poem from *Insectlopedia* and monitored their sharing in small groups. Next, they chose poems, created sketches, and shared with another pair. Finally, we had a whole-class discussion about how Sketch to Stretch helps our reading.

Poem: Florian, D. (1999). "The Black Widow Spider." *Insectlopedia.* New York: Scholastic.

Teacher-Guided Small-Group Instruction

In a small group, I began by reviewing the comprehension strategies I had taught and then revisited visualization and Sketch to Stretch. I read a poem and guided the students to sketch what it meant to them. They shared their sketches and interpretations. Next, I provided a number of poems from which students made a selection. I guided the students to read it independently and then sketch what the poem made them think about. Realizing that not all students are talented illustrators, I praised sketching efforts and reminded them to use some of the techniques I had suggested in whole-group instruction. I offered assistance when it was requested. Then the students shared their sketches. We ended by reflecting on the importance of visualization and how Sketch to Stretch helped them to create their own interpretations. The students enjoyed discussing the various interpretations they had for the poem.

Poem: Schertle, A. (2001). "The Barn." *A lucky thing.* Ill. W. Minor. New York: Scholastic.
Sketch to Stretch response: Erin drew a house with clouds and rain drops. When it was her turn to comment on her sketch, she said, "There was a storm, and the house was ruined." John drew a building with two animals crashing into it. When commenting on it, he said, "Two animals crashed down a big building after running in a storm."

Poem: Sierra, J. (1998). "My Father's Feet." *Antarctic antics: A book of penguin poems.* Ill. J. Aruego & A. Dewey. San Diego, CA: Gulliver Books/Harcourt Brace.
Sketch to Stretch response: Charlene drew a picture of a large animal's feet with fur on them. She said this represented warmth.

GUIDED COMPREHENSION: VISUALIZATION—SKETCH TO STRETCH

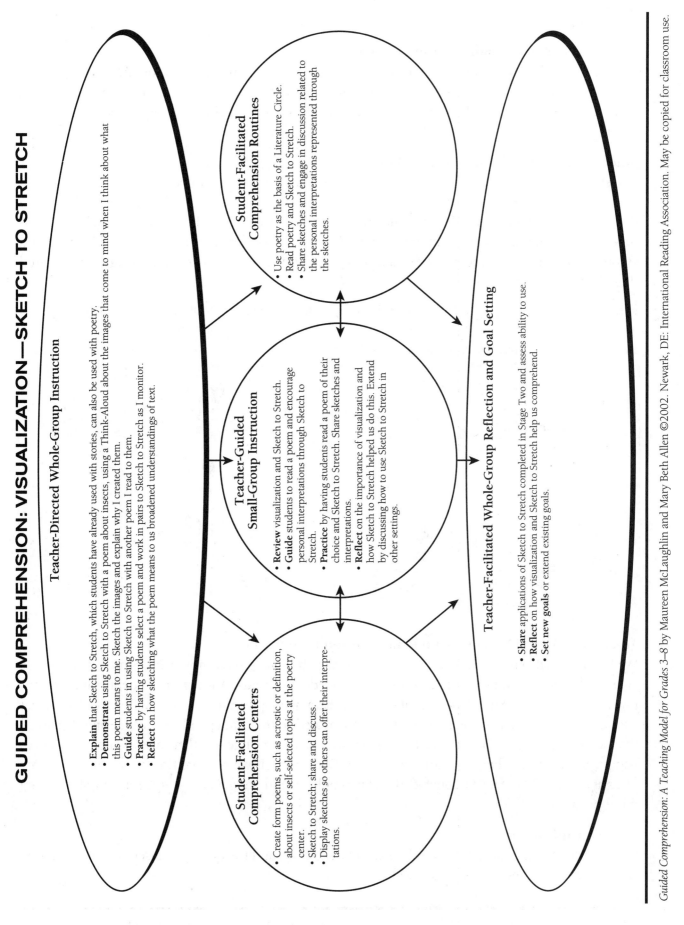

Teacher-Directed Whole-Group Instruction

- **Explain** that Sketch to Stretch, which students have already used with stories, can also be used with poetry.
- **Demonstrate** using Sketch to Stretch with a poem about insects, using a Think-Aloud about the images that come to mind when I think about what this poem means to me. Sketch the images and explain why I created them.
- **Guide** students in using Sketch to Stretch with another poem I read to them.
- **Practice** by having students select a poem and work in pairs to Sketch to Stretch as I monitor.
- **Reflect** on how sketching what the poem means to us broadened understandings of text.

Student-Facilitated Comprehension Routines

- Use poetry as the basis of a Literature Circle.
- Read poetry and Sketch to Stretch.
- Share sketches and engage in discussion related to the personal interpretations represented through the sketches.

Teacher-Guided Small-Group Instruction

- **Review** visualization and Sketch to Stretch.
- **Guide** students to read a poem and encourage personal interpretations through Sketch to Stretch.
- **Practice** by having students read a poem of their choice and Sketch to Stretch. Share sketches and interpretations.
- **Reflect** on the importance of visualization and how Sketch to Stretch helped us do this. Extend by discussing how to use Sketch to Stretch in other settings.

Student-Facilitated Comprehension Centers

- Create form poems, such as acrostic or definition, about insects or self-selected topics at the poetry center.
- Sketch to Stretch; share and discuss.
- Display sketches so others can offer their interpretations.

Teacher-Facilitated Whole-Group Reflection and Goal Setting

- **Share** applications of Sketch to Stretch completed in Stage Two and assess ability to use.
- **Reflect** on how visualization and Sketch to Stretch help us comprehend.
- **Set new goals** or extend existing goals.

Guided Comprehension: A Teaching Model for Grades 3–8 by Maureen McLaughlin and Mary Beth Allen ©2002. Newark, DE: International Reading Association. May be copied for classroom use.

Student-Facilitated Comprehension Centers

Students visited the poetry center and wrote form poems—acrostic or definition. After writing their poems, students engaged in Sketch to Stretch, sharing their drawings with other students working on independent practice. These poems and the sketches will be included in one of our class poetry books.

Student-Facilitated Comprehension Routines

The students worked in small groups for this activity, and each chose a poem as the basis for Sketch to Stretch. They read their poems silently, sketched their interpretations, and then shared them with their peers in a Literature Circle. After the group members had commented on each sketch, the illustrator commented on his or her interpretation. Examples of students' work are featured below. For a second application, the students wrote a group poem and created individual drawings. They shared these by using Sketch to Stretch.

Poem: Volavkova, H. (Ed.). (1993). "The Butterfly." *I never saw another butterfly*. New York: Shocken Books.

Sketch to Stretch responses from Katherine and Ryan:

Teacher-Facilitated Whole-Group Reflection and Goal Setting

We began by reflecting on how visualization and sketching help us comprehend. Students seemed to agree that it helps because it lets us show what's inside our heads. A lot of the students said they enjoyed using Sketch to Stretch because it provided them with opportunities to draw. Then students met with a partner and shared the sketches they had created in their independent practice and explained the messages they thought the sketches conveyed. Finally, we came together to assess our progress in using visualization to help our comprehension. Everyone felt we were getting better and had more ideas about how to use it. We concluded that we could extend our goal to include learning about open mind portraits.

Assessment Options

Observation, the messages conveyed by students' sketches, and the quality of discussion were among the informal assessment measures I used.

Knowing How Words Work: Concept of Definition Map

The books described in this Guided Comprehension plan were nonfiction texts with photograph illustrations by Seymour Simon.

Teacher-Directed Whole-Group Instruction

I reminded students about the comprehension strategies we've been using and focused on Knowing How Words Work. Then I introduced the Concept of Definition Map and shared copies of the visual representation with the class. Before reading the book for this lesson, I used an overhead and a Think-Aloud to explain and model a Concept Map using the word *dogs*. Then I engaged students in brainstorming what we knew about wolves and discussed responses. We used that information to complete a Concept Map about wolves. I intentionally left one example blank and explained to the students that we would look for more examples when reading the text. I explained that we would use the book to change or add information to the Concept of Definition Map. I read aloud the book *Wolves*, and the students and I added or changed information after the reading. The students were eager to complete the map by helping to find information in the text. We added the species "tundra wolves" as the example I had intentionally left blank. The students recognized that "gray" and "timber" described the same wolf. So we deleted "gray" and added "Mexican wolf." Then we reflected on how Concept of Definition Maps help us understand what we read.

Book: Simon, S. (1993). *Wolves*. New York: HarperCollins.

Teacher-Guided Small-Group Instruction

In small groups I revisited the comprehension strategies and the teaching idea of the day. After reviewing the Concept Map, I guided students in completing one on snakes. I reminded them to consider the information on the map as they were reading. I previewed the text and worked with students to generate questions we thought the text might answer. Then I guided the students to read the text independently. After reading, we discussed students' personal responses and updated our Concept Map based on what we had learned from reading. Then in pairs, students completed Concept Maps on animals of their choice and discussed how brochures they read added to their knowledge of these animals. Finally, we reflected on how Concept Maps helped us to read and when we could use them again.

Book: Simon, S. (1992). *Snakes*. New York: Scholastic.

Student-Facilitated Comprehension Centers

Some students visited the poetry center. They used their completed Concept of Definition Maps to create and illustrate form poems including acrostics, cinquains, definition poems, and diamantes. Some students visited the writing center and used their completed Concept of Definition Maps to write stories. Other students visited the research center and used their Concept of Definition Maps to develop research questions at multiple levels. A few used the Questions Into Paragraph (QuIP) graphic organizer to facilitate their research (see Appendix A, page 161).

Student-Facilitated Comprehension Routines

The students worked in small groups to complete Concept of Definition Maps related to books they were reading for Literature Circles or Questioning the Author. They also collaborated about why and

GUIDED COMPREHENSION: KNOWING HOW WORDS WORK—CONCEPT OF DEFINITION MAP

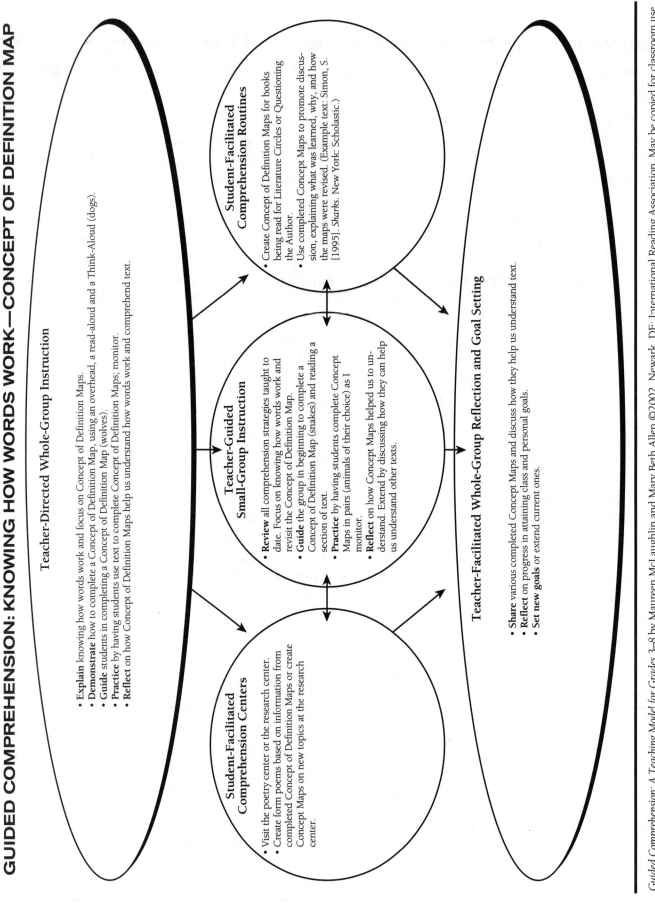

Teacher-Directed Whole-Group Instruction

- **Explain** knowing how words work and focus on Concept of Definition Maps.
- **Demonstrate** how to complete a Concept of Definition Map, using an overhead, a read-aloud and a Think-Aloud (dogs).
- **Guide** students in completing a Concept of Definition Map (wolves).
- **Practice** by having students use text to complete Concept of Definition Maps; monitor.
- **Reflect** on how Concept of Definition Maps help us understand how words work and comprehend text.

Student-Facilitated Comprehension Centers

- Visit the poetry center or the research center.
- Create form poems based on information from completed Concept of Definition Maps or create Concept Maps on new topics at the research center.

Teacher-Guided Small-Group Instruction

- **Review** all comprehension strategies taught to date. Focus on knowing how words work and revisit the Concept of Definition Map.
- **Guide** the group in beginning to complete a Concept of Definition Map (snakes) and reading a section of text.
- **Practice** by having students complete Concept Maps in pairs (animals of their choice) as I monitor.
- **Reflect** on how Concept Maps helped us to understand. Extend by discussing how they can help us understand other texts.

Student-Facilitated Comprehension Routines

- Create Concept of Definition Maps for books being read for Literature Circles or Questioning the Author.
- Use completed Concept Maps to promote discussion, explaining what was learned, why, and how the maps were revised. (Example text: Simon, S. [1995]. *Sharks*. New York: Scholastic.)

Teacher-Facilitated Whole-Group Reflection and Goal Setting

- **Share** various completed Concept Maps and discuss how they help us understand text.
- **Reflect** on progress in attaining class and personal goals.
- **Set new goals** or extend current ones.

how they revised their webs and summarized this information in their Guided Comprehension Journals.

Book: Simon, S. (1995). *Sharks*. New York: Scholastic.
Concept of Definition Map:

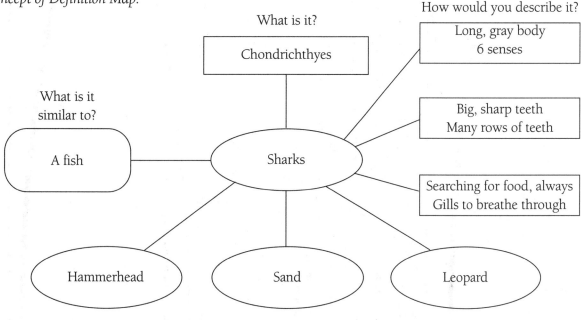

What is it?

How would you describe it?

Chondrichthyes

Long, gray body
6 senses

What is it
similar to?

Big, sharp teeth
Many rows of teeth

A fish

Sharks

Searching for food, always
Gills to breathe through

Hammerhead

Sand

Leopard

What are some examples?

Teacher-Facilitated Whole-Group Reflection and Goal Setting

The students shared the concept maps they had completed independently and then in small groups they described how the maps contributed to their understanding of how words work. Both of these information sources informed our class discussion about how well we had achieved our class goal and what our new goal would be.

Assessment Options

I used a lot of observation to assess students' understanding. I also reviewed and commented on many of the Concept Maps the students completed. Discussion was another factor in assessment. The quality of the response and the reasoning used to refine the Concept Map were among the information sources.

Monitoring: INSERT

Teacher-Directed Whole-Group Instruction

I began by explaining what monitoring is and how it helps us to comprehend. Then I introduced and explained the INSERT method using an article related to our content area of study, the branches of government. I engaged in direct instruction of this technique to assure that students would know not only what INSERT was and how it worked, but would also see me model it. I made a brainstormed list of what I already knew and used a chart to share the notation system with the class. I used an overhead so the students could follow along as I read and see how I inserted the notations. I demonstrated how to mark

GUIDED COMPREHENSION: MONITORING—INSERT

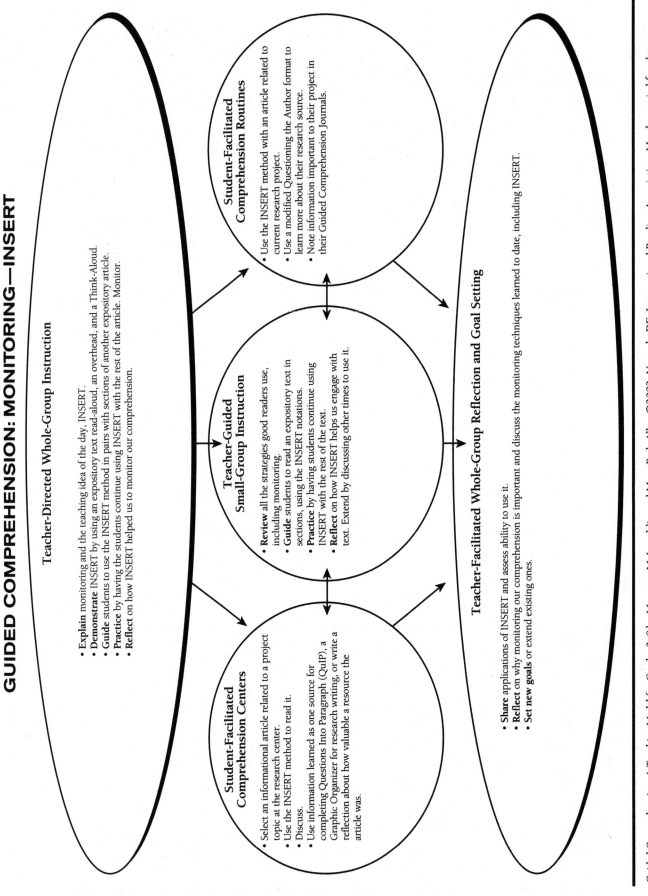

Teacher-Directed Whole-Group Instruction

- **Explain** monitoring and the teaching idea of the day, INSERT.
- **Demonstrate** INSERT by using an expository text read-aloud, an overhead, and a Think-Aloud.
- **Guide** students to use the INSERT method in pairs with sections of another expository article.
- **Practice** by having the students continue using INSERT with the rest of the article. Monitor.
- **Reflect** on how INSERT helped us to monitor our comprehension.

Student-Facilitated Comprehension Centers

- Select an informational article related to a project topic at the research center.
- Use the INSERT method to read it.
- Discuss.
- Use information learned as one source for completing Questions Into Paragraph (QuIP), a Graphic Organizer for research writing, or write a reflection about how valuable a resource the article was.

Teacher-Guided Small-Group Instruction

- **Review** all the strategies good readers use, including monitoring.
- **Guide** students to read an expository text in sections, using the INSERT notations.
- **Practice** by having students continue using INSERT with the rest of the text.
- **Reflect** on how INSERT helps us engage with text. Extend by discussing other times to use it.

Student-Facilitated Comprehension Routines

- Use the INSERT method with an article related to current research project.
- Use a modified Questioning the Author format to learn more about their research source.
- Note information important to their project in their Guided Comprehension Journals.

Teacher-Facilitated Whole-Group Reflection and Goal Setting

- **Share** applications of INSERT and assess ability to use it.
- **Reflect** on why monitoring our comprehension is important and discuss the monitoring techniques learned to date, including INSERT.
- **Set new goals** or extend existing ones.

the text for information that confirmed (✓), supplemented (+), refuted (–), or was confusing (?) while reading. I stopped periodically and summarized my understanding of the article. Then I discussed the process with my students. Next, I guided them to use the INSERT method in pairs with an article about the presidency. I provided individual copies of descriptions of INSERT, including the notations. After previewing the text, we brainstormed our lists and read the first section of the text, inserting the notations as we read. We discussed where we placed the notations and why. Then the students read the rest of the text in sections, inserting the notations as they read. I monitored their practice and we stopped periodically to discuss our understandings and use of notations. When we had finished reading, we used the notations to facilitate discussion, answer questions, and generate new ones. Finally, we reflected about what we learned from using INSERT.

Teacher-Guided Small-Group Instruction

I reminded students of the comprehension strategies good readers use and then reviewed comprehension monitoring and INSERT. Then I guided students' reading of sections of an article about the executive branch of the government. We brainstormed lists about what we already knew and students used INSERT charts as references to insert the notation system as they read the first section of text. Then students read the text in sections, stopping to share understandings and our use of the notation system. We concluded by discussing ways the students can use INSERT in Guided Comprehension centers and routines.

Student-Facilitated Comprehension Centers

At the research center, students applied INSERT to an article related to their research project. They reflected in their journals about their understanding of the article, how INSERT helped them to learn, and how informative the resource was. For example, Aurora, whose research project was about John Adams, used an article that contained an excerpt from *John Adams* by David McCullough. The following is a portion of her evaluation of the article as a research resource:

> On a scale of 1 to 10 with 10 being the highest rating, I would give this article a 9. There was a lot of information in the article that I didn't know before. The writer of the article was very clear about his purpose and where the information came from. A lot of the article came from a book about John Adams's life and that author used a lot of family letters as sources for the book. I learned a lot and used a lot of pluses in my INSERT because so much of the article had things that were new to me. I didn't use many question marks because not much confused me.

Student-Facilitated Comprehension Routines

Students used the INSERT method with articles they were reading for their research projects. They shared project updates and their use of INSERT in discussion groups. Then the students used a modified Questioning the Author format to gain insights about the source behind the research article. They used their Guided Comprehension Journals to record information that supported their projects.

Teacher-Facilitated Whole-Group Reflection and Goal Setting

We talked about how monitoring and INSERT help us comprehend. In small groups, students shared INSERTs they had completed in various settings to support their learning. It was interesting to hear them talking about the wide variety of applications. Then we returned to whole-class discussion and analyzed our progress in effectively monitoring our comprehension. We decided to stay with this goal and extend our understanding by focusing on a new technique called "Say Something."

Assessment Options

I used informal assessments including observation, student writing, and discussion. I also learned a lot about students' knowledge and ability to apply it when we assessed our progress in attaining our class goal.

Summarizing: Lyric Summaries

Teacher-Directed Whole-Group Instruction

I began by reminding students of our class goal. Instead of having my students retell another story using the all too familiar story map, I decided it would be more challenging and interesting to create Lyric Summaries. I reviewed the story elements with my students. Then I asked the students to listen for these components as I read *The True Story of the Three Little Pigs*. Afterward we discussed the characters, setting, problem, main events, and solution. Using a PowerPoint presentation, I had the students listen to the music of "Jingle Bells," and they sang along. Next I used a Think-Aloud to demonstrate how to rewrite the lyrics of "Jingle Bells" to retell the story of *The True Story of the Three Little Pigs*. (I had it prepared ahead of time but walked my students through the process of creating it.) After I created my version of the song, we had fun singing it. We discussed if I had written an effective summary. I then guided my students in small groups to begin writing a Lyric Summary of this story using "Twinkle, Twinkle, Little Star." When they appeared to be comfortable with this technique, students completed their Lyric Summaries, and I monitored their practice. Then we made sure our Lyric Summaries included all the essential components, and the students sang their summaries. Finally, we reviewed what makes a good summary and how to use Lyric Summaries to help us summarize. The students were very excited about using music in this way.

Song: "Jingle Bells"
Book: Sciezka, J. (1996). *The true story of the three little pigs.* New York: Penguin Putnam.
Summary: The Wolf tells his version of what happened between him and the three little pigs.
Lyric Summary:

> Alexander T. Wolf,
> Had no sugar for his cake.
>
> To his neighbors he did go,
> Sneezing all the way.
>
> Huff! Snuff! Huff!
>
> Straws and sticks fell down,
> Two little piggies died.
>
> "I was framed!" said the wolf.
> "In jail I'll sleep tonight."
>
> Huff and Puff, Huff and Puff,
> Hear what I have to say.
>
> Oh how great it is to eat
> Two ham dinners in one day!

GUIDED COMPREHENSION: SUMMARIZING—LYRIC SUMMARIES

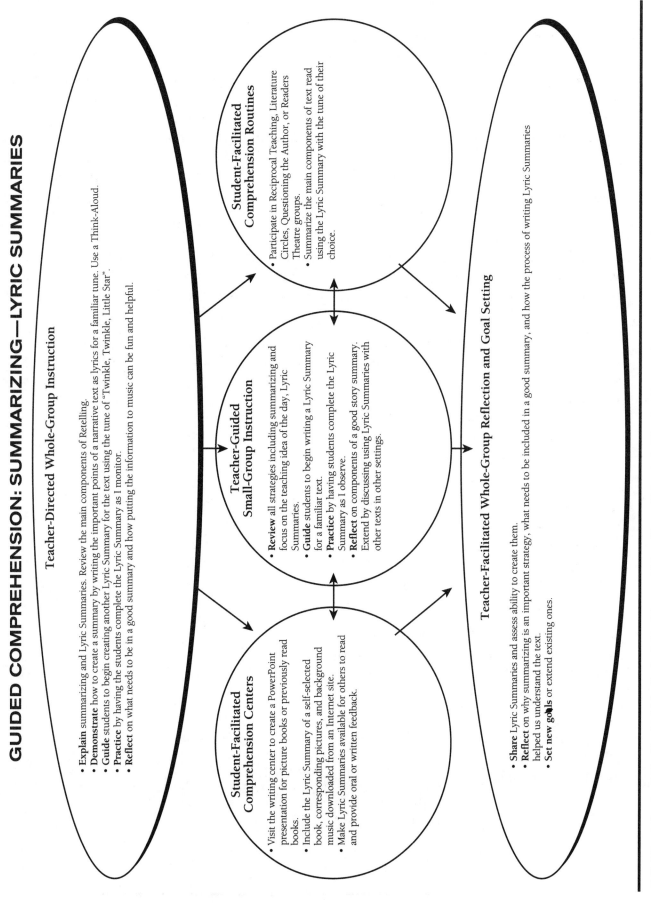

Teacher-Directed Whole-Group Instruction

- **Explain** summarizing and Lyric Summaries. Review the main components of Retelling.
- **Demonstrate** how to create a summary by writing the important points of a narrative text as lyrics for a familiar tune. Use a Think-Aloud.
- **Guide** students to begin creating another Lyric Summary for the text using the tune of "Twinkle, Twinkle, Little Star".
- **Practice** by having the students complete the Lyric Summary as I monitor.
- **Reflect** on what needs to be in a good summary and how putting the information to music can be fun and helpful.

Student-Facilitated Comprehension Routines

- Participate in Reciprocal Teaching, Literature Circles, Questioning the Author, or Readers Theatre groups.
- Summarize the main components of text read using the Lyric Summary with the tune of their choice.

Teacher-Guided Small-Group Instruction

- **Review** all strategies including summarizing and focus on the teaching idea of the day, Lyric Summaries.
- **Guide** students to begin writing a Lyric Summary for a familiar text.
- **Practice** by having students complete the Lyric Summary as I observe.
- **Reflect** on components of a good story summary. Extend by discussing using Lyric Summaries with other texts in other settings.

Student-Facilitated Comprehension Centers

- Visit the writing center to create a PowerPoint presentation for picture books or previously read books.
- Include the Lyric Summary of a self-selected book, corresponding pictures, and background music downloaded from an Internet site.
- Make Lyric Summaries available for others to read and provide oral or written feedback.

Teacher-Facilitated Whole-Group Reflection and Goal Setting

- **Share** Lyric Summaries and assess ability to create them.
- **Reflect** on why summarizing is an important strategy, what needs to be included in a good summary, and how the process of writing Lyric Summaries helped us understand the text.
- **Set new goals** or extend existing ones.

Teacher-Guided Small-Group Instruction

My students could not wait to write their own Lyric Summaries. I never saw so much excitement about summarizing a story before. We reviewed the strategies readers use to comprehend and then we focused on the concept of using Lyric Summaries to retell a story. Next, I gave the students the opportunity to compose a song that would summarize *The Hoboken Chicken Emergency* with my support. We had just finished reading this book together. First, we listed all the major components of the story. Then, I guided students in creating the first verse. We talked about how to make our ideas fit with the tune. Next, students finished writing the Lyric Summary. I assisted when necessary, although the help they needed was mostly rephrasing to fit the tune. After creating the Lyric Summary, we checked to make sure we had included all the components of a story summary. Then we reflected on how this helped us to create a summary and set goals for writing summaries this way in other settings.

During whole-group reflection and goal setting, the students sang the song for the whole class. We reviewed the components of an effective story summary and the class listened to determine if the song was a good summary for this book. They agreed it was. We had a lot of fun with this.

Song: "Up on the Housetop"
Book: Pinkwater, D.M. (1984). *The Hoboken chicken emergency.* New York: Simon & Schuster.
Summary: A 266-pound chicken invades the town of Hoboken until everyone decides to treat him
      nicely.
Lyric Summary:

Up in the treetop Cluck, Cluck, Cluck!
Here comes a man with a big fire truck!
Down the ladder Henrietta comes,
With Arthur at her side saying Hup, Hup, Hup.

Cluck, Cluck, Cluck!
Who wouldn't know?
Cluck, Cluck, Cluck
Who wouldn't know?
That Henrietta runs around at night,
Don't be screaming you will give her a fright.

The mayor got a chicken snatcher
Who made the wrong trap and didn't catch her,
Another chicken snatcher came and said
"Don't you treat her like she's dead!"

Cluck, Cluck, Cluck!
Henrietta was good.
Cluck, Cluck, Cluck
Like she should.

Now Henrietta lives with Arthur,
She won't live with any other!!!

Student-Facilitated Comprehension Centers

Students visited the writing center to create PowerPoint presentations that included Lyric Summaries for picture books that they read at the center or for a book they had read previously. In addition to the lyrics, they included corresponding pictures and the background music downloaded from an Internet site. These summaries were available for other classmates to read and they gave verbal and written responses to the authors. Students were reminded to keep all the story elements in mind. Needless to say, these were a big hit! The following is an example of one of those Lyric Summaries.

Song: "Grandma Got Ran Over by a Reindeer"
Book: Dorris, M. (1994). *Guests*. New York: Hyperion.
Summary: The first Thanksgiving is restated through the eyes of a young Algonquin boy and girl.
Lyric Summary:

> Moss was upset about the strangers,
> He wanted to run very far away.
>
> On his way he met a girl named Trouble,
> She dared him to go into the woods.
>
> He accepted it and went inside
> Now he talks to a porcupine.
>
> The porcupine showed him something to
> Eat and a good place to sleep!

Student-Facilitated Comprehension Routines

Students used the stories from their Literature Circle, Reciprocal Teaching, Questioning the Author, and Readers Theatre groups to write Lyric Summaries of the books they had just finished discussing. Melodies that students used ranged from "Old MacDonald Had a Farm" to the disco hit "I Will Survive" and they asked to perform them for the whole class. We did this in Stage Three.

Teacher-Facilitated Whole-Group Reflection and Goal Setting

We began by reviewing the components of a good story summary. Then groups of students shared their Lyric Summaries. The students critiqued one another based on the group's ability to incorporate each of the story elements into their lyrics. We reflected on why summarizing is an important strategy, what needs to be included in a good story summary, and how the process of writing Lyric Summaries helped us make sense of a story. Students used a self-reflection and goal-setting form (see Appendix E, pages 223–224) to record personal strengths and weaknesses in their ability to write story summaries and set goals for future learning. I noted the students' great enthusiasm for writing summaries this way and planned to use Lyric Summaries again.

Assessment Options

I used observation and students' Lyric Summaries as the primary assessments. I also noted the high level of student engagement this activity provided.

GUIDED COMPREHENSION PLANNING FORM

Strategy: _____

Teaching Idea: _____

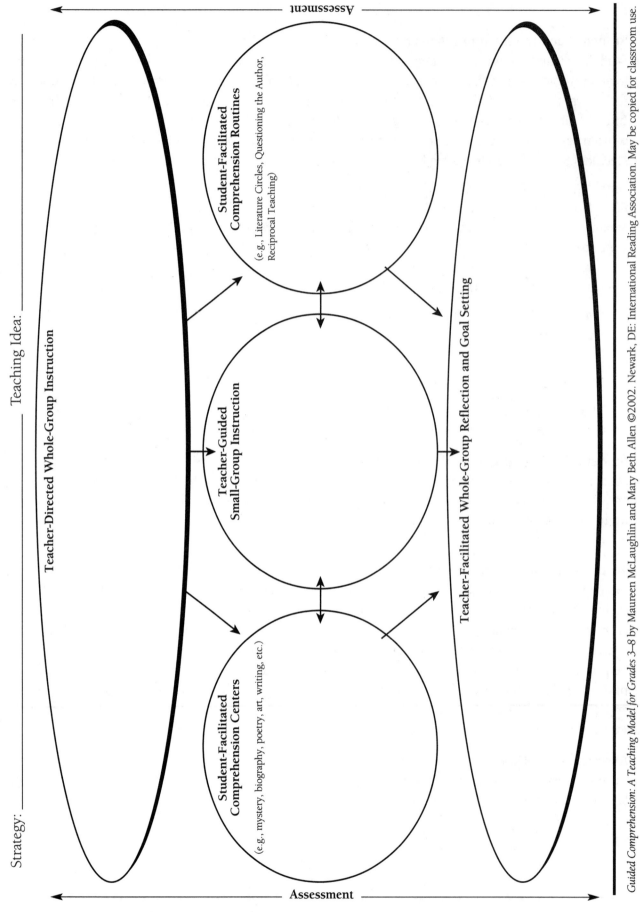

Assessment

Teacher-Directed Whole-Group Instruction

Student-Facilitated
Comprehension Routines

(e.g., Literature Circles, Questioning the Author,
Reciprocal Teaching)

Teacher-Guided
Small-Group Instruction

Student-Facilitated
Comprehension Centers

(e.g., mystery, biography, poetry, art, writing, etc.)

Teacher-Facilitated Whole-Group Reflection and Goal Setting

Assessment

GUIDED COMPREHENSION PLANNING OUTLINE

Whole Group

Comprehension Strategy: _____

Class Goal: _____

Teaching Idea: _____

Text: _____

Direct Instruction:

• Explain: _____

_____

• Demonstrate: _____

_____

• Guide: _____

_____

• Practice: _____

• Reflect: _____

Guided Comprehension Group 1

Comprehension Strategy: _____

Teaching Idea: _____

Text: _____

Process:

• Review: _____

_____

• Guide: _____

_____

• Practice: _____

_____

• Reflect and Extend: _____

_____

_____

Comprehension Centers:

Comprehension Routines:

Reflection and Goal Setting:

Assessment Options:

SAMPLE 60- AND 90-MINUTE GUIDED COMPREHENSION SCHEDULES

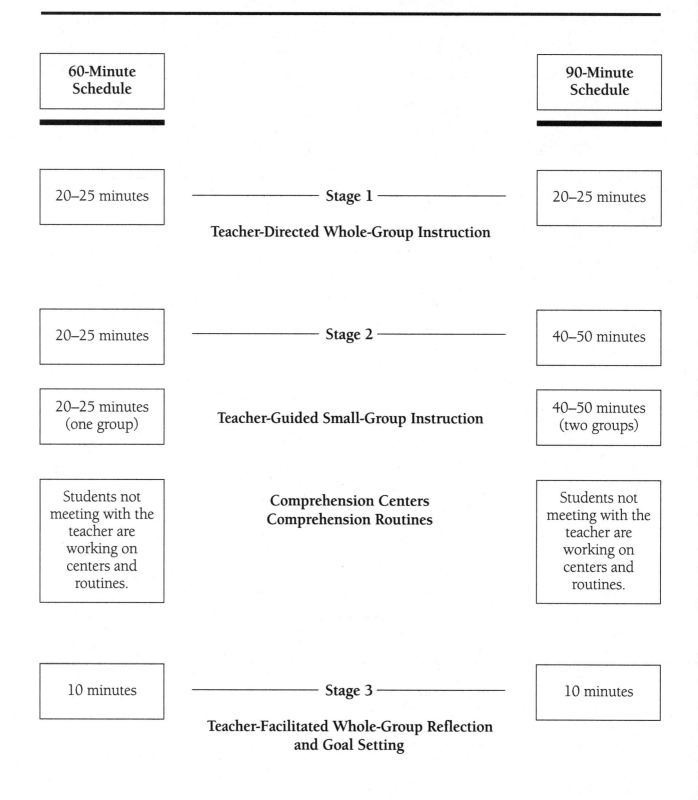

| 60-Minute Schedule | | 90-Minute Schedule |

| 20–25 minutes | —————— Stage 1 —————— | 20–25 minutes |

Teacher-Directed Whole-Group Instruction

| 20–25 minutes | —————— Stage 2 —————— | 40–50 minutes |

| 20–25 minutes (one group) | Teacher-Guided Small-Group Instruction | 40–50 minutes (two groups) |

| Students not meeting with the teacher are working on centers and routines. | **Comprehension Centers** **Comprehension Routines** | Students not meeting with the teacher are working on centers and routines. |

| 10 minutes | —————— Stage 3 —————— | 10 minutes |

Teacher-Facilitated Whole-Group Reflection and Goal Setting

REFERENCES

Almasi, J.F. (1996). A new view of discussion. In L.B. Gambrell & J.F. Almasi (Eds.), *Lively discussions! Fostering engaged reading* (pp. 2–24). Newark, DE: International Reading Association.

Alvermann, D. (1991). The discussion web: A graphic aid for learning across the curriculum. *The Reading Teacher, 45,* 92–99.

Anderson, R.C. (1994). Role of reader's schema in comprehension, learning, and memory. In R.B. Ruddell, M.R. Ruddell, & H. Singer (Eds.), *Theoretical models and processes of reading* (4th ed., pp. 469–482). Newark, DE: International Reading Association.

Anderson, R.C., & Pearson, P.D. (1984). A schema-theoretic view of basic processes in reading comprehension. In P.D. Pearson, R. Barr, M.L. Kamil, & P. Mosenthal (Eds.), *Handbook of reading research* (Vol. 1, pp. 225–253). New York: Longman.

Askew, B.J., & Fountas, I. (1998). Building an early reading process: Active from the start! *The Reading Teacher, 52,* 126–134.

Au, K.H., Carroll, J.H., & Scheu, J.A. (1997). *Balanced literacy instruction: A teacher's resource book.* Norwood, MA: Christopher-Gordon.

Au, K.H., & Raphael, T.E. (1998). Curriculum and teaching in literature-based programs. In T.E. Raphael & K.H. Au (Eds.), *Literature-based instruction: Reshaping the curriculum* (pp. 123–148). Norwood, MA: Christopher-Gordon.

Baker, L., Afflerbach, P., & Reinking, D. (1996). Developing engaged readers in school and home communities: An overview. In L. Baker, P. Afflerbach, & D. Reinking (Eds.), *Developing engaged readers in school and home communities* (pp. xiii–xxvii). Hillsdale, NJ: Erlbaum.

Baker, L., & Wigfield, A. (1999). Dimensions of children's motivation for reading and their relations to reading activity and reading achievement. *Reading Research Quarterly, 34,* 452–481.

Barrentine, S.J. (1999). *Reading assessment: Principles and practices for elementary teachers.* Newark, DE: International Reading Association.

Baumann, J.F., & Kameenui, E.J. (1991). Research on vocabulary instruction: Ode to Voltaire. In J. Flood, J.M. Jensen, D. Lapp, & J.R. Squire (Eds.), *Handbook on teaching the English language arts* (pp. 604–632). New York: Macmillan.

Bean, T.W. (1997). ReWrite: A music strategy for exploring content area concepts. *Reading Online* [Online]. Available: http://www.readingonline.org/literacy/bats/index.html.

Bean, T.W. (2000). Music in the content areas. In M. McLaughlin & M.E. Vogt (Eds.), *Creativity, innovation, and content area teaching* (pp. 91–103). Norwood, MA: Christopher-Gordon.

Beck, I.L., & McKeown, M.G. (1991). Conditions of vocabulary acquisition. In R. Barr, M.L. Kamil, P. Mosenthal, & P.D. Pearson (Eds.), *Handbook of reading research* (Vol. 2, pp. 789–814). White Plains, NY: Longman.

Beck, I.L., McKeown, M.G., Hamilton, R.L., & Kucan, L. (1997). *Questioning the author: An approach for enhancing student engagement with text.* Newark, DE: International Reading Association.

Blachowicz, C.L. (1986). Making connections: Alternatives to the vocabulary notebook. *Journal of Reading, 29,* 643–649.

Blachowitcz, C.L., & Fisher, P. (2000). Vocabulary instruction. In M.L. Kamil, P.D. Pearson, & R. Barr (Eds.), *Handbook of reading research* (Vol. 3, pp. 503–523). Mahwah, NJ: Erlbaum.

Blachowicz, C.L., & Lee, J.J. (1991). Vocabulary development in the whole literacy classroom. *The Reading Teacher, 45,* 188–195.

Bottomley, D.M., Henk, W.A., & Melnick, S.A. (1997/1998). Assessing children's views about themselves as writers using the Writer Self-Perception Scale. *The Reading Teacher, 51,* 286–296.

Brabham, E.G., & Villaume, S.K. (2000). Continuing conversations about literature circles. *The Reading Teacher, 54,* 278–281.

Brooks, J.G., & Brooks, M.G. (1993). *In search of understanding: The case for constructivist classrooms.* Alexandria, VA: Association for Supervision and Curriculum Development.

Brown, K.J. (1999/2000). What kind of text—for whom and when? Textual scaffolding for beginning readers. *The Reading Teacher, 53,* 292–307.

Brown, L.A. (1993). Story collages: Help for reluctant writers. *Learning, 22*(4), 22–25.

Buehl, D. (2001). *Classroom strategies for interactive learning* (2nd ed.). Newark, DE: International Reading Association.

Busching, B.A., & Slesinger, B.A. (1995). Authentic questions: What do they look like? Where do they lead? *Language Arts, 72,* 341–351.

Chiardello, A.V. (1998). Did you ask a good question today? Alternative cognitive and metacognitive strategies. *Journal of Adolescent & Adult Literacy, 42,* 210–219.

Clay, M.M. (1985). *The early detection of reading difficulties: A diagnostic survey with recovery procedures* (3rd ed.). Portsmouth, NH: Heinemann.

Clay, M.M. (1991). Introducing a new storybook to young readers. *The Reading Teacher, 45,* 264–273.

Clemmons, J., Laase, L., Cooper, D., Areglado, N., & Dill, M. (1993). *Portfolios in the classroom.* Jefferson City, MO: Scholastic.

Cooper, J.D., & Kiger, N.D. (2001). *Literacy assessment: Helping teachers plan instruction.* Boston: Houghton Mifflin.

Courtney, A.M., & Abodeeb, T.L. (2001). *Journey of discovery: Building a classroom community through diagnostic-reflective portfolios.* Newark, DE: International Reading Association.

Covey, S.R. (1989). *The 7 habits of highly effective people.* New York: Simon & Schuster.

Cunningham, P. (1995). *Phonics they use.* New York: HarperCollins.

Cunningham, P., & Allington, R. (1999). *Classrooms that work: They can all read and write* (2nd ed.). New York: Addison-Wesley.

Dahl, K.L., & Farnan, N. (1998). *Children's writing: Perspectives from research.* Newark, DE: International Reading Association.

Daniels, H. (1994). *Literature circles: Voice and choice in the student-centered classroom.* York, ME: Stenhouse.

Darling-Hammond, L.D., Ancess, J., & Falk, B. (1995). *Authentic assessment in action: Studies of schools and students at work.* New York: Teachers College Press.

Davey, B. (1983). Think-aloud—modeling the cognitive processes of reading comprehension. *Journal of Reading, 27,* 44–47.

Dewey, J. (1933). *How we think: A restatement of reflective thinking to the educative process.* Lexington, MA: D.C. Heath.

Dixon-Krauss, L. (1996). *Vygotsky in the classroom: Mediated literacy instruction and assessment.* White Plains, NY: Longman.

Duffy, G.G., Roehler, L.R., Sivan, E., Rackliffe, G., Book, C., Meloth, M., Vavrus, L.G., Wesselman, R., Putnam, J., & Bassiri, D. (1987). Effects of explaining the reasoning associated with using reading strategies. *Reading Research Quarterly, 22,* 347–368.

Durkin, D. (1978/1979). What classroom observations reveal about reading comprehension instruction. *Reading Research Quarterly, 14,* 481–533.

Fawson, P.C., & Reutzel, D.R. (2000). But I only have a basal: Implementing guided reading in the early grades. *The Reading Teacher, 54,* 84–97.

Fielding, L.G., & Pearson, P.D. (1994). Reading comprehension: What works. *Educational Leadership, 51*(5), 62–68.

Forman, E.A., & Cazden, C.B. (1994). Exploring Vygotskian perspectives in education: The cognitive value of peer interaction. In R.B. Ruddell, M.R. Ruddell, & H. Singer (Eds.), *Theoretical models and processes of reading* (4th ed., pp. 391–413). Newark, DE: International Reading Association.

Fountas, I.C., & Pinnell, G.S. (1996). *Guided reading: Good first teaching for all children.* Portsmouth, NH: Heinemann.

Fountas, I.C., & Pinnell, G.S. (1999). *Matching books to readers: Using leveled books in guided reading, K–3.* Portsmouth, NH: Heinemann.

Gambrell, L.B. (1996a). Creating classroom cultures that foster reading motivation. *The Reading Teacher, 50,* 14–25.

Gambrell, L.B. (1996b). What research reveals about discussion. In L.B. Gambrell & J.F. Almasi (Eds.), *Lively discussions! Fostering engaged reading* (pp. 25–38). Newark, DE: International Reading Association.

Gambrell, L.B. (2001). *It's not either/or but more: Balancing narrative and informational text to improve reading comprehension.* Paper presented at the 46th Annual Convention of the International Reading Association, New Orleans, Louisianna.

Gambrell, L.B., & Almasi, J.F. (Eds.). (1996). *Lively discussions! Fostering engaged reading.* Newark, DE: International Reading Association.

Gambrell, L.B., Palmer, B.M., Codling, R.M., & Mazzoni, S.A. (1996). Assessing motivation to read. *The Reading Teacher, 49,* 518–533.

Gaskins, I.W., Ehri, L.C., Cress, C., O'Hara, C., & Donnelly, K. (1996). Procedures for word learning: Making discoveries about words. *The Reading Teacher, 50,* 2–18.

Gilles, C. (1998). Collaborative literacy strategies: "We don't need a circle to have a group." In K.G. Short & K.M. Pierce (Eds.), *Talking about books: Literature discussion groups in K–8 classrooms* (pp. 55–68). Portsmouth, NH: Heinemann.

Goldman, S.R., & Rakestraw, J.A. (2000). Structural aspects of constructing meaning from text. In M.L. Kamil, P.D. Pearson, & R. Barr (Eds.), *Handbook of reading research* (Vol. 3, pp. 311–335). Mahwah, NJ: Erlbaum.

Goodman, Y.M. (1997). Reading diagnosis—Qualitative or quantitiative? *The Reading Teacher, 50,* 534–538.

Goodman, Y.M., Watson, D.J., & Burke, C. (1987). *Reading miscue inventory.* Katonah, NY: Richard C. Owen.

Griffin, P.E., Smith, P.G., & Burrill, L.E. (1995). *The American literacy profile scales: A framework for authentic assessment.* Portsmouth, NH: Heinemann.

Gunning, T.G. (1998). *Best books for beginning readers.* Boston: Allyn & Bacon,

Guthrie, J.T., & Alvermann, D. (Eds.). (1999). *Engaged reading: Processes, practices, and policy implications.* New York: Teachers College Press.

Guthrie, J.T., & Wigfield, A. (1997). *Reading engagement: Motivating readers through integrated curriculum.* Newark, DE: International Reading Association.

Guthrie, J.T., & Wigfield, A. (2000). Engagement and motivation in reading. In M.L. Kamil, P.D. Pearson, & R. Barr (Eds.), *Handbook of reading research* (Vol. 3, pp. 403–422). Mahwah, NJ: Erlbaum.

Haggard, M.R. (1986). The vocabulary self-collection strategy: Using student interest and world knowledge to enhance vocabulary growth. *Journal of Reading, 29,* 634–642.

Hansen, J. (1998). *When learners evaluate.* Portsmouth, NH: Heinemann.

Harris, T.L., & Hodges, R.E. (Eds.). (1995). *The literacy dictionary: The vocabulary of reading and writing.* Newark, DE: International Reading Association.

Harvey, S. (1998). *Nonfiction matters: Reading, writing, and research in grades 3–8.* Portland, ME: Stenhouse.

Harvey, S., & Goudvis, A. (2000). *Strategies that work: Teaching comprehension to enhance understanding.* York, ME: Stenhouse.

Henk, W.A., & Melnick, S.A. (1995). The Reader Self-Perception Scale (RSPS): A new tool for measuring how children feel about themselves as readers. *The Reading Teacher, 48,* 470–482.

Hiebert, E.H. (1994). Becoming literate through authentic tasks: Evidence and adaptations. In R.B. Ruddell, M.R. Ruddell, & H. Singer (Eds.), *Theoretical models and processes of reading* (pp. 391–413). Newark, DE: International Reading Association.

Hiebert, E.H., Pearson, P.D., Taylor, B.M., Richardson, V., & Paris, S.G. (1998). *Every child a reader.* Ann Arbor, MI: Center for the Improvement of Early Reading Achievement (CIERA).

Hill, B.C., & Ruptic, C.A. (1994). *Practical aspects of authentic asessment: Putting the pieces together.* Norwood, MA: Christopher-Gordon.

Hill, B.C., Ruptic, C.A., & Norwick, L. (1998). *Classroom based assessment.* Norwood, MA: Christopher-Gordon.

Houghton Mifflin. (2001). Leveled reading passages assessment kit. Boston: Author.

Hoyt, L., & Ames, C. (1997). Letting the learner lead the way. *Primary Voices, 5,* 16–29.

Hunt, L.C. (1996/1997). The effect of self-selection, interest, and motivation upon independent, instructional, and frustration levels. *The Reading Teacher, 50,* 278–282.

International Reading Association. (1999). *Using multiple methods of beginning reading instruction: A position statement of the International Reading Association.* Newark, DE: Author.

International Reading Association. (2000). *Excellent reading teachers: A position statement of the International Reading Association.* Newark, DE: Author.

Johnson, D.D., & Pearson, P.D. (1984). *Teaching reading vocabulary* (2nd ed.). New York: Holt, Rinehart and Winston.

Kamil, M.L., Mosenthal, P.B., Pearson, P.D., & Barr, R. (Eds.). (2000). *Handbook of reading research* (Vol. 3). Mahwah, NJ: Erlbaum.

Kaywell, J. (Ed.). (1993). *Adolescent literature as a complement to the classics.* Norwood, MA: Christopher-Gordon.

Keene, E., & Zimmermann, S. (1997). *Mosaic of thought: Teaching comprehension in a reader's workshop.* Portsmouth, NH: Heinemann.

Klein, A. (1995). Sparking a love for reading: Literature circles with intermediate students. In B.C. Hill, N.J. Johnson, & K.L. Noe (Eds.), *Literature circles and response.* Norwood, MA: Christopher-Gordon.

Langer, J. (1981). From theory to practice: A prereading plan. *Journal of Reading, 25,* 152–156.

Lasear, D. (1991). *Seven ways of teaching: The artistry of teaching with multiple intelligences.* Palatine, IL: Skylight.

Leslie, L., & Caldwell, J.A. (2000). *Qualitative Reading Inventory–3.* New York: Longman.

Lewin, L. (1998). *Great performances: Creating classroom-based assessment tasks.* Alexandria, VA: Association for Supervision and Curriculum Development.

Lindquist, T. (1995). *Seeing the whole through social studies.* Portsmouth, NH: Heinemann.

Lipson, M.Y. (2001). *A fresh look at comprehension.* Paper presented at the Reading/Language Arts Symposium, Chicago, Illinois.

Lipson, M.Y., & Wixson, K. (1997). *Assessment and instruction of reading and writing disability: An interactive approach* (2nd ed.). New York: Longman.

Macon, J.M. (1985, November). *Ideas for literature response.* Paper presented at the Annual Meeting of the California Reading Association, Anaheim, California.

Macon, J.M. (1991). *Literature Response.* Paper presented at the Annual Literacy Workshop, Anaheim, CA.

Maring, G., Furman, G., & Blum-Anderson, J. (1985). Five cooperative learning strategies for mainstreamed youngsters in content area classrooms. *The Reading Teacher, 39,* 310–313.

McGinley, W., & Denner, P. (1987). Story impressions: A prereading/prewriting activity. *Journal of Reading, 31,* 248–253.

McKeown, M.G., Beck, I.L., & Worthy, M.J. (1993). Grappling with text ideas: Questioning the author. *The Reading Teacher, 46,* 560–566.

McLaughlin, E.M. (1987). QuIP: A writing strategy to improve comprehension of expository structure. *The Reading Teacher, 40,* 650–654.

McLaughlin, M. (1995). *Performance assessment: A practical guide to implementation.* Boston: Houghton Mifflin.

McLaughlin, M. (2000a). Assessment for the 21st century: Performance, portfolios, and profiles. In M. McLaughlin & M.E. Vogt (Eds.), *Creativity and innovation in content area teaching* (pp. 301–327). Norwood, MA: Christopher-Gordon.

McLaughlin, M. (2000b). Inquiry: Key to critical and creative thinking in the content areas. In M. McLaughlin & M.E. Vogt (Eds.), *Creativity and innovation in content area teaching* (pp. 31–54). Norwood, MA: Christopher-Gordon.

McLaughlin, M. (2002). Dynamic assessment. In B. Guzzetti (Ed.), *Literacy in America: An encyclopedia.* Santa Barbara, CA: ABC.

McLaughlin, M., & Vogt, M.E. (1996). *Portfolios in teacher education.* Newark, DE: International Reading Association.

McLaughlin, M., & Vogt, M.E. (Eds.). (2000). *Creativity and innovation in content area teaching.* Norwood, MA: Christopher-Gordon.

McMillan, J.H. (1997). *Classroom assessment: Principles and practice for effective instruction.* Needham Heights, MA: Allyn & Bacon.

McTighe, J., & Lyman, F.T. (1988). Cueing thinking in the classroom: The promise of theory-embedded tools. *Educational Leadership, 45*(7), 18–24.

Miholic, V. (1994). An inventory to pique students' metacognitive awareness of reading strategies. *Journal of Reading, 38,* 84–86.

Minick, N. (1987). Implications of Vygotsky's theories for dynamic assessment. In C.S. Lidz (Ed.), *Dynamic assessment: An interactional approach for evaluating learning potential* (pp. 116–140). New York: Guilford.

Morrow, L.M. (1985). Retelling stories: A strategy for improving children's comprehension, concept of story, and oral language complexity. *The Elementary School Journal, 85*(5), 647–661.

Mowery, S. (1995). *Reading and writing comprehension strategies.* Harrisburg, PA: Instructional Support Teams Publications.

National Commission on Teaching and America's Future. (1997). *Doing what matters most: Investing in quality teaching* [Online]. Available: http://www.tc.columbia.edu/-teachingcomm.

National Reading Panel. (2000). *Teaching children to read: An evidence-based assessment of the scientific research literature on reading and its implications for reading instruction.* Washington, DC: National Institutes of Health.

Newmann, F.M., & Wehlage, G.G. (1993). Five standards for authentic instruction. *Educational Leadership, 50,* 8–12.

Noe, K.L., & Johnson, N.J. (1999). *Getting started with literature circles.* Norwood, MA: Christopher-Gordon.

Ogle, D. (1986). K-W-L: A teaching model that develops active reading of expository text. *The Reading Teacher, 39,* 564–570.

Ogle, D. (2000). Making it visual: A picture is worth a thousand words. In M. McLaughlin & M.E. Vogt (Eds.), *Creativity and innovation in content area teaching* (pp. 55–71). Norwood, MA: Christopher-Gordon.

Palincsar, A.S., & Brown, A.L. (1984). Reciprocal teaching of comprehension-fostering and monitoring activities. *Cognition and Instruction, 1,* 117–175.

Palincsar, A.S., & Brown, A.L. (1986). Interactive teaching to promote independent learning from text. *The Reading Teacher, 39,* 771–777.

Pearson, P.D. (2001). *Comprehension strategy instruction: An idea whose time has come again.* Paper presented at the annual meeting of the Colorado Council of the International Reading Association, Denver, Colorado.

Pennsylvania Department of Education. (1998). *Reading rubric for student use* [Online]. Available: http://www.pde.psu.edu/connections.

Peterson, R., & Eeds, M. (1990). *Grand conversations: Literature groups in action.* New York: Scholastic.

Pinciotti, P. (2001a). *Art as a way of learning: Explorations in teaching.* Bethlehem, PA: Northampton Community College.

Pinciotti, P. (2001b). *Book arts: The creation of beautiful books.* East Stroudsburg, PA: East Stroudsburg University of Pennsylvania.

Raphael, T. (1986). Teaching children Question-Answer Relationships, revisited. *The Reading Teacher, 39,* 516–522.

Rasinski, T.V. (1999). Making and writing words using letter patterns. *Reading Online* [Online]. Available: http://www.readingonline.org/articles/words/rasinski_index.html.

Readence, J., Bean, T., & Baldwin, R. (2000). *Content area reading: An integrated approach* (7th ed.). Dubuque, IA: Kendall Hunt.

Richard-Amato, P.A. (1988). *Making it happen: Interaction in the second language classroom.* New York: Longman.

Richardson, J.S. (2000). *Read it aloud! Using literature in the secondary content classroom.* Newark, DE: International Reading Association.

Rigby. (2001). PM benchmark introduction kit. Crystal Lake, IL: Author.

Roehler, L.R., & Duffy, G.G. (1984). Direct explanation of comprehension processes. In G.G. Duffy, L.R. Roehler, & J. Mason (Eds.), *Comprehension instruction: Perspectives and suggestions* (pp. 265–280). New York: Longman.

Roehler, L.R., & Duffy, G.G. (1991). Teachers' instructional actions. In R. Barr, M.L. Kamil, P. Mosenthal, & P.D. Pearson (Eds.), *Handbook of reading research* (Vol. 2, pp. 861–883). White Plains, NY: Longman.

Rosenblatt, L.M. (1978). *The reader, the text, and the poem: The transactional theory of the literary work*. Carbondale, IL: Southern Illinois University Press.

Ruddell, M.R. (2001). *Teaching content reading and writing* (3rd ed.). New York: John C. Wiley.

Ruddell, R.B. (1995). Those influential literacy teachers: Meaning negotiators and motivation builders. *The Reading Teacher, 48*, 454–463.

Samway, K.D., & Wang, G. (1996). *Literature study circles in a multicultural classroom*. York, ME: Stenhouse.

Schmitt, M.C. (1990). A questionnaire to measure children's awareness of strategic reading processes. *The Reading Teacher, 43*, 454–461.

Schon, D. (1987). *Educating the reflective practitioner*. San Francisco: Jossey-Bass.

Schwartz, R. & Raphael, T. (1985). Concept of definition: A key to improving students' vocabulary. *The Reading Teacher, 39*, 198–205.

Short, K.G., & Burke, C. (1996). Examining our beliefs and practices through inquiry. *Language Arts, 73*, 97–103.

Short, K.G., Harste, J.C., & Burke, C. (1996). *Creating classrooms for authors and inquirers*. Portsmouth, NH: Heinemann.

Sippola, A.E. (1995). K-W-L-S. *The Reading Teacher, 48*, 542–543.

Smith, F. (1997). *Reading without nonsense*. New York: Teachers College Press.

Snow, C.E., Burns, M.S., & Griffin, P.G. (Eds.). (1998). *Preventing reading difficulties in young children*. Washington, DC: National Academy Press.

Stahl, S., & Kapinus, B. (1991). Possible sentences: Predicting word meaning to teach content area vocabulary. *The Reading Teacher, 45*, 36–43.

Stauffer, R. (1975). *Directing the reading-thinking process*. New York: Harper & Row.

Szymusiak, K., & Sibberson, F. (2001). *Beyond leveled books*. Portland, ME: Stenhouse.

Tierney, R.J. (1990). Redefining reading comprehension. *Educational Leadership, 47*(6), 37–42.

Tierney, R.J. (1998). Literacy assessment reform: Shifting beliefs, principled possibilities and emerging practices. *The Reading Teacher, 51*, 374–390.

Tierney, R.J., & Pearson, P.D. (1994). A revisionist perspective on learning to learn from text: A framework for improving classroom practice. In R.B. Ruddell, M.R. Ruddell, & H. Singer (Eds.), *Theoretical models and processes of reading* (pp. 514–519). Newark, DE: International Reading Association.

Tierney, R.J., & Readence, J.E. (2000). *Reading strategies and practices* (5th ed.). Needham Heights, MA: Allyn & Bacon.

Tompkins, G.E. (1997). *Literacy for the 21st century: A balanced approach*. Upper Saddle River, NJ: Merrill.

Tompkins, G.E. (2001). *Literacy for the 21st century: A balanced approach* (2nd ed.). Upper Saddle River, NJ: Prentice Hall.

Vacca, R.T., & Vacca, J.L. (1999). *Content area reading: Literacy and learning across the curriculum* (6th ed.). New York: Longman.

Vaughn, J., & Estes, T. (1986). *Reading and reasoning beyond the primary grades*. Boston: Allyn & Bacon.

Vogt, M.E. (1996). Creating a response-centered curriculum with literature discussion groups. In L.B. Gambrell & J.F. Almasi (Eds.), *Lively discussions! Fostering engaged reading* (pp. 181–193). Newark, DE: International Reading Association.

Vogt, M.E. (2000). Active learning: Dramatic play in the content areas. In M. McLaughlin & M.E. Vogt (Eds.), *Creativity and innovation in content area teaching* (pp. 55–71). Norwood, MA: Christopher-Gordon.

Vygotsky, L.S. (1978). *Mind in society: The development of higher psychological processes.* (M. Cole, V. John-Steiner, S. Scribner, & E. Souberman, Eds. and Trans.). Cambridge, MA: Harvard University Press. (Original work published 1934)

Waldo, B. (1991). Story pyramid. In J.M. Macon, D. Bewell, & M.E. Vogt (Eds.), *Responses to literature: Grades K–8* (pp. 23–24). Newark, DE: International Reading Association.

Weaver, B.M. (2000). *Leveling books K–6: Matching readers to text.* Newark, DE: International Reading Association.

Wood, K. (1984). Probable passages: A writing strategy. *The Reading Teacher, 37,* 496–499.

CHILDREN'S LITERATURE CITED

Abercrombie, B. (1995). *Charlie Anderson.* New York: Aladdin.

Adler, D.A. (1981). *Cam Jansen and the mystery of the dinosaur bones.* New York: Scholastic.

Adler, D.A. (1994). *A picture book of Anne Frank.* New York: Holiday House.

Angelou, M. (1994). "On the Pulse of Morning." In *The collected poems of Maya Angelou.* New York: Random House.

Archambault, J., & Martin, B. Jr. (1987). *Knots on a counting rope.* New York: Henry Holt.

Base, G. (1996). *Animalia.* New York: Puffin Books.

Brown, M.W. (1990). *The Important Book.* New York: Harper Trophy.

Bulla, C.R., & Williams, R. (1990). *Squanto: Friend of the Pilgrims.* New York: Scholastic.

Bunting, E. (1995). *Terrible things: An allegory of the Holocaust.* New York: Jewish Publication Society.

Charlip, R. (1993). *Fortunately.* New York: Aladdin.

Cohlene, T., & Reasoner, C. (1991). *Little firefly: An Algonquin legend.* New York: Troll.

Demi. (1990). *The empty pot.* New York: Henry Holt.

Dorris, M. (1994). *Guests.* New York: Hyperion.

Dorris, M. (1997). *Sees behind trees.* New York: Hyperion.

Dorris, M. (1999). *Morning girl.* New York: Hyperion.

Fleischman, S. (1990). *The whipping boy.* New York: Troll.

Florian, D. (1999). *Insectlopedia.* New York: Scholastic.

Gardiner, J.R. (1988). *Stone fox.* New York: Harper Trophy.

George, E., & Speare, G. (1984). *The sign of the beaver.* New York: Bantam Doubleday Dell.

Gibbons, G. (1992). *Stargazers.* New York: Scholastic.

Goodrich, F. (1993). *The diary of Anne Frank.* San Diego, CA: HBJ School.

Henkes, K. (1991). *Chrysanthemum.* New York: Greenwillow.

Howe, J. (1982). *Howliday Inn.* New York: Macmillan.

Kettleman, H. (2000). *Armadillo tattletale.* New York: Scholastic.

Konigsburg, E.L. (1998). *The view from Saturday.* New York: Aladdin.

Levitt, M. (1990). *The weighty word book.* Boulder, CO: Manuscripts LTD.

Lowry, L. (1990). *Number the stars.* Boston: Houghton Mifflin.

McDonough, Y.Z. (1997). *Anne Frank.* New York: Henry Holt.

Nickle, J. (1998). *The ant bully.* New York: Scholastic.

Paulsen, G. (1987). *Hatchet.* New York: Simon & Schuster.

Perl, L., & Lazan, M.B. (1999). *Four perfect pebbles.* New York: Camelot.

Pinkwater, D.M. (1984). *The Hoboken chicken emergency.* New York: Simon & Schuster.

Polacco, P. (1998). *Thank you, Mr. Falkner.* New York: Philomel.

Schertle, A. (2001). *A lucky thing.* New York: Scholastic.

Sciezka, J. (1996). *The true story of the three little pigs.* New York: Penguin Putnam.

Sierra, J. (1998). *Antarctic antics: A book of penguin poems.* San Diego, CA: Gulliver Books, Harcourt Brace.

Simon, S. (1979). *Animal fact/Animal fable.* New York: Crown.

Simon, S. (1992). *Snakes.* New York: Scholastic.

Simon, S. (1993). *Wolves.* New York: HarperCollins.

Simon, S. (1995). *Sharks.* New York: Scholastic.

Teague, M. (1994). *Pigsty*. New York: Scholastic.

Van Allsburg, C. (1984). *The mysteries of Harris Burdick*. Boston: Houghton Mifflin.

Viorst, J. (1981). *If I were in charge of the world and other worries*. New York: Atheneum.

Volavkova, H. (Ed.). (1993). *I never saw another butterfly*. New York: Shocken Books.

Yolen, J. (1990). *The devil's arithmetic*. New York: Penguin.

INDEX

Note: Page numbers followed by *f* indicate figures.

A

B

T